Russia's Ekranoplans

The Caspian Sea Monster and other WIG Craft

Sergey Komissarov

Midland Publishing

Russia's Ekranoplans
© 2002 Sergey Komissarov
ISBN 1 85780 146 6

Published by Midland Publishing
4 Watling Drive, Hinckley, LE10 3EY, England
Tel: 01455 254 490 Fax: 01455 254 495
E-mail: midlandbooks@compuserve.com

Midland Publishing is an imprint of
Ian Allan Publishing Ltd

Worldwide distribution (except North America):
Midland Counties Publications
4 Watling Drive, Hinckley, LE10 3EY, England
Telephone: 01455 254 450 Fax: 01455 233 737
E-mail: midlandbooks@compuserve.com
www.midlandcountiessuperstore.com

North American trade distribution:
Specialty Press Publishers & Wholesalers Inc.
39966 Grand Avenue, North Branch, MN 55056, USA
Tel: 651 277 1400 Fax: 651 277 1203
Toll free telephone: 800 895 4585
www.specialtypress.com

© 2002 Midland Publishing
Design concept and layout
by Polygon Press Ltd. (Moscow, Russia)
Line drawings by G.F.Petrov and S.D.Komissarov

This book is illustrated with photos from the archives of Yefim Gordon, Gennadiy Petrov, Sergey Komissarov, Dmitriy Griniuk, Helmut Walther, Central Hydrofoil Design Bureau, Amphibious Transport Technologies JSC, Wingships Airlines JSC and the Russian Aviation Research Trust

Printed in England by
Ian Allan Printing Ltd
Riverdene Business Park, Molesey Road,
Hersham, Surrey, KT12 4RG

All rights reserved. No part of this publication may be reproduced, stored in a retrieval system, transmitted in any form or by any means, electronic, mechanical or photo-copied, recorded or otherwise, without the written permission of the publishers.

Contents

Introduction 3

1. Alexeyev, the Pioneer:
   Standard-Setting Designs 11
2. Bartini: Bold Ideas
   Italian-Born Designer's Projects ... 43
3. Beriyev's Activities:
   Hydroplane Versus *Ekranoplan* 59
4. Sukhoi Diversifies:
   WIG Vehicles on the Agenda 65
5. Enthusiasts Make Their
   Contribution 69
6. Free Enterprise: Enter New Firms .. 81
   Line drawings 97
   Colour photographs 113

Title page: The VVA-14 aircraft with WIG properties was typical of Robert Bartini's unorthodox designs. It was later converted into the 14M1P 'true' WIG vehicle.

Below: A nice air-to-air of the Orlyonok, probably the best-known Soviet WIG vehicle.

Introduction

The purpose of this book is to show Russia's role and achievements in the development of *ekranoplans*, or wing-in-ground-effect (WIG) craft – a new means of transportation which remains a fairly exotic domain to this day. These achievements, quite justifiably, attract much interest in many countries. After all, it was in Russia (represented in the shape of the now-defunct Soviet Union) that pioneering work in this field of technology brought about highly impressive results that have yet to be surpassed. From the 1960s onwards Russia has been occupying a leading position in the world as far as construction of large WIG craft is concerned. The author's intention is to present a general review of the work accomplished by Russian design bureaux and production plants in this field of technology (see below in this chapter) and to give a description of specific designs (they will be covered in subsequent chapters).

To begin with, a few words about the subject of this book. Wing-in-ground-effect craft making use of a dynamic air cushion are vehicles operating in close proximity to a supporting surface. This is usually water, but basically it makes no difference whether a WIG craft is operating over water or over land – provided that the ground surface is sufficiently even and flat.

A feature common to an aircraft and a WIG craft is wings generating lift due to aerodynamic forces. However, in the case of the WIG craft this lift is augmented owing to the ground effect created by compression of the ram air stream between the wings and the supporting surface. A higher lift/drag ratio enables a WIG craft to obtain the same lift at lower speeds and lower engine power compared to aircraft. As a result, the WIG craft are, in principle, more fuel-efficient compared to aircraft.

Since large flat areas on land are not a common occurrence, WIG craft are in most cases intended for use over water. Operation from the surface of lakes, rivers or seas of necessity introduces some features of waterborne vessels into the design of WIG vehicles. Historically, a number of WIGs emerged as a kind of attempt to lift water-borne craft out of the water for the purpose of achieving greater speeds, and in many cases WIG craft were built at shipyards. Small wonder that the question is posed sometimes whether one should regard these new craft as very low-flying aircraft or as ships that have lifted themselves out of the water.

WIG vehicles come in every shape and size. Some, like the famous Alexeyev KM shown here, use booster engines to assist take-off; others, like Beriyev's tiny Be-1, use hydrofoils for the same purpose.

It would appear that both definitions might be appropriate, since the concept of WIG vehicles embraces a wide variety of craft featuring quite substantial differences. They may tend to be closer to one or the other of the two extremes, but, generally speaking, they are always something of a hybrid. On the one hand, a WIG vehicle in cruise flight is subjected to aerodynamic forces, much in common with conventional aircraft, while the hydrodynamic forces act on it only during take-off and landing – or rather alighting. On the other hand, WIG craft operating in close proximity to the water surface in a marine environment have to be subjected to the same rules and requirements as conventional marine vessels in terms of traffic safety.

The latter consideration has played an important role when it came to establishing a formal classification of WIG vehicles with a view to adopting rules concerning their certification and safety regulations. Three basic categories have been formally adopted for this purpose.

The first of them **(Type A)** encompasses vehicles that can be operated only within the height of the surface effect. They usually feature wings of low aspect ratio (up to 1) and are fitted only with a rudder, there being no elevator; the 'driver' (or should we say helmsman?) does not have to possess piloting skills and steers the vehicle in much the same way as an ordinary speedboat. In Russian parlance, such vehicles are termed Dynamic Air Cushion Vessels, or WIG vessels (*ekranoplan* boats). Among Russian designs, such examples may be cited as the Volga-2, Amphistar and Raketa-2 (described in other chapters).

The second category **(Type B)** includes vehicles which are capable of leaving the surface effect zone for a short while and making brief 'hops'. The altitude of such a 'hop' shall not exceed the minimum safe altitude of flight for aircraft, as prescribed by International Civil Aviation Organisation (ICAO) regulations (150 m/500 ft). In Russian parlance such vehicles are regarded as WIG craft (*ekranoplans*) proper; they feature wings with an aspect ratio of up to 3 and are provided with elevators. They are controlled by pilots. Among Russian designs this category is represented by the Orlyonok, KM, Strizh, ESKA-1 etc.

The third category **(Type C)** covers WIG vehicles capable of flying outside the surface effect zone for a considerable time and of climbing to altitudes in excess of the minimum safe flight altitude for aircraft, as prescribed by ICAO regulations.

This classification subdividing the WIG vehicles into types A, B and C was formulated by Russian organisations and submitted by Russia to the International Marine Organisation (IMO) and ICAO for their consideration. Thanks in no small degree to determined efforts of the Russian side it has proved possible to reach within the framework of IMO an agreement on a number of basic issues pertaining to legal, technical and operational aspects of WIG craft. For the first time international documents were evolved that provide rules for commercial operation of WIG craft and for their safety. These documents (shortly to take effect) represent an important milestone. For the first time they have given an expression at a high level for an international recognition of WIG craft as a new and promising means of maritime transport and provided a legal basis for its further development and commercial operation on international sea routes.

Against this background, let us take a look at the story of WIG craft design and production in Russia.

The early research on ground effect and of efforts aimed at creating practicable WIG vehicles dates back to the 1920s and 1930s when work in this field was started in several countries (as is well known, the first self-propelled WIG vehicle was built by T. Kaario, a Finnish engineer, in 1935). The Soviet Union was among these countries. Theoretical and experimental work in this direction was started in the USSR in the 1920s (experimental work by B. N. Yur'yev, 1923). Further work followed in the late 1930s, when a whole set of theoretical studies and experiments in the field of ground effect research was performed by Yakov M. Serebriyskiy and Sh. A. Biyachuyev. The results of this work were published in specialised literature.

In the late 1930s the first steps in practical design of WIG craft in the USSR were made by Pavel Ignat'yevich Grokhovsky, an aviation engineer and inventor renowned for his energy and innovative ideas.

However, it is Rostislav Yevgen'yevich Alexeyev (1916-1980), an outstanding scientist and designer, who must be credited with having played a paramount, decisive role in shaping the course of research, design and construction of WIG vehicles in Russia. His was the conceptual approach and design philosophy; he may truly be regarded as the founder of the Russian wingship construction. Alexeyev started his activities as a builder of hydrofoil ships in his capacity of the chief of the Central Hydrofoil Design Bureau (TsKB po SPK – *Tsentrahl'noye konstrooktorskoye byuro po soodahm na podvodnykh kryl'yakh*) set up in Nizhniy Novgorod. An impressive range of highly successful hydrofoil vessels designed under his guidance was developed and put into operational service. Yet, it was precisely his work on WIG craft – work veiled in utmost secrecy for many years – that was destined to become the most prominent and significant part of his creative activities and represented a major contribution to the world's technical progress.

The Central Hydrofoil Design Bureau has been actively engaged in WIG craft design since the early 1960s. The work was based on the concept of autostabilisation of the wing of a WIG vehicle relative to the interface between the supporting water surface and the air. This concept proved sound and was subsequently incorporated in all WIG projects issued by the design bureau. On its basis a search was initiated for suitable aero-hydrodynamical layouts; initially, one of these featured two sets of wings arranged in tandem. The first 3-ton (6,600-lb) ekranoplan built in 1961 was fitted with two sets of wings. Research revealed that the tandem layout is practicable only in a very close proximity to the surface and is unable to ensure the necessary measure of stability and safety, once the craft leaves this close proximity. Experiments with one of these tandem-wing machines ended in a crash. R. Alexeyev arrived at the decision to make use of a classic aircraft layout (one set of wings and a tail unit) which was to be subjected to modifications designed to ensure stability and controllability during cruise flight in ground effect. In particular, low-set or mid-set wings of much lower aspect ratio (around 3) were adopted. An important feature was the use of an outsize horizontal tail; it was to be placed sufficiently far aft and high up relative to the main wings so as to minimise the influence of downwash induced by the wings depending on the flight altitude and pitch angle. Ten experimental WIG vehicles featuring this layout were built by the Central Hydrofoil design Bureau, their weight and dimensions growing with every successive machine. These were the machines in the SM series (SM stands for *samokhodnaya model'* – self-propelled model), with an all-up weight of up to 5 tonnes (11,000 lb).

Design experience gained by R. Alexeyev in developing these machines enabled him to take a bold decision to initiate the design of gigantic WIG vehicles with an all-up weight of more than 400 t (880,000 lb). In 1962 the Central Design Bureau was engaged in project work on a combat WIG craft intended for ASW weighing 450 t (990,000 lb); two years later the design team in Nizhniy Novgorod started designing the T-1 troop transport and assault WIG craft.

It should be noted that the very considerable scope attained by the activities of the Central Hydrofoil Design Bureau was due to the fact that the new means of transport had attracted much interest on the part of the military. As a consequence, for many years this work was highly classified. Thus, construction of WIG vehicles in the Soviet Union got a boost from military programmes. In the opinion of military specialists both in the Soviet Union (and nowadays in Russia) and in the West, large WIG vehicles can be employed for a wide range of missions in the armed forces, notably in the Navy. These include troop transportation, anti-submarine warfare (ASW), anti-shipping strikes with guided missiles etc. The most ambitious projects envisaged the use of WIG craft as flying aircraft carriers! An inherent advantage of WIG vehicles when used in warfare is their ability to remain undetected by enemy radar thanks to the low altitude of their flight; the lack of contact with the sea surface makes them undetectable by acoustic means (sonar devices). WIG vehicles are capable of operating not only over water expanses but also over snow-covered stretches of land and over ice fields. This makes them eminently suitable for use in Polar regions. Their high speed ensures their quick response to the changing battlefield situation, and their high load-carrying capacity enhances their capability for accomplishing various missions and carrying a wide range of weapons.

In assessing the suitability of WIG craft for ASW, one should bear in mind that, owing to their low flight altitude, WIG vehicles cannot be equipped with sonobuoys. However, they possess a wider range of capabilities for making use of a dunking sonar when afloat. Moreover, thanks to their big dimensions they can, in principle, be fitted with ASW weapons normally carried by surface ships, to be used without getting airborne.

WIG vehicles are superior to amphibious aircraft in sea-going capabilities and endurance; they can be armed with more potent missiles possessing longer range. However, they have their limitations associated with the need for target designation from an external source (amphibious seaplanes can provide target designation for their weapons when flying at high altitude).

The projects of an ASW WIG vehicle and the T-1 troop-carrying WIG vehicle never left the drawing board. On the other hand, in 1966 the Design Bureau built, in response to an order from the Navy, the KM WIG craft (KM stands *korahbl'-maket* – a 'mock-up', ie, prototype ship). With its fuselage length of nearly 100 m (330 ft), wing span of nearly 40 m (130 ft) and all-up weight of 430 t (948,000 lb), this gigantic machine was a unique piece of engineering. In a record-setting flight its weight reached 540 t (1,190,000 lb), which was an unofficial world record for flying machines at the time. The KM *ekranoplan*, dubbed 'Caspian Sea Monster' in the West, underwent comprehensive testing in the

Above: Robert Bartini's unorthodox VVA-14 vertical take-off amphibious aircraft in level flight with the rubberised fabric floats inflated. The 14-engined (!) aircraft with two cruise engines and 12 lift-jets possessed certain WIG properties.

Later in its test career the VVA-14 was converted into the 14M1P vehicle – a true *ekranoplan*. Clearly visible in this view are the two turbofan engines flanking the flight deck; these exhausted under the wing centre section, creating a static air cushion.

A prototype of the Volga-2 WIG craft on the bank of the river from which it derived its name. This elegant vehicle is a product of the Central Hydrofoil Design Bureau.

course of 15 years of operation. It marked the completion of a whole range of research and practical design tasks associated with approbation of the WIG concept as a whole and evolving the scientific basis for their design, construction and testing. The results of this work made it possible to create a theoretical and methodological basis for designing and building practicable examples of WIG vehicles.

One of these was the *Orlyonok* (Eaglet) troop transport/assault *ekranoplan* with a take-off weight of 140 t (309,000lb). It was capable of transporting a 20-tonne (44,000-lb) cargo at a speed of 400 km/h (248 mph) to a distance of up to 1,500 km (930 miles). Three examples of the Orlyonok (Project 904) were delivered to the Navy for evaluation. Their service career proved to be far from an unqualified success. Normal operation was hampered, above all, by circumstances of bureaucratic nature. The WIG machines were operated by the Navy, yet their crews had to include pilots because in certain operational modes they had to be piloted like aircraft. However, neither the Air Force nor the Naval Aviation showed any enthusiasm for these machines and sought to 'prove' in every possible way that they could not be regarded as flying machines – unabashed by the fact that provision was made for operating them also out of surface effect and there were plans for long-range ferrying flights at high altitude. Yielding to this pressure, the Navy top brass then decided that WIG craft should be classed as 'ships with aircraft-like properties'. In turn, the Central Hydrofoil Design Bureau clearly underestimated the 'aviation' aspect of the matter and had failed to consult the Air Force on the methods of testing, which gave rise to justifiable complaints. Arrangements required to facilitate operational use of the machines delivered to the Navy suffered setbacks and delays. Series production of WIG craft for the Navy was expected to amount to several dozens of examples, but these plans failed to materialise. Introduction of new types of weaponry in the USSR, following a pattern common to many countries, depended heavily on lobbying on the part of this or that person in the top echelon. The Soviet Minister of Defence, Marshal of the Soviet Union Dmitriy F. Ustinov supported the idea of WIG vehicle construction, but he died in 1985. Sergey L. Sokolov, the new Minister of Defence, influenced by the newly appointed Commander-in-Chief of the Navy V. N. Chernavin, ordered that all the funds available to the Navy be used for the construction of submarines. A crash suffered in 1992 by one of the Orlyonok machines was hardly conducive to improving the atmosphere around their integration into the armed forces. This was further aggravated by the transfer of the WIG machines from ordinary Naval units to the Naval Aviation – airmen were not overly enthusiastic about the new hardware. Deprived of the necessary attention and supplies, the base where the WIG craft were stationed began to fall into decay. Eventually the three surviving machines (two *Orlyonok*s and one *Loon'*) were struck off charge on the pretext of difficulties associated with maintenance and repairs. That marked, for the time being, the end of operational use of transport and combat WIG vehicles in the Russian Navy.

There is an episode in the story of the Orlyonok which eloquently bears witness to the character of both the machine and its creator, Rostislav Alexeyev. During one of the test flights Alexeyev was on board. The pilot, who had little experience with this type of vehicles, impacted the machine heavily right on the crest of a wave. The crew did not grasp the situation. Only Alexeyev, who had taken a look from the upper hatch, knew what had happened. Without a word, he took over the controls, gave full throttle to the nose-mounted booster engines and steered the machine to its base which was situated 40 km (25 miles) away. Only then could the crew take a look at the machine. They were stunned by the sight: the vehicle had lost its tail! The rear fuselage complete with the tail unit and main engine had simply broken off on impact and sunk! The fact that the Orlyonok still made it safely back to base bore witness both to the designer's presence of mind and to the machine's qualities. However, this episode placed a welcome tool in the hands of Alexeyev's detractors and those who were intent on closing down the work on WIG vehicles. The episode was followed by 'administrative measures' (ie, repercussions) which boiled down to victimising the designer. He was deprived of the possibility to make full use of his creative potential, which affected very adversely the development of the WIG-vehicle construction in the USSR and present-day Russia.

An important stage in the activities of the Central Hydrofoil Design Bureau was marked the creation of the Loon' (Hen harrier) – a 400-tonne missile carrier armed with *Moskit* (Mosquito) anti-shipping missiles. It was launched in 1987. Construction of a second example of this machine was envisaged, but the collapse of the Soviet Union drastically affected the programme (see Chapter 1 for details of the 'service career' of the Loon' and Orlyonok WIG vehicles). The second example, already under construction, was to be completed as a search-and-rescue machine. Accordingly, conversion work was started (progress reports appeared in the press in 1994), but this project, too, stranded for a long time due to various political and economic reasons. Only quite recently was the conversion work resumed and, hopefully, has a prospect of successful completion which would result in creating an unorthodox and highly effective maritime SAR vehicle.

Rostislav Alexeyev died in 1980. Earlier, after the crash of the prototype Orlyonok, he had to relinquish the post of chief of the Central Design Bureau of Hydrofoils, and then of Chief Designer. For many years the Design Bureau was led by V. V. Ikonnikov, later by B. V. Choobikov. At present this organisation is headed by General Director I. M. Vasilevskiy.

The Central Hydrofoil Design Bureau, now named after R. Alexeyev and transformed into a joint-stock company, continues to actively pursue the designing of WIG vehicles. The emphasis has shifted to machines intended for commercial uses. Among these, such machines as the Volga-2 eight-passenger WIG boat and a series of Strizh (Swift, the bird) WIG vehicles have fairly good prospects for service introduction. The Design Bureau is engaged in developing a whole range of different machines including heavy sea-going transport *ekranoplans*. Some of the projects are being developed with a view to foreign markets and partnership schemes with investors from abroad.

The Central Hydrofoil Design Bureau in Nizhniy Novgorod has retained its position as Russia's leading developer of heavy sea-going WIG craft, but it is not a monopolist in its field. In the course of the last four decades and especially the last decade questions of WIG research and practical design have been dealt with by quite a number of organisations, big and small, including design bureaus, scientific institutions, commercial firms, student design teams and individual enthusiasts. Here are some of them:

WIG vehicles have occupied important place in the activities of **Robert Lyudvigovich Bartini**, a well-known Soviet aircraft designer who made a significant contribution to evolving the theory of dynamic air cushion vehicles and prepared a number of designs which failed to reach the hardware stage, with the exception of the 14M1P (they are described in detail in Chapter 2).

At a certain stage in his career Bartini continued his activities within the framework of **Gheorgiy Mikhaïlovich Beriyev's design bureau** (now the **Taganrog Aviation Scientific and Technical Complex named after G. M. Beriyev**). This is where his 14M1P was built. Also other Beriyev engineers and design teams were engaged in WIG vehicle design; in 1965 they designed and built the Be-1 experimental WIG vehicle. During the last decade engineers of the Taganrog firm have been working with designs of large (even gigantic) aircraft of this type combining the features of a WIG vehicle and a traditional amphibious flying boat.

The **Sukhoi Design Bureau** has been cooperating with the Central Hydrofoil Design Bureau; in the course of the recent 10 to 15 years it developed several WIG projects such as the S-90, S-90-8 and S-90-200.

The **A. N. Krylov Shipbuilding Research Institute** in St. Petersburg has been actively engaged in theoretical studies and, to some extent, practical design of WIG craft; it acquired a branch in Nizhniy Novgorod. That city is the place of activity for a number of small firms established in the early 1990s. These include the **Technology and Transport** joint-stock society (now renamed **Amphibious Transport Technologies**) which has developed the Amphistar passenger WIG speedboat; **Amphicon** (a Russian acronym meaning *amfibeeynyye konstrooktsii* – amphibious designs), **Transal** (an abbreviation of *Trahnsport Alexeyeva* – Alexeyev's Transport). In Moscow the **Roks-Aero** company was working with WIG designs in the early 1990s; the **KOMETEL** company is active there at present.

In the course of the recent decades (from the 1960s onwards) a whole series of light WIG vehicles was designed and built by young designers working within enthusiast designer groups or so-called student design bureaus that had been established at a number of aviation institutes (colleges). Here mention must be made of such teams within **TsLST** (*Tsentrahl'naya laboratoriya spasahtel'noy tekhniki* – Central Laboratory for SAR Technology), **MVTU** (*Moskovskoye vyssheye tekhnicheskoye oochilischche* – Moscow Higher Technical College named after Nikolay E. Bauman), **MIIGA** (*Moskovskiy institoot inzhenerov grazhdahnskoy aviahtsii* – Moscow Institute of Civil Aviation Engineers), **MAI** (*Moskovskiy aviatsionnyy institoot* – Moscow Aviation Institute), **RKIIGA** (*Rizhskiy krasnoznamyonnyy institoot inzhenerov grazhdahnskoy aviahtsii* – Riga Red Banner Institute of Civil Aviation Engineers), **KnAPI** (*Komsomol'skiy-na-Amoore politekhnicheskiy institoot* – Komsomolsk-on-Amur Polytechbical Institute) etc. Problems pertaining to WIG vehicles are studied by such scientific institutions as **TsAGI** (*Tsentrahl'nyy aero- i ghidro-dinamicheskiy institoot* – Central Aero- and Hydrodynamical Institute) in Moscow and Zhukovskiy, **SibNIIA** (*Sibeerskiy naoochno-issledovatel'skiy institoot aviahtsii* – Siberian Aviation Research Institute) in Novosibirsk, the **Irkutsk State University** in cooperation with the **Russian Academy of Sciences**.

What are the general trends and prospects in the activity of Russian organisations in the field of WIG design and production at present?

As to military applications, it would appear that the need for WIG vehicles in the Armed Forces of Russia has fallen dramatically. One of the reasons for this is presumably the radical change in the world situation as compared to the Soviet period. The confrontation between social systems and military alliances has given way to partnership and co-operation between Russia and the West, entailing a revision of the scope and character of Russian military programmes. Another factor is the marked worsening of the economic situation in Russia in the 1990s. Budgetary limitations drastically reduced the resources that could be used by the Armed Forces for funding the development and acquisition of new military hardware. Publications in the popular press generally avoid the subject of possible plans for resurrection of WIG vehicles intended for military applications. In early 2000 the well-informed weekly *Nezavisimoye Voyennoye Obozreniye* (Independent Military Review) carried a small article which, with reference to Chief of the Navy Headquarters Admiral Viktor Kravchenko, briefly charted plans for the development of the Navy up to the year of 2010. Only traditional ships were listed for acquisition, while WIG vehicles were mentioned only as potential export articles.

In these circumstances design bureaux engaged in WIG vehicle design were compelled to stake on designing machines intended for commercial application. The prospects of commercial use of WIG craft, however, remain unclear to this day. To win a secure place in the world transport system, the new means of transportation has to overcome many obstacles. The competition between WIG craft and traditional means of transport (aircraft, ships) can, inter alia, take the form of covert opposition from certain quarters to introduction of WIG vehicles on lucrative sea routes. However, the main thing is the objective factor – namely the ability of WIG vehicles to demonstrate economic advantages over traditional air and sea transport. Here WIG vehicles have on the credit side their far superior speeds as compared to displacement vessels and greater load-carrying capacity per unit of engine power or thrust as compared to aircraft. Research on transport economics undertaken by a number of organisations in Russia and in the West revealed a niche which could be filled by WIG vehicles. It is passenger and cargo transportation on transoceanic trunk routes, as well as transport communications between islands in an archipelago and between islands and the mainland. WIG craft are presumed to have no need for a pier (as distinct from ships) or an airfield (as distinct from aircraft). This is important, since it is uneconomical to build a sea port or an airport in areas with low traffic intensity.

In practice, the economic efficiency of WIG craft has not yet established itself as something indisputable. One of the factors affecting it is the relatively low payload to all-up weight ratio of the first-generation military WIG vehicles built to date (due in part to the use of shipbuilding, rather than aircraft technologies in construction).

Be it as it may, at the end of 1980 and the beginning of 1990s the Russian design bureaux specialising in WIG vehicles set about designing machines intended for commercial application both at home and abroad. In 1993 designer V. V. Sokolov, a disciple of

R. Alexeyev, voiced an optimistic opinion: *'Research done by specialised institutes show that the expected high productivity of ekranoplans leading to their profitability fully meets the demands of potential buyers and the trends in the development of transport systems; therefore, commercial ekranoplans can become a reality already in the nearest future'*.

There was no prospect of obtaining the necessary funding from the State budget, so the design bureaux and companies in question pinned their hopes on establishing co-operation with foreign partners which were expected to make the necessary investments. International co-operation was expected to provide the basis not only for the introduction of WIG craft into cargo and passenger transportation, but also for the employment of this new means of transport in systems for aerial launch of space shuttles, in international maritime SAR systems etc.

These plans and intentions had, generally speaking, a certain realistic foundation. Russia is universally recognised to have far outstripped other countries in design and construction of WIG vehicles, especially large sea-going craft. A noteworthy comment on this score was made by Vladimir Kirillovykh, Chief Designer of the Central Hydrofoil Design Bureau. In December 2001 he said in an interview to a Russian magazine that Russia was some twenty years ahead of other countries as far as the technology of WIG vehicle construction was concerned. *'There are many amphibious craft in the world today, but all of them are unsuitable for use at sea,* – says he. – *Nowadays only Russia is in possession of technology required for the construction of precisely the sea-going* ekranoplans*.'*

Several countries displayed an interest in getting access to the advanced Russian know-how in WIG design. In 1992 an authoritative group of US specialists visited the *ekranoplan* base in Kaspiysk to obtain firsthand impressions of the Russian achievements and assess prospects of co-operation. In the USA interest was shown for making use of the Russian experience in connection with some plans for gearing WIGs to military tasks.

In 1990s the Sukhoi Design Bureau signed an agreement with a Singapore company on the joint development of a WIG vehicle for cargo and passenger transportation in South-East Asia. Unfortunately the agreement foundered for financial reasons. This and other similar efforts brought no results – not a single joint project has been brought to fruition. The main reason is the lack of the necessary funding by the Russian partners.

At present the following trends can be observed as regards the practical use of WIG vehicles in Russia. Firstly, it is the relatively cheap smaller size craft carrying 8 to 12 passengers that are used as an initial step in the introduction of the new means of cargo and passenger transportation. This is due both to a cautious approach of carriers to the new technology and to a lack of financial means for developing, buying and operating bigger and costlier machines. Secondly, many projects developed earlier by Russian design bureaux or currently under development represent Type B and C WIG vehicles, yet the emphasis is placed on the introduction of Type A machines (DAC vessels) intended for operation only within ground effect. In Russia the introduction of WIG craft is associated first and foremost with the development of river transport in shipping agencies of inland waterways, such as the rivers of Volga, Oka, Kama, Ob', Irtysh, Yenisey, Amur, Lena etc. The reason is simple. Type A WIG vehicle are certified according to requirements for river-going and sea-going ships, while certification of vehicles capable of operation out of ground effect is effected according to requirements for aircraft. This makes the certification procedure in the latter case far more complicated and costly – an important consideration for operators with limited resources. Therefore introduction of Type B and C WIG vehicles into commercial operations in Russia can be expected only when some experience in the operation of Type A machines has been accumulated and potential operators have considerably improved their financial situation.

This does not mean that work on designing large WIG craft has stopped for the time being. In 1996 the Central Hydrofoil Design Bureau was engaged in projecting passenger and cargo versions based on a modified layout of the Orlyonok. A project of a WIG vehicle with an all-up weight of 50 t (110,000 lb) is to serve as a baseline model for a whole range of versions intended for various missions. This project, as well as some other projects evolved in the Central Hydrofoil Design Bureau, are regarded as a matter of considerable importance by the Russian Government which is providing support for them. This is intended to ensure that Russia remains at the forefront of development in this field of transport technology. The State Duma (the lower house of the Russian parliament) adopted a special resolution 'On the development of *ekranoplan* construction', and the Russian government issued appropriate directives.

As for the construction and operational use of WIG vehicles in the super-heavy class (1,000 t/2,200,000 lb and more), implementation of such projects by the Russian industry alone (without cooperating with foreign companies) seems quite Utopian in the nearest future, bearing in mind the huge expenses involved in designing, testing, development and construction of such monsters.

Further work of the Russian design bureaux will presumably proceed under the conditions of tough competition from Western countries having greater financial resources at their disposal. To quote Dr. Sc. A. Maskalik, one of the designers of the Amphistar WIG vehicle: *'Yes, we still retain advanced positions in the construction of* ekranoplans, *but Western contenders are now making their presence more and more acutely felt. If no urgent measures are taken, we can lose this advantage completely'*. Hopefully this is not going to happen.

In the following chapters the reader will find a description of the most significant designs of WIG vehicles created in Russia (when dealing with the Soviet period, mention is made of designs evolved in other republics of the USSR, notably in the Ukraine and the Baltic republics). Separate chapters are devoted to the most prominent design bureaux in this field, while the concluding two chapters deal with designs emanating from enthusiasts, scientific institutions and less important design bureaux. However, the range of types covered here is by no means exhaustive.

The author feels that a few words are called for to explain the terminology used in this book. The terminology pertaining to the subject under consideration, both in English and in Russian, is still in the making, showing a number of variations of some basic terms. In some cases, Russian terms have no direct equivalent in English. Therefore the author deems it necessary to mention here his personal preferences in translating some basic definitions and notions.

The subject of this book is a new means of transport associated with ground effect, or surface effect. Accordingly, the generally accepted English term for the machines in question is 'wing-in-ground-effect vehicle', with such variations as 'wing-in-surface-effect vehicle', 'wing-in ground (surface) effect craft'. These terms are often abbreviated to WIG vehicles (craft), less frequently WIGE vehicles. However, we also have the American term 'wingship', and one can encounter such variations as 'WIG aircraft', reflecting the uncertainty as to whether one should regard the new means of transport as *fish* or *fowl*. In addition, the Russian term 'ekranoplan', (pronounced *ekranoplahn*), sometimes spelled 'ekranoplane', has received a measure of currency in some English-language publications. Its use in Russian publications reveals some variations in the understanding of the word by different authors. Generally it is understood to cover all types of WIG vehicles, but sometimes it is used restrictively with reference to vehicles operating in ground effect only, as distinct from the Russian term '*ekranolyot*' which refers to WIG vehicles capable of operating also out of ground effect and especially to those capable of high-altitude flying.

The author has chosen to make use basically of the term 'wing-in-ground-effect vehicle', or 'WIG vehicle', with variations as appropriate, but occasionally the reader will encounter the Russian words '*ekranoplan*' and '*ekranolyot*' reflecting the style and usage of Russian official documents. Some difficulty arises in translating the term '*ekranolyot*'. Translating it as 'WIG **aircraft**', while technically correct, can be ambiguous, since this term sometimes covers the general notion of WIG vehicles. Therefore it was considered wise to adapt translation to the context and to make use, where appropriate, of the modern IMO classification of Type A, B and C vehicles.

Much emphasis has been placed in the recent years on putting the simplest WIG vehicles operating exclusively in ground effect (Type A vehicles) on the same footing with ships in terms of certification. This has resulted in Russian terminology such as '***kahter-ekranoplahn***' (WIG boat) or '***soodno na dinamicheskoy vozdooshnoy podooshke***' (dynamic air cushion vessel), as distinct from a '*real ekranoplan*' which is supposed to possess at least a measure of ability to fly out of ground effect.

In describing the powerplants of WIG vehicles, the Russian terminology makes wide use of the word '*poddoov*' which means 'blowing' and is usually rendered descriptively as directing (deflecting) streams of air or jet efflux gases beneath the wings for the purpose of forming a static air cushion under them for take-off. In Western parlance, this is often rendered by such terms as power-augmented ram air cushion (PAR) etc. Engines installed in a WIG vehicle specially for this purpose are termed variously as assisted take-off engines, lift engines or booster engines (the latter term is used in the book). These are only examples of the variations that can be encountered.

With all the aforesaid in mind, I hope the reader will forgive minor inconsistencies in terminology that may eventually be found in this book.

Acknowledgements

The author would like to thank Keith Dexter, Sergey M. Ganin, the EKIP Concern, the ATT and ATTK Joint Stock Companies and the Wingship Airlines Joint Stock Company for the materials used in the making of this book, and Yefim I. Gordon, Gennady F. Petrov and Pavel G. Tkachenko for the photos they kindly supplied.

Special thanks go to Gennady Petrov for his line drawings, to Dmitriy V. Griniuk for the excellent photos on pp. 29, 113-119 and 124 and to Helmut Walther for his valuable photos from Nizhniy Novgorod (pp. 34-36, 40, 121-122 and 126-127).

Finally, the author thanks his son Dmitriy for his assistance in the technical preparation of the manuscript for publishing.

The SM-6 experimental *ekranoplan*, another Alexeyev product.

The famous Orlyonok, one of only two military WIG types so far to reach operational service. Note the similarity in layout to the SM-6 on the preceding page which was a proof-of-concept vehicle for the Orlyonok.

Chapter 1

Alexeyev, the Pioneer

Standard-Setting Designs

The history of the establishment and development of this design bureau has been presented in the introductory chapter. Here follows a description of its designs.

Vehicles in the SM series
At the initial stage of the work on WIG vehicles in the Central Hydrofoil Design Bureau several light machines were built under the common designation SM (*samokhodnaya model'*, self-propelled model), individual designs bearing a succession of numbers from 1 to 8. They were proof-of-concept vehicles used to check the surface effect and evolve technical features which came into use later when design was started of WIG vehicles intended for practical operation.

SM-1
This machine was built in 1961, making its first flight on 22nd July. It had two sets of wings arranged in tandem and fitted with endplates. The front wings of rectangular shape had ailerons/flaps, the aft wings were of trapezoidal planform and were mounted at virtually the same height as the front wings. The aft wings were fitted with an elevator on their trailing edges. The vehicle had a length of 20 m (65 ft 7½ in), the wing span being 10.3 m (33 ft 9½ in), and a take-off weight of 2,830 kg (6,240 lb). A turbojet engine with no cowling but with a funnel-shaped air intake was mounted on top of the fuselage behind a three-seat open cockpit. Successful tests of the SM-1 corroborated the basic concept of flight in close proximity of a supporting surface. A speed of 200 km/h (124 mph) was reached; stability and controllability characteristics during flight close to the supporting surface (water, snow-covered stretches of land) proved to be satisfactory. Yet the tests revealed insufficient seaworthiness and excessively high take-off and landing speeds. The latter may be regarded as one of the main drawbacks of the tandem layout, another being the vehicle's excessive sensitivity to unevenness of the supporting surface.

Above: The SM-1 during trials. Note the open cockpits, the uncowled engine and the auxiliary fin immediately ahead of it.

In January 1962, during one of the test flights, the SM-1 soared into the air of its own accord, leaving the ground effect zone, and then 'fell through', impacting the ice, when the pilot shut down the engine. The machine was damaged and the crew sustained minor injuries. That brought the SM-1's testing to an end – the machine was not repaired.

SM-2
This machine built in 1962 was initially fitted with two wing sets arranged in tandem. It was damaged by a hangar fire before the trials could begin and reworked in the process of

The SM-2 skims along the water surface before becoming airborne. Note the pitot intake of the forward engine. The vertical tail appears disproportionately large in this view.

Above and below: The SM-2 in wing-borne flight, showing the nozzle of the rear-mounted cruise engine. The curved strakes on the aft fuselage underside were probably meant to improve the hydrodynamic properties.

restoration to feature an aircraft layout. This aero-hydrodynamical layout with one set of wings, a T-tail and a device for power-augmented take-off was adopted for all subsequent vehicles designed in the Central Hydrofoil Design Bureau. The SM-2 served for studying the influence of take-off booster blowing devices on the take-off performance of WIG vehicles (such a device was used by R. Alexeyev on the SM-2 for the first time in the world practice). The booster engine located in the forward fuselage was fitted with bifurcated flattened nozzle extensions placed wide apart on both sides of the fuselage; they directed the jet efflux under the wings. Initially it also served as a cruise engine, but the thrust of the bifurcated nozzles proved insufficient, and a separate cruise engine was fitted in the aft fuselage under the fin. Both engines were 900-kgp (1,984-lb st) Tumanskiy RU19-300 turbojets in a 'marine' version featuring enhanced corrosion protection.

The WIG vehicle had a length of 20 m (65 ft 7½ in), a wing span of 11,5 m (37 ft 8¾ in), a take-off weight of 3,200 kg (7,055 lb) and a maximum speed of 270 km/h (167 mph). On completion of the testing the vehicle was upgraded: the swept-back wing leading edges were replaced by straight leading edges to improve the effect from blowing, resulting in a rectangular wing planform. In this version the vehicle was redesignated **SM-2P** (the P presumably stands for *priamougol'nyoye krylo* – rectangular wings).

Thanks to the lift augmentation (blowing) the take-off performance of the SM-2 was considerably improved as compared to the SM-1.

SM-3

This single-seat experimental machine built in 1962 was used for studying the aerodynamic layout with low aspect ratio wings. The wings of this WIG vehicle had a chord twice as big as on the previous machines, the aspect ratio being a mere 0.48. An unorthodox device for blowing under the wing was used: the air bled from the compressor of the RU19-300 engine placed in the forward fuselage was ejected through nozzles located along the wing's leading edge on its lower surface. Thereby an efflux curtain was created along the entire leading edge. The machine with an all-up weight of 3,400 kg (7,500 lb) had a cruising and maximum speed of 140 and 180 km/h (87 and 112 mph) respectively.

SM-4

This three-seat machine built in 1963 as a derivative of the SM-3, differed in having two engines – a booster engine and a cruise engine. The booster engine located in the front fuselage was fitted with steerable nozzles for directing the jet efflux under the wings. The flattened nozzles stood proud of the fuselage sides. The cruise engine was located in the aft fuselage; placed in its efflux was a gas rudder for directional control at low speeds. The tail unit featured a fin of reduced area with a small rudder. An additional all-movable vertical control surface was mounted on the forward fuselage. The wings fitted with endplates were attached to the boat hull-type fuselage in its centre portion; they were rectangular in planform and had an aspect ratio of 2. The wing flaps were divided into two sections and were spring-loaded to reduce the loads created during contact with the water. Two pilots sat in two separate cockpits staggered vertically; a third open cockpit in the rear was intended for a test engineer. The machine had an all-up weight of 4,800 kg (10,580 lb) and developed a speed of 140 km/h (87 mph) in cruise flight, the maximum speed reaching 230 km/h (143 mph).

SM-5

Built in 1963, this machine was a 1/4th scale analogue of the giant KM WIG vehicle. The SM-5 had wings of rectangular shape with endplates and spring-loaded flaps divided into several sections. The boat-type fuselage had planing steps on its lower surface and was hydrodynamically shaped with a view to ensuring good seaworthiness. The enclosed crew cockpit was located in the front fuselage; placed behind it was a booster engine with pivoting nozzles on both sides of the hull which directed the jet efflux under the wings. The cruise engine was placed ahead of the fin, its air intake occupying a position above the fuselage over the wing centre section The engine's bifurcated jet nozzle flanked the sides of the fin. The tail unit was T-shaped. The rudder ran along the whole of the fin's height and its lower portion placed below the waterline served as a water rudder. The vehicle had an AUW of 7,300 kg (16,100 lb); the cruising and maximum speeds were 140 and 230 km/h (87 and 143 mph) respectively.

In August 1965 the SM-5 crashed after being caught in a powerful head-on gust of wind. The vehicle banked abruptly and pitched up. Instead of throttling back the engines, the pilots gave them full throttle for climb, but the machine, leaving the ground effect zone, lost stability, banked and impacted the water surface. The crew were killed. This was the first fatal crash of a WIG vehicle in the SM family.

SM-6

Despite its sequence number, this experimental machine was built after the SM-2P7 and the SM-8 machines, making its appearance in 1972. It was intended for studying the problems of aero- and hydrodynamics and strength, as well as for developing technical features for the Orlyonok heavy troop-carrier/assault WIG vehicle which was later evolved from the SM-6. Its powerplant comprised three engines: an Ivchenko AI-20 turboprop engine driving a four-bladed AV-68 propeller for cruise, mounted atop the fin, and two booster/cruise turbojet engines in the nose. Their location anticipated precisely the powerplant layout of the future Orlyonok. Like its bigger stablemate, the SM-6 featured a normal aerodynamic layout of a boat-hulled low-wing aircraft with a T-tail. As distinct from other machines in the SM series, it had more harmonious aircraft-like contours. The airframe was made of steel and AMG-61 aluminium/magnesium alloy and was protected from corrosion by a special coating and by electrochemical devices. The fuselage was of beam-and-stringer construction. The hull

The SM-3 moves across a snow-covered field. Like most of the vehicles in the SM series, it looked pretty hair-raising! This view illustrates well the extremely wide chord of the wings.

Above: The SM-6 was, in effect, a subscale prototype for the future Orlyonok. It is seen probably just before touchdown; the hydroskis (equipped with wheels for taxying on the ground) are visible under the forward fuselage and wing centre section.

Despite the fact that the SM-6 sports a different side number (6M79) in this view, it is still the same craft; the number was changed to 6M80 to confuse would-be spies. And the last two digits do NOT denote the year, the sole SM-6 having been first flown in 1972!

Above: Of all the vehicles in the SM series the SM-6 had the most aesthetically pleasing, aircraft-like forms. This view shows well the powerplant arrangement with the dorsal 'nostrils' of the booster engine air intakes and the dorsal exhaust of the AI-20 cruise engine. Note how the turbojets are angled outwards.

The SM-6 in cruise flight. Note how the pressure of the dynamic air cushion 'irons out' the waves while the vortices from the wingtips generate characteristic trails on the water.

Above: The SM-6 in relatively high-altitude flight (for a WIG vehicle of this class); the tell-tale wake on the water surface is almost gone. Note that the booster engines are equipped with special six-lobe nozzles – probably serving the same purpose as the 'hushkits' on the BAC One-Eleven.

The SM-6 comes out onto the shore under its own power, waves washing over the top of the wings.

The SM-8 was a subscale analogue of the KM vehicle. Except for the dorsal excrescences, from a distance it looked extremely similar to its 'big brother'. The purpose of the 'smokestack' mounted above the wing leading edge remains unknown. The full-length rudder acts as a water rudder when afloat.

bottom was shaped by steps and by two hydro-skis to which the main and nose undercarriage units were attached. At an all-up weight of 26,500 kg (58,430 lb) the vehicle had a cruising speed of 350 km/h (218 mph).

SM-2P7

This single-seat vehicle was built in 1964 for studying take-off and landing performance, problems of stability of flight over a supporting surface and the possibilities of optimising the aerodynamic layout of a single-engined WIG vehicle. The SM-2P7 was a development of the earlier SM–2P in which the nose-mounted RU19-300 engine was replaced by an Izotov KR-7-300 turbojet with a thrust of up to 2,000 kgp (4,409 lb st). It served both as a booster and a cruise engine. Hot gases generated by the engine passed through a row of nozzles placed parallel to the wings' leading edge within approximately half of the span. Nozzle deflectors served for directing the jet efflux under the wings in the blowing mode during take-off. The rectangular wings of the SP-2P7 had an aspect ratio of more than 2.4; they were fitted with spring-loaded multi-section flaps and endplates. The machine had an all-up weight of 6,300 kg (13,890lb); the performance included a cruising speed of 130km/h (80 mph) and a maximum speed of 270 km/h (168mph).

SM-8

The SM-8 WIG vehicle built in 1967 became the second 1/4th scale analogue of the KM *ekranoplan*; it reflected the changes introduced into the layout of the KM in the course of its design. The SM-8 became the last in the family of SM experimental flying vehicles, the tests of which furnished results essential for the creation of theory and for evolving the methods of designing and developing new models of heavy WIG vehicles for military and civil applications. The testing of the SM-8 proceeded in parallel with the testing of the KM; the analogue served for checking the methods of testing its bigger stablemate.

The SM-8, having an all-up weight of 8,100 kg (17,860 lb), was powered by one turbojet located in the upper part of the fuselage ahead of the fin. Its air intake was protected from spray by a special U-shaped guard. To emulate the blowing (booster) engines of the KM, the SM-8 was provided with a special nozzle device in the front fuselage intended to direct part of the gases bled from the engine under the wings. The vehicle had a cruising speed of 220 km/h (137 mph).

The construction and testing of the SM series (SM-1 through SM-8) were directly connected with the creation of designs that marked the apex of the Central Hydrofoil Design Bureau's achievements – the vehicles known as KM, Loon' and Orlyonok. Therefore it would be logical to give the description of these designs here. Descriptions of later machines in the SM series will be given separately.

KM

In 1963, in response to an order placed by the Navy, construction was started at the 'Volga' shipyard near Gor'kiy (now Nizhny Novgorod) of a gigantic WIG vehicle which was designated KM (*korahbl'-maket* – 'mock-up ship', or rather prototype ship). It was a machine of staggering dimensions, the length of the hull exceeding 90 m (295 ft). It was launched in March 1966 and the first flight took place on 18th October of that year. Further testing of the WIG vehicle took place on the Caspian Sea. Its optimum flight altitude in ground effect proved to be 4 to 14 m (13 to 46 ft). At that time the KM (sometimes referred to as KM-1 in Western sources) was the biggest flying vehicle in the world – its weight in one of the flights reached 544 tonnes (1,299,300 lb)! Small wonder that it was nicknamed 'Caspian Sea Monster' in the West (later some Russian journalists, too, deciphered KM as *Kaspeeyskiy monstr*). This huge machine was powered by 10 Dobrynin VD-7 turbojets with a thrust of 13,000 kgp

Above and below: The SM-8 in cruise flight. These photos show clearly the massive spray guard on the engine air intake, the bifurcated engine nozzle, the 'garden rake' immediately aft of the cockpit with nozzles emulating the KM's booster engines, the flap actuator fairings and the extreme dihedral of the tailplane.

The legendary Caspian Sea Monster – the mighty KM as originally flown with tail-mounted cruise engines. Note the tail number 04 White, one of several identities which the KM had during its flying career.

apiece; of these, two engines located at the fin leading edge served as cruise engines, while the remaining eight engines were mounted in two packages of four on the forward fuselage sides, performing the role of booster engines for power-augmented take-off. The machine reached a maximum speed of 500 km/h (310 mph), the cruising speed being 430 km/h (267 mph).

The KM had good manoeuvrability, stability and controllability; it could perform tight turns with large bank angles, the wingtip float touching the sea surface. This machine flew for 15 years and earned a reputation for being a very reliable means of transport. Unfortunately, in 1980 the KM crashed due to pilot error. The pilot, who had not been at the controls of the big machine for a long time, over-did the pitching-up at take-off. The machine began to rise steeply. Losing his head, the pilot throttled back abruptly and applied the elevator in a fashion contrary to flight manual. The winged ship started banking to port, impacted the water surface and sank; the crew escaped unhurt.

In the course of its testing the KM underwent a number of modifications some of which were rather substantial. For example, in 1979 the cruise engines placed on the fin were transferred to a pylon mounted over the forward fuselage so as to lessen spray ingestion. The cruise engines were provided with spray deflectors on the intakes.

Orlyonok (Project 904)

This troop-carrier/assault WIG vehicle designed in response to an order from the Navy made its first flight from one of the channels of the Volga river in 1972. After this, disguised as a Tupolev Tu-134 airliner, the prototype was transported on a barge to Kaspiysk (a naval base on the Caspian Sea) to be tested in sea conditions. It was the first WIG vehicle intended for speedy transportation of troops and materiel. Its cargo hold measuring 21 m (68 ft 11 in) in length, 3.2 m (10 ft 6 in) in height and 3.0 m (9 ft 10 in) in width made it possible to transport self-propelled vehicles that were on the strength of the Soviet Marines.

The Orlyonok features an aircraft layout. It is an all-metal cantilever monoplane with a fuselage provided with hydrodynamic elements in its lower portion (planing steps, hydroskis etc.); it has low-set wings and a T-tail with a horizontal tail of considerable dimensions. Its powerplant comprises two Kuznetsov NK-8-4K booster turbofans rated at 10,500 kgp (23,148 lb st) for take-off (provision was made for their eventual replacement with 13,000-kgp/28,660-lb st NK-87 turbofans) and one 15,000-ehp NK-12MK cruise turboprop (a version of the NK-12M used on the Tu-95 bomber) driving AV-90 eight-blade contra-rotating propellers. All the engines are maritime versions of the respective aircraft engines. The booster engines are fitted with special pivoting nozzles and used not only for creating an air cushion on take-off by directing their efflux under the wings (blowing mode) but also for acceleration to cruising speed. The air intakes of the NK-8-4K engines are blended into the contours of the forward fuselage, which reduces drag and helps protect the engines from corrosive sea spray. The cruise engine is located at the junction of the fin and horizontal tail; being placed so high, it is less vulnerable to spray ingestion at take-off and landing and to salt contamination from aerosols whose density depends on the height over the sea surface.

The fuselage of the Orlyonok is of beam-and-stringer construction; it is divided into three sections – forward, centre and aft. The centre fuselage accommodates the cargo hold accessed by swinging the hinged forward fuselage 92° to starboard. The hinged part of the fuselage houses the flight deck, the booster engines and a radar in a 'thimble' radome. The aft fuselage houses a compartment for auxiliary power units and accessories required for starting the main engines and operating the vehicle's electrical and

Above: The KM at a later stage of the trials, now sporting the tail number 07 White. Note the hinged flaps on the booster engine nozzles directing the efflux under the wings during take-off and the heat-resistant panels at the top of the rudder protecting the skin from the hot efflux of the cruise engines.

The KM cruises at full speed, kicking up almighty plumes of spray. Interestingly, the cruise engines are fitted with spray guards while the booster engines are not at this stage of the programme.

Above: WIGs of a feather flock together? The SM-6 and the KM off the Caspian Sea coast, with the latter craft's cruise engines uncowled for maintenance. The people crawling over both machines like ants illustrate the sheer bulk of the KM; note that the tail number has been changed *again* (to 08 White).

A harbour tug tows the KM in its ultimate configuration to the pier. This picture shows the cruise engines relocated to a pylon above the flight deck, as well as the large span of the horizontal tail. Note that the booster engines have been retrofitted with spray guards.

hydraulic systems. Placed dorsally on the hull are a turret with twin cannons, the antenna of a navigation radar, direction finder aerials, communication and navigation equipment aerials. To reduce shock loads in the take-off and landing mode the designers introduced hydroskis shaped as simple deflectable panels. The craft is equipped with a wheeled undercarriage intended for beaching the machine and rolling it along paved taxiways on the shore.

The low-set wings of trapezoidal planform comprising an integral centre section and outer wing panels of torsion-box construction are fitted with flaperons. The lower surface of the wings along the leading edge, closer to the wing tips, incorporates special hinged panels which are deflected 70° during take-off. The wingtips carry floats doubling as endplates. The wing high-lift devices are used for creating an air cushion which lifts the vehicle out of the water. During take-off the efflux of the jet engines is directed under the wings; the pilot lowers the flaps and leading-edge panels, thus barring the way for the gas tending to escape fore and aft. The increased gas pressure under the wings lifts the machine out of the water. The main part of the wings, with the exception of the flaps and leading-edge panels, is manufactured watertight. The wing is divided into 14 watertight bays, two of which are used for fuel.

The sharply swept T-tail comprises a fin/rudder assembly and large-span stabilisers with elevators.

Here are some basic characteristics and performance figures: the machine measures 58.1 m (190 ft 7 in) in length and 31.5 m (103 ft 4 in) in wing span, the width and height of the hull being 3.8 m (12 ft 6 in) and 5.2 m (17 ft) respectively; it has an all-up weight of 125,000 kg (275,600 lb) and an empty weight of 100,000 kg (220,500 lb). The Orlyonok's maximum speed is 400 km/h (249 mph), the cruising speed being 360 km/h (224 mph). The height of flight over the supporting surface can vary from 0.5 m to 5 m (1 ft 8 in to 16 ft), the optimum height being 2 m (6 ft).

To relieve the crew workload in flight, provision is made for automatic stabilisation of the altitude (by deflecting the flaps), the pitch angle (by deflecting the elevators), the heading (by deflecting the rudder) and the bank angle (by deflecting the ailerons).

In addition to the first prototype which crashed in 1975 (see details below), an initial batch of three Orlyonoks was manufactured; they were adopted for squadron service by the Navy and underwent evaluation from 1979 onwards. Each of the three examples had its own factory designation; these three Project 904 machines were designated S-21, S-25 and S-26 (as can be seen on photos, the machines were serialled 21 White, 25 White

Above: The prototype of the Orlyonok assault/transport WIG vehicle in cruise mode. The booster engine intakes are well visible, as is the large span of the horizontal tail.

Unlike all subsequent Orlyonoks, the prototype sported a civil-style blue/white colour scheme.

Above: A full frontal of the Orlyonok prototype on its hardstand. From this angle the vehicle has a squat and rather ungainly look. The photo shows well the eight-bladed AV-90 contraprop of the cruise engine and the wing leading edge camber.

and 26 White for the greater part of their service career). In the Navy they were known as the MDE-150, MDE-155 and MDE-160 respectively (MDE presumably means *morskoy desahntnyy ekranoplahn* – sea-going transport and assault WIG vehicle). They were taken on charge by the Navy on 3rd November 1979, 27th October 1981 and 30th December 1981 respectively. The Naval Command presumed that the WIG vehicles would demonstrate high effectiveness (considerable speed and ensuing capability for surprise actions, capability for overcoming anti-assault obstacles and minefields) and would ensure the seizure of bridgeheads at a coastline defended by the enemy. There were plans in hand for manufacturing 11 Orlyonok (Project 904) machines during the 12th and 13th five-year plan periods (1981-1990), to be followed by the construction of transport and assault WIG craft of a new type (with a new project number) possessing greater cargo carrying capacity. Preparations were made for establishing a WIG vehicle-operating unit in the Red Banner Baltic Fleet. However, for several reasons these plans did not come to fruition. The Orlyonok WIG craft were doomed never to leave the Caspian Sea.

Initially they were operated by the specially established 236th Squadron of WIG vehicles within the brigade of transport and assault ships of the Red Banner Caspian Flotilla. Later an idea cropped up of transferring the WIG vehicles under the authority of headquarters of the Naval Aviation, but these plans met with much opposition on the part of the latter. An end to these disputes was formally put by Order No. 0256 issued by the Minister of Defence on 12th November 1986

This is how the Orlyonok's forward fuselage swings open for loading and unloading. Note the folding vehicle loading ramps, the twin-cannon dorsal turret immediately forward of the fuselage break point, the weather radar in a thimble radome and the pylon-mounted 'saucer' of the navigation radar.

Above: The Orlyonok prototype before touchdown with the rear hydroski fully deployed. Interestingly, the entry doors are not marked externally.
Below: The prototype caught by the camera in a banking turn. Note that the Soviet Navy flag has been painted on the tail, revealing the craft's true owner.

Above and below: Two fine air-to-air studies of the Orlyonok in its element. Note the APU exhaust at the base of the rudder, the HF aerial 'sting' pointing aft from the fin top and the phoney circular markings around the entry doors (which in reality are not circular at all).

Above: The Orlyonok prototype sweeps past a Soviet Navy frigate (side number GKS-13) standing at anchor.
Below: The Orlyonok puts to sea in a flurry of spray... and comes out onto a sandy beach to disgorge troops (opposite page, bottom).

Above: A Soviet BTR-60PB eight-wheel armoured personnel carrier is about to roll off the Orlyonok. This view shows the design of the double-hinged loading ramps, the overhead actuating cylinder and the many securing clamps around the hatch perimeter; the latter is natural, considering the high stresses in the area.

Above: 'Eagle eyrie' at Kaspiysk, with two of the three production Orlyonoks undergoing routine maintenance (the one nearest to the camera wears its original serial 610 White). Note the open overwing entry doors; the doors probably served for troop disembarkation during assault operations.

under the terms of which *ekranoplans* became part of the aviation element of the Navy's Fleets. The document prescribed that WIG vehicles, as well as aircraft and helicopters, must be regarded as a class of the Naval Aviation's weaponry. In accordance with directive No. DF-035 dated 21st April 1987 the WIG craft operating unit, renamed 11th Air Group, was formally placed under the command of the Black Sea Fleet, albeit it retained its former base on the Caspian Sea – the town of Kaspiysk.

The incorporation of the WIG vehicles into the normal activities of the armed forces was not trouble-free and was not pursued all too vigorously. Much time was spent on repairs and modernisation (albeit the machines were almost brand-new!). There were difficulties with crew training. By 1983 four crew captains had received sufficient training; all of them had previously flown the Beriyev Be-12 Chaika ASW amphibian. Up to 1984 crew training was undertaken in accordance with the 'Temporary course for training the crews of *ekranoplan* ships' prepared by the combat training section of the Navy. Later the manual was reworked with participation of the combat training section of the Naval Aviation.

In 1983 GNII-8 VVS (State Research Institute No. 8 of the Air Force) joined in the test-

The same base at a later date, with all three production Orlyonoks on the hardstand; left to right, the S-26 (26 White), S-25 (25 White) and the ill-starred S-21 (21 White). Interestingly, the S-25 and S-26 are painted a lighter shade of grey than the first production machine.

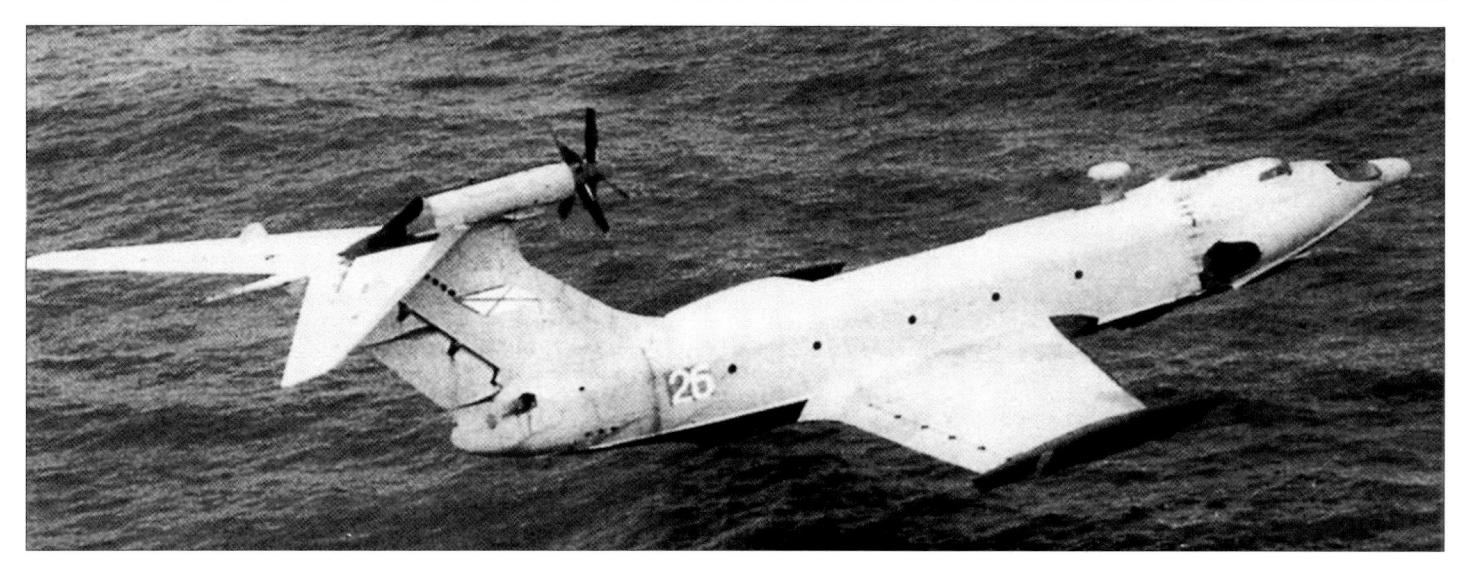

Three shots of Orlyonok '26 White' in action sometime in the 1990s; note the Russian Navy's St. Andrew's flag on the tail replacing the original Soviet Navy flag.

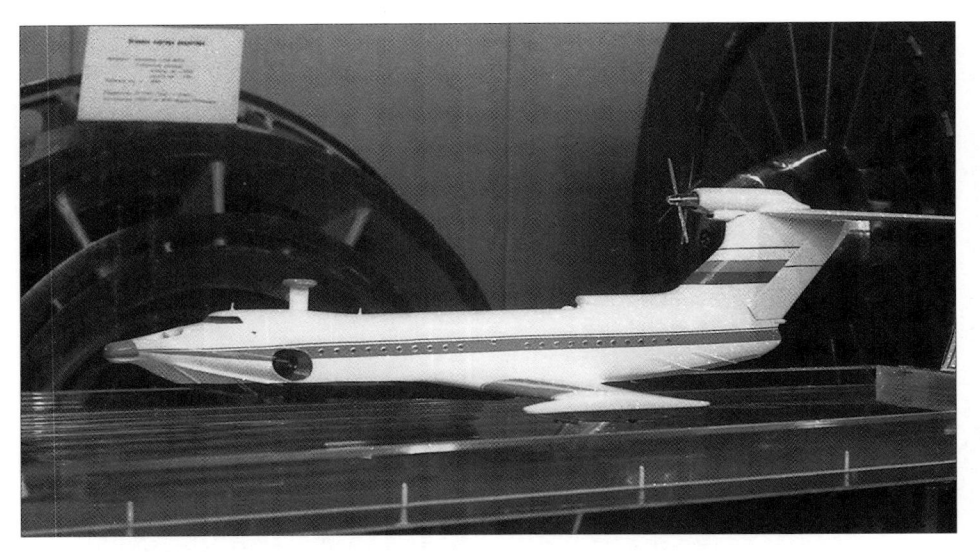

Above and below: This model of a passenger version of the Orlyonok was displayed at the MAKS-93 airshow, complete with water basin with artificial waves. Note the fat dorsal fairing ahead of the fin.

ing of one of the Orlyonoks. This was done in response to a request from the Naval Aviation headquarters, albeit without much enthusiasm. The institute justifiably reproached the developers of the WIG vehicle for having prepared an operation manual for the crew without the participation of test pilots. Its form and contents were quite out of keeping with the standards to which operation manuals for crews of aircraft and helicopters were prepared. There were also other complaints and remarks.

Unfortunately, mastering the new hardware was not free from incidents and crashes.

In 1975 the prototype *ekranoplan* undergoing tests beached on a rocky sand-bank. Blowing from the booster engines made it possible to lift it off from the rocks and safely return to base, but the episode did not go unpunished. The hull of the prototype machine was made of K282T1 alloy which, while possessing sufficient strength, was on the fragile side. Obviously the contact with the rocks left its traces – cracks in the aft fuselage which went unnoticed at the time. In the course of one of the subsequent trials, when the craft made a touch-down in rough seas, the aft fuselage broke off. Chief Designer Rostislav Ye. Alexeyev, who was on board, reacted instantly by taking over the controls and managed to bring the crippled machine in planing mode safely back to base (the consequences of this episode for the Chief Designer are described in the introductory chapter).

On 12th September 1992 another crash occurred, this time accompanied by a loss of life. The first production Orlyonok with the factory designation S-21 left its base in Kaspiysk to take part in preparations for a demonstration of Russian WIG craft to foreign guests who were to include representatives from the US Aerocon company. While cruising at 350 km/h (217 mph), the Orlyonok suddenly began to pitch down. To parry this, the crew captain gave full throttle to the cruise engine and hauled back on the control stick. As a result, the machine soared in a steep climb. Having reached a height of 40 m (130 ft), it stalled and crashed into the sea, bounced, pulled up a second time and impacted again, sustaining severe damage. Of the ten crew on board nine persons survived, albeit with injuries, and were eventually rescued. The tenth crew member – a flight engineer – was killed. The crippled Orlyonok drifted 110 km (60 nm) and was eventually blown up – the Russian Navy could not afford the price asked for its retrieval by salvage companies. It was presumed that the crash had been caused by a failure of the automatic stability system, although pilot error is also cited.

After this the remaining WIG complement of the Navy came to include two Project 904 machines (Orlyonok) and one Project 903 craft (Loon') which is described later in this chapter. Quite clearly, for many they were a thorn in their flesh. Gradually, the *ekranoplans* began to sink into oblivion – there were many other things to think of. The vehicles gradually fell into disrepair to the point of no longer being airworthy. Finally, in 1998 the command of the Russian Navy issued an order requiring the Orlyonok WIG vehicles to be written off on account of their alleged unsuitability for repairs and refurbishment.

The Orlyonok served as a basis for several versions intended for civil applications. These include the following projects.

Sea-going passenger WIG vehicle
This variant fully retained the basic configuration of the baseline Orlyonok, differing only in being demilitarised and fitted out in accordance with the new tasks. Here are its basic performance characteristics: normal take-off weight, 125 t (275,000 lb); maximum TOW, 140 t (308,000 lb), payload, up to 20 t (44,100 lb) in cargo configuration, 150 passengers in passenger configuration or 30 passengers and 17 t (37,480 lb) of cargo in a mixed configuration; cruising speed, 350 km/h (217 mph); range, up to 1,500 km (930 miles); wave height during take-off and landing, 1.5 m (5 ft) at normal TOW or 0.5 m (1 ft 8 in) at maximum TOW.

A.90.150
This designation has been applied loosely in Western sources to both a projected passenger version and to the baseline Orlyonok. As a passenger version, according to Russian sources, it is intended to carry 100 to 150 passengers in single-deck configuration and 300 passengers in a double-deck variant. It was presumed that it could serve regular passenger routes, transporting up to 150 passengers, or be used as a passenger/cargo transport for speedy delivery of goods and shift crews to offshore oil rigs, fishing vessels and Polar research stations (the latter case involved landing on ice). With a powerplant identical to that of the baseline version, it has a take-off weight of 110-125 t (242,500-

Above: An artist's impression of a projected geological prospecting version of the Orlyonok known as Gheofizik (Geophysicist) or MAGE (the acronym means 'sea-going Arctic prospecting WIG vehicle').

The Gheofizik in action, moving at low speed and towing what appears to be a submerged sensor array supported by buoys. Note the rear doors used for loading and deploying the sensors.

275,000 lb), a cruising speed of 400 km/h (249 mph) and a range of 2,000 km (1,240 miles).

Orlyonok-P

This is a passenger version of Orlyonok with new composite wings ('P' presumably stands for *passazheerskiy* – passenger, used attributively). A model of the craft shows new outer wing panels of smaller chord and higher aspect ratio added to the main wings outboard of the endplates/floats. This is expected to give the Orlyonok-P a lift/drag ratio that is one-third higher than that of the basic model; its fuel consumption will be on a level with that of advanced aircraft now under development.

The basic specifications and performance of the Orlyonok-P are as follows: displacement (take-off weight), up to 140 t (308,640 lb); payload, 40 t (88,180 lb); range, 2,000 km (1,240 miles); speed, 375 km/h (233 mph), seaworthiness at take-off and landing, sea state 4; crew, 6.

Sea-going cargo WIG vehicle

This was a 'demilitarised' version of the baseline troop transport and assault Orlyonok, retaining its loading feature – the forward fuselage swinging to starboard. It is capable of transporting 30 t (66,000 lb) of cargo to a distance of 1,000 km (620 miles), the maximum range being 2,000 km (1,240 miles). Cruising speed is 400 km/h (249 mph).

MAGE

This sea-going Arctic prospecting WIG vehicle (MAGE = *morskoy arkticheskiy gheologorazvedyvatel'nyy ekranoplahn*) differs from the baseline Orlyonok not only in having the armament and troop-carrying equipment deleted, but also in some structural details. The aft fuselage houses a propelling device for slow-speed motion when afloat – a propeller screw in an annular duct driven by a diesel engine. The aft fuselage features clamshell doors and houses special equipment which permits the machine to take samples of ground from the sea bed and perform prospecting with the use of seismoacoustic, magnetometric and gravimetric methods.

The MAGE is also known as Gheofizik (Geophysicist).

SAR WIG vehicle

This version is intended for search and rescue work for the benefit of the merchant fleet and the Navy, for delivering rescue teams to accident and natural disaster sites in the vicinity of offshore drilling rigs, platforms and inhabited places at the coastline, as well as for rendering assistance to people affected by these disasters and evacuating them from those places. With a crew of 16, including pilots, rescue workers and medical attendants, the machine can take on board 95 rescuees (up to 150 in an emergency).

Mriya/Orlyonok Aviation and Maritime Search-and-Rescue System

This SAR system was evolved by the Alexeyev Central Hydrofoil Design Bureau together with the Antonov Design Bureau. Its task consists in detecting the accident site on the sea surface, performing rescue work and rendering the necessary assistance to people in distress. The system comprises the An-225 Mriya (Dream) carrier aircraft and the Orlyonok WIG vehicle carried on top of its fuselage. The overall weight of the system is 610 t (1,345,000 lb).

Once an accident has been reported, the An-225 with the Orlyonok attached to it 'piggy-back' takes off, heading for the area where the accident has happened. In the vicinity of the accident site the Orlyonok starts its engines and detaches itself from the carrier aircraft, making a gliding descent to the water surface where it alights. According to the project plan, the Orlyonok was to be fitted out with special equipment enabling it to render urgent medical aid and accommodate up to 70 survivors. In accordance with the designers' concept five systems making part of a unified SAR complex would be located in different areas of the world's oceans. This international complex was expected to cover virtually all major maritime traffic routes, fishery areas and areas of off-shore oil and gas extraction. Since both component parts of the SAR complex had already been created and had undergone operational trials, it was presumed that creation of such a system would be less costly than establishing other similar systems. However, a prerequisite for putting such a plan into effect was the setting up of an international rescue service. Unfortunately, this project was not put into practice.

Loon'

In the late 1980s the work of the Central Hydrofoil Design Bureau on WIG vehicles intended for military application led to the creation of a unique machine – a missile strike *ekranoplan*. Bearing the manufacturer's designation 'Project 903', it was subsequently named *Loon'*, which means 'hen-harrier' (according to some sources, it was initially named *Ootka* – 'duck', but this sounded totally unwarlike and could also be interpreted as 'canard', ie, something bogus). This machine with an all-up weight of 380 t (838,000 lb), a hull length of 73 m (240 ft) and a wing span of 45 m (148 ft) was launched in 1987. Its design was based on the layout which had already been tried and tested on such vehicles as the KM and the Orlyonok, that is to say, the 'aircraft' layout – that of a monoplane with wings of trapezoidal planform and a T-tail.

The Loon', however, differed a lot from its predecessors – the entire powerplant comprising eight 13,000-kgp (28,660-lb st) Kuznetsov NK-87 turbofans was located on the forward fuselage. Thus, the engines served both as booster (blower) engines and cruise engines. This was apparently associated with another special feature of the machine – the placement of its offensive armament. Mounted dorsally on the fuselage were six launch containers for 3M80 *Moskit* (Mosquito) supersonic anti-shipping missiles (NATO code name SS-N-22) developed under the guidance of Aleksandr Ya. Berezniak. During the launch of these missiles there was a risk of the combustion products being ingested by engines previously placed high on the tail unit, which could cause the engines to flame out. Transferring all the engines into the forward fuselage eliminated this danger.

As distinct from the low-wing Orlyonok, the Loon' had mid-set wings; otherwise, they were similar to those of its predecessor and were of multi-spar metal construction which was made watertight. Placed on the bottom of

This reasonably accurate artist's impression of the Loon' appeared in the *Soviet Military Power* brochure published by the US Department of Defense.

Above: The Loon' missile strike WIG vehicle in cruise flight, clearly showing the three paired launch tubes for 3M80 Moskit anti-shipping missiles with associated blast deflectors and the fin-mounted guidance system array. The defensive armament, complete with gunner's stations, was borrowed from the IL-76M transport.

the hull was a hydroski device intended to cushion the impact when alighting on water.

The Loon' was equipped with a radar for air and surface targets detection and with a navigation radar, as well as with an ECM suite. The defensive armament consisted of two gunner's stations borrowed directly from the Il'yushin IL-76M military transport, each with a UKU-9K-502 turret mounting two 23-mm (.90 calibre) Gryazev/Shipoonov GSh-23 double-barrelled cannons.

The machine's performance included a maximum speed of 500 km/h (310 mph), a cruising altitude of 5 m (15 ft) and a range of 2,000 km (1,240 miles). It had an endurance of 5 days when afloat. The vehicle had a crew of 15.

Armed with Moskit anti-shipping missiles, the WIG vehicle flying at ultra-low level at a speed of 350-400 km/h (218-249 mph) could deal a devastating blow to the potential enemy's naval units and leave the scene unimpeded. According to Russian press reports, *'the Project 903 ekranoplan No. S-31 underwent operational testing in 1990-1991'*. In the course of this trial operation live missile launches were made from the onboard launch tubes, as testified by available photos. The machine met the design requirements, but it was ill-fated. Initially, in line with the provisions of directive No. 252-73 issued by the Communist Party Central Committee and the Soviet Council of Ministers on 26th March 1980, the programme of warship construction envisaged the completion of four Project 903 machines in the 12th and 13th five-year plan periods (1981-1990); later the planned figures were increased. Plans were in hand for the construction of six Project 903 WIG vehicles

The Loon' fires a Moskit missile in cruise flight. It is easy to see why the designers chose to mount all eight engines on the forward fuselage.

Above: A model showing a project version of the Spasatel' search and rescue WIG vehicle based on the Loon'. Note the fin root fillet, fuselage spine and the fin top location of the navigation radar.

Above: A cutaway model of the Spasatel' as actually built, showing the straight fin leading edge. It was displayed at one of the Hydro Aviation Shows in Ghelendzhik.

The former second Loon' in the assembly shop of the Volga shipyard in Nizhniy Novgorod, nearing completion as the prototype of the Spasatel' SAR craft.

up to 1995 and another four machines of this type before 2000. However, in the late 1980s there came a change of heart towards the WIG vehicles in the command of the Navy. In 1989 it was decided to limit the construction of the attack WIG machines to just one example. A decision was taken to convert the second example of the Loon', then under construction, into a SAR vehicle.

As for the sole example of the Loon' combat *ekranoplan*, it was withdrawn from service and is stored in Kaspiysk. According to one document, *'in order to preserve the missile-armed* ekranoplan, *the Commander-in-Chief of the Navy took a decision providing for its preservation at the territory of the 11th Air Group and for transforming it into an air base (for storage of the* ekranoplan), *with one crew complement to be retained at the base'*.

Spasatel' (Rescue Worker)

The second example of the Loon' attack *ekranoplan* ordered by the military was 80 per cent complete when the work was stopped and the machine was preserved with an imminent prospect of being scrapped. However, it was saved from that fate through a conversion for civil use. Research performed on the Loon' airframe in 1990-91 confirmed that this machine possessed a considerable potential for conducting search and rescue work. In 1992 a plan cropped up in the Ministry of Defence, providing for the conversion of this machine into a SAR WIG vehicle for the benefit of the Navy. A technical project was prepared, and work was started at the 'Volga' shipyard in Nizhniy Novgorod with a view to converting the second Loon', then under construction, into the Spasatel' (rescue worker, pronounced *spasahtel'*).

The equipment suite of this machine (Project 9037) enabled it to transport anything between 150 and 500 persons. The volume of internal compartments was such that it could take 700 to 800 persons on board and remain afloat in a stormy sea waiting for aid to come. This vehicle can take off and alight in sea state 5; the rescue means can be deployed directly on its wings. The project provides for an onboard hospital with a surgery room and an intensive therapy ward, as well as a separate place for special treatment needed by those affected by radiation during nuclear power-plant accidents, or by fire or chemical burns. The idea was that improved WIG craft of the 'Spasatel' type could become the basis of a world-wide SAR system that could be set up under the auspices of the United Nations.

Seven crew members (apart from the medical personnel) had their accommodation in a cockpit in forward fuselage, while the navigator and a team of rescue workers sat in an aft compartment at the top of the fin affording an excellent, nearly all-round view. The crew was to be provided with inflatable boats, ladders and other rescue means suited for actions under the conditions of a stormy sea. It was envisaged that the Spasatel' would leave the assembly shop in 1994, but the work tempo was slowed down owing to insufficient funding from the Ministry of Defence, and for some time the project was, in fact, 'put on ice'. In December 2001 a press report appeared stating that construction of the Spasatel' was approaching its completion – under the influence of a number of tragic accidents such as the demise of the SNS *Komsomolets* (K-178) and RNS *Kursk* (K-141) nuclear submarines and of the M/V *Estonia* car ferry a decision was taken to speed up the construction of this vehicle capable of providing urgent relief in the event of a marine disaster. According to reports, the testing of the Spasatel' was expected to begin at Lake Ladoga as early as 2002, given a favourable course of events.

Further Designs in the SM series

SM-9 Ootka (Duck, or canard)

This was an experimental WIG vehicle featuring a canard (tail-first) layout with the horizontal tail mounted on the front part of the hull. A photo shows it to be a single-seat machine with an open cockpit and a tractor propeller in an annular shroud located in the elongated nose part of the fuselage. The fuselage rests on wings of rectangular shape and low aspect ratio, each outer wing panel being supported by a float attached at mid-span rather than at the tip. In addition to the canard horizontal

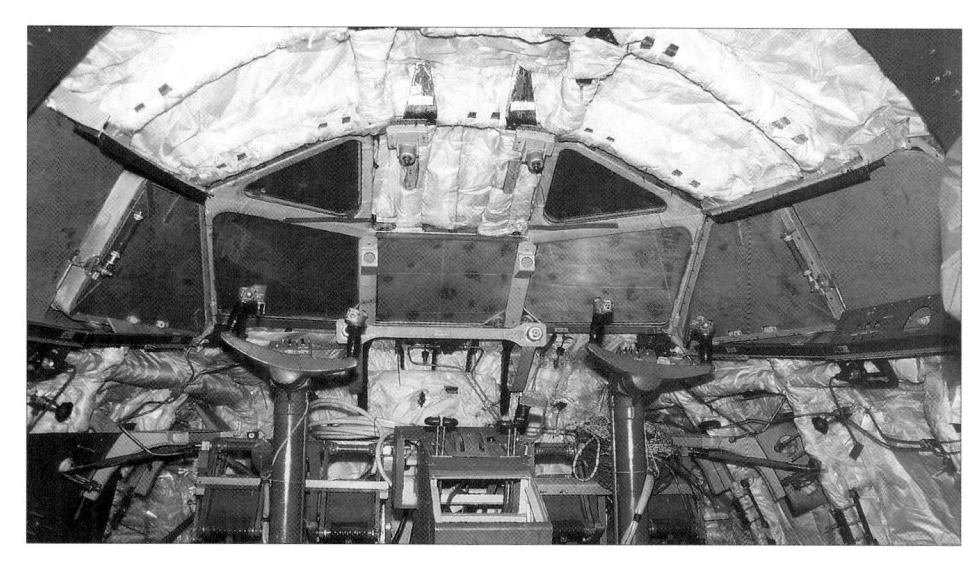

Above: The flight deck of the unfinished Spasatel', showing the aircraft-type control columns. All avionics and instrument panels have yet to be installed.

Above: The outer wing panels of the Spasatel' are temporarily attached to the top of the fuselage and temporary floats mounted on the wing stubs, allowing the craft to be towed through narrow channels.

The tail unit of the Spasatel' (minus the outer portions of the horizontal tail), showing the fin-top navigator's station/'crow's nest'. Note the upward-hinged tailcone allowing rescue rafts to be launched.

Above: Poachers beware! ...or what? The SM-9 experimental WIG vehicle bore Rybnadzor *(Fisheries Control Agency) titles. Too bad the agency still does not have fast craft of this kind in its inventory.*

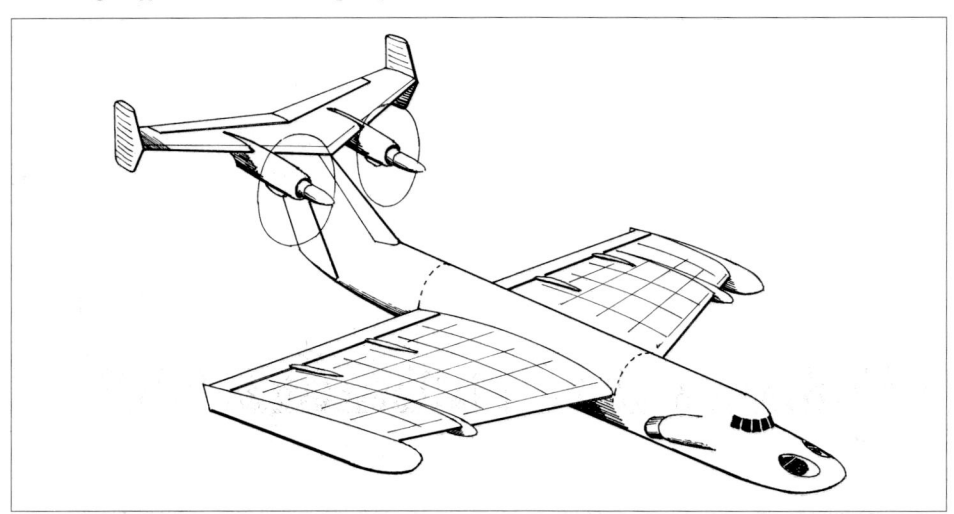

An artist's impression of the T-1 transport/assault WIG vehicle. The drawing does not reveal the location of the loading door, though the same solution as on the Orlyonok was probably envisaged.

surfaces, the machine is provided with a normal horizontal tailplane with endplates resembling turned-down tips. Placed atop the horizontal tailplane are two fins with rudders. The vehicle carries the inscription '*Rybnadzor*' (Fisheries control). According to the IMO classification, the SM-9 is a Type B vehicle capable of operating out of surface effect for brief periods for the purpose of avoiding obstacles.

The SM-9 was designed and built in 1977. R. Alexeyev used this vehicle, and later the SM-11, for research aimed at enhancing the lift/drag ratio of WIG vehicles. He took the 'flying wing' layout featuring a wing with an aspect ratio that was rather high for a WIG vehicle (around 5). By selecting an optimum airfoil section and making use of automatic oscillation damping and stabilisation systems he tried to solve the problems of stability of flight in ground effect for this new layout. However, a positive solution for 'flying-wing' WIG vehicles was not reached at the time.

The main specifications of the SM-9 are as follows: crew, 1; length, 11.14 m (36 ft 7 in); span, 9.85 m (32 ft 4 in); height, 2.57 m (8 ft 5 in); all-up weight, 1,750 kg (3,860 lb); cruising speed, 120 km/h (75 mph).

SM-11
Little is known about this machine, designed and built in 1985. According to some sources this was a Type B WIG vehicle capable of leaving the surface effect zone for brief periods. In its layout it was similar to a prospective 'flying wing' WIG vehicle with double sweepback on the leading edges but featured a T-tail of modest span with a cruise engine at the top and two tilting propellers (driven by another engine) on the forward fuselage sides. The machine was tested in the late 1980s, shortly before the break-up of the Soviet Union.

Here are some specifications: crew, 1; length, 6.96 m (22 ft 10 in); span, 9.94 m (32 ft 7 in); all-up weight, 600 kg (1,320 lb); cruising speed, 110 km/h (68 mph).

WIG Vehicles for Military Purposes – Projects that Failed to Materialise

ASW WIG vehicle
Project work on this machine weighing 450 t (990,000 lb) was started in 1962, but the design did not reach the hardware stage. No other information is available.

T-1
This project of a troop transport and assault WIG vehicle was under development in 1964. Judging by a published drawing, it was a big machine featuring an aircraft layout. The wings fitted with endplate floats had a fairly high (for a WIG vehicle) aspect ratio; the tail unit was T-shaped. The powerplant comprised two booster engines in the forward fuselage arranged in the same fashion as those of Orlyonok, and two cruise turboprop engines. The latter were located in an unorthodox manner – they were mounted at mid-span on the leading edges of the two halves of the horizontal tail which was fitted with small endplates.

Patrol WIG vehicle
This machine of moderate size featured an aircraft layout and was powered by two turbojets mounted in the forward fuselage. They performed the double role of booster engines during take-off and cruise engines in forward flight.

Projects 1133 and 905
As noted in a Russian reference book on he country's arms, 1996-1997, an armament programme envisaged at one time the development of strike, ASW and troop-carrier WIG vehicles (Projects 903, 1133 and 905 respectively). Of these, only the Project 903 (Loon', see above) was built.

Joint Project of the Central Hydrofoil Design Bureau and the Aerocon Company (USA)

In early 1992 negotiations took place between the Alexeyev Central Hydrofoil Design Bureau and the American Aerocon company on joint development of a new WIG vehicle. The Aerocon company had been set up at the initiative of DARPA (Defense Advanced Research Project Agency) – an agency working for the US military. Aerocon was tasked with establishing co-operation with the Russian organisation holding leading positions in WIG vehicle construction, with the intention of borrowing advanced Russian technology. Aerocon had

An artist's impression of a projected fast patrol craft using WIG technology – one of several projects developed by the Central Hydrofoil Design Bureau which never reached the hardware stage.

received from DARPA a contract worth US$ 546,000 for investigating the concept of a WIG vehicle.

At that time the experts of the US Central Command (CENTCOM) seriously considered the possibility of employing a WIG vehicle in combat. To bring down the cost of creating the WIG machines, US military specialists made a provision for the development of a civil version. The project envisaged the construction of a giant machine possessing an all-up weight of 5,000 t (11,000,000 lb) and a cargo-carrying capacity of 1,500 t (3,310,000 lb), which would be able to transport 3,000 passengers or 2,000 troops with full military equipment and materiel. The powerplant comprising 20 turbojets with a static thrust of 395 kN each was expected to give the machine a cruising speed of 800 km/h (497 mph) and a range of 16,000 km (9,900 miles) in cruise flight at a height of 2-10 metres (6-33 ft) above the water surface.

This cooperation did not progress far and was terminated without resulting in the emergence of a detailed project.

Chaika-2 (Seagull II)

This is a project for a sea-going multipurpose WIG vehicle. Its baseline model was to be developed into a family of shore- or water-based WIG vehicles intended for various duties. Their possible missions include border control, patrolling the 200-mile maritime economic zone, SAR work, passenger and cargo transportation, ecological and legal maritime monitoring.

The machine shares the 'aircraft' layout characteristic for the progeny of the Alexeyev Design Bureau, a novel feature being the composite wings with swept outer wing panels of narrower chord – an unusual arrangement. The powerplant comprises two 4,500-kgp (9,900-lb st) Tumanskiy (Gavrilov) R-195 booster turbojets and two 2,500-ehp Klimov (Izotov) TV7-117S turboprop engines for cruise, each driving an Aerosila SV-34 six-bladed propeller. The booster engines used for blowing under the wings during take-off are arranged in a fashion similar to that of the Orlyonok. The cruise engines feature an

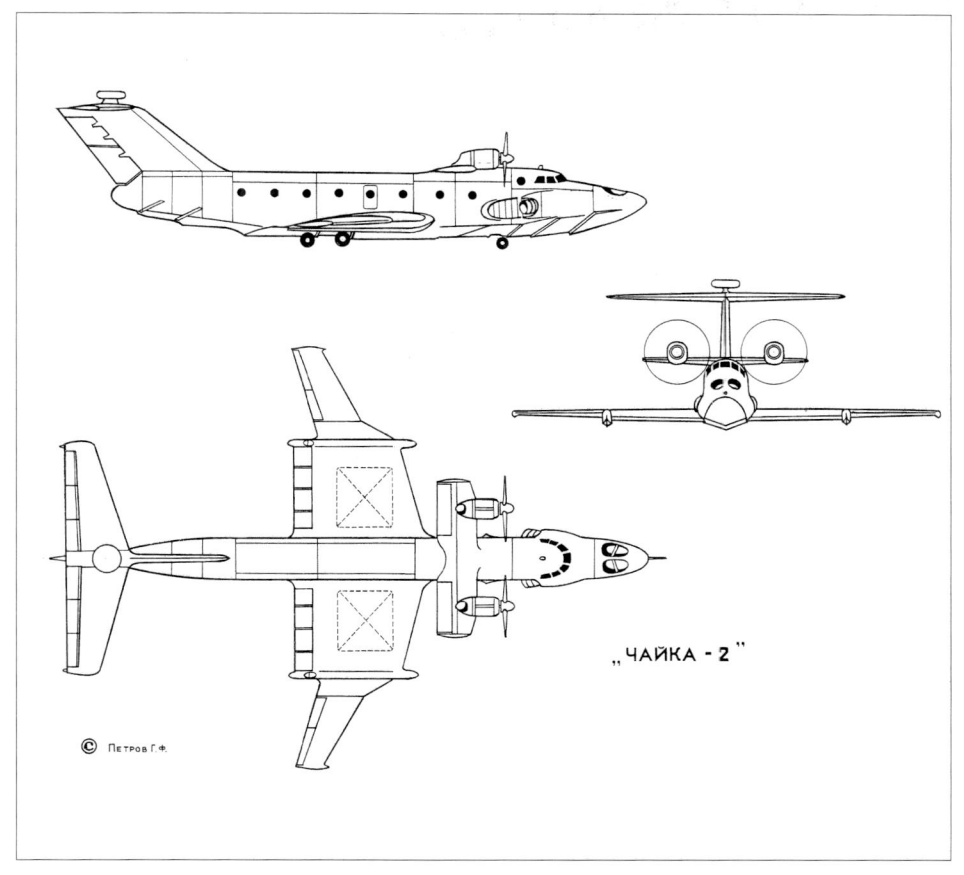

One of the possible configurations of the Chaika-2 multi-purpose WIG vehicle.

Above: An artist's impression of a large ocean-going passenger craft similar to the Loon' in general arrangement – the WIG equivalent of a Boeing 747.

This projected 'WIG airliner' has an unusual arrangement, combining Orlyonok-type buried cruise engines and fin-top cruise turboprops with additional nose-mounted turbofans à la Loon'.

unusual arrangement: instead of being placed on the fin they are carried on small foreplanes mounted on top of the forward fuselage. Specifications include an all-up weight of 40 to 50 t (88,200 to 110,250 lb), a payload of 4 t (8,800 lb), a seating capacity of 100 passengers, a speed of 350 km/h (218 mph) and a range of 3,500 km (2,175 miles). A different project configuration has an almost biplane-like layout, featuring vertically staggered tandem wings, the tips of which are connected by endplates, and two booster/cruise turbofans pylon-mounted on the forward fuselage sides.

Projects for Sea-going Passenger WIG Vehicles

In addition to passenger versions of the baseline Orlyonok design described above the Central Hydrofoil Design Bureau prepared several more projects of sea-going passenger ekranoplans. Details follow of some of these projects.

Chaika (Seagull)

This project is described as 'the first passenger WIG vehicle design' of the Alexeyev Design Bureau and is known only from a published drawing which shows a machine generally similar in its layout to the Orlyonok with its low-set wing and a T-tail. A notable difference is the absence of a cruise engine on top of the fin; it appears that two engines buried in the forward fuselage are intended to serve both as booster engines at take-off and as cruise engines, their nozzles rotating to suit the flight mode.

MPE

The Central Hydrofoil Design Bureau worked on a number of projects bearing a common designation MPE (*morskoy passazheerskiy ekranoplahn* – sea-going passenger ekranoplan). They include a project of a machine designed to carry 250 passengers and adaptable to various uses; also envisaged was the development of a 450-passenger machine possessing a speed of 550 km/h (342 mph), a range of 6,000 km and a capacity for operating at a sea state with waves 3 m (10 ft) high. It appears that some of these projects were 'inherited' by a new design bureau known initially as 'Technology and Transport' which broke away from the 'mother' organisation in 1993. Projects developed now under the name of this new organisation include the MPE-100, MPE-200, MPE-300, MPE-400 etc. (see Chapter 6, a section dealing with this company under its new name 'Amphibious Technologies and Transport').

In 1996 mention was made in the Russian press of a baseline project of a sea-going WIG vehicle weighing some 50 t (110,250 lb) which was being developed in the Central Hydrofoil Design Bureau with a view to subsequent construction on its basis of various versions intended both for state agencies and for commercial operation (this may well be a reference to the Chaika-2 design).

Type A WIG Vehicles (*ekranoplan Boats*, DAC Boats) designed by R. Alexeyev and the Central Hydrofoil Design Bureau

In the late 1970s R. Alexeyev realised that for a number of reasons it was not possible to launch series production of full-fledged *ekranoplans* (Type B and C craft, in the modern classification) for commercial service. Instead, he suggested to his associates that they take up design work on simpler craft – dynamic air cushion (DAC) ships which, as distinct from the 'true' WIG vehicles, are intended for motion only in the horizontal plane, their vertical motion being reduced to the barest minimum (in modern classification they are designated Type A WIG vehicles). To study some basic questions pertaining to vehicles of this type, Alexeyev designed a small single-seat craft which was in fact a platform flanked by inflatable pontoons. The use of inflatable pontoons was a novel design feature which had some advantages as compared to rigid skegs or the flexible 'skirt' employed by ACV. The machine was propelled by a tractor airscrew mounted ahead of the driver's seat.

Research vehicle for testing the layout of the future SM-10 WIG craft

One more machine intended purely for research purposes was required in connection with the design of WIG vehicles certified as ships (Type A). To study the basic layout of such a vehicle, a prototype machine (apparently without a special designation) was built. A photo shows this single seat vehicle to possess rectangular wings of very small aspect ratio, fitted with inflatable pontoons at the wingtips; placed in an open position above the wings was the pilot's seat protected by a nose fairing and a windshield. It was flanked by two engines buried in the wings and transmitting their torque through extension shafts to two tractor airscrews placed ahead of the wing leading edge and above it. The propellers had annular shrouds fitted with deflectors which directed the air stream under the wings during take-off. The twin fins were topped by a horizontal tail. Discernible in the picture is some sort of installation between the fins (possibly a third engine with a tractor propeller). The vehicle made a series of successful flights.

SM-10 (forerunner of the Volga-2)

The vehicle described above was developed into a bigger craft designated SM-10 and intended for carrying eight passengers and a driver. It was designed and built in 1985 as an analogue of the future production model – the Volga-2. Its specifications include: length, 11.43 m (37 ft 6 in); span, 7.63 m (25 ft); height, 3.32 m (10 ft 11 in); all-up weight, 2,200 kg (4,850 lb); cruising speed, 120 km/h (75 mph); range, 300 km (186 miles).

Volga-2 ekranoplan boat

This eight-passenger dynamic air cushion amphibious boat designed in the Central Hydrofoil Design Bureau and built at the 'Volga' shipyard in Nizhniy Novgorod in 1986 featured only minor differences from the SM-10. The vehicle is powered by two engines placed on the wings on both sides of the hull. These are series-produced 140 hp VAZ-413 Wankel-type gasoline engines with a mixed air/water cooling system. They transmit their power through extension shafts to four-blade shrouded propellers. The shrouds are fitted at their rear plane with remote-controlled horizontal deflector vanes which direct the airflow under the wings in the take-off mode. The vehicle features rectangular wings of low aspect ratio (1.0) fitted with endplates and inflatable pontoons at the tips which are provided with an inflation system and a pressure control device. Thanks to these pontoons the vehicle can be operated all year round: in the summer it operates from water and in the winter from splintered ice and sludge.

A T-tail serves for control and stabilisation of the vehicle. As distinct from the prototypes, the strut-braced stabilisers have small swept extra fins installed at approximately three quarters span on the production model. The wings are provided with flaps and spoilers.

The streamlined hull houses a passenger compartment with seats for eight passengers and a driver; the seats are of aircraft type.

The Volga-2 has the same dimensions as the SM-10 (see above). Other specifications include an all-up weight of 2,500 kg (5,500 lb), a top speed of 120 km/h (75 mph) and a range of 500 km (310 miles).

Above: An experimental dynamic air cushion boat, apparently with no separate designation, seen during trials on the Volga River. This craft was intended to test features developed for commercial DAC vessels.

Above: A proof-of-concept vehicle built for testing the wing/powerplant concept of the Volga-2 commercial DAC vessel. The German magazine Flieger Revue called it Ur-Wolga ('the ancestor of the Volga').

A Volga-2 – possibly the prototype – in cruise flight.

Above: Another prototype of the Volga-2 (or the same craft following modifications), featuring recontoured engine cowlings, though this is not yet the definitive shape. The tail unit is still unmodified.

Above: 07 Red, a production Volga-2, 'parked' on the bank of the Volga River in 2001 (note the Russian flag on the fin). The production version has additional vertical tail surfaces and reshaped engine cowlings.

In defiance of superstition this vehicle, a subscale analogue of the projected Raketa-2 passenger WIG, was designated SM-13. The three engines are well visible here.

The Volga-2 WIG vehicle was put into production at the 'Sokol' aircraft factory in Nizhniy Novgorod to meet an order from RAO Gazprom (a natural gas industry concern in Russia). By 2001 several machines had been delivered. In 1996 the Central Hydrofoil Design Bureau was engaged in designing various versions of the Volga-2, including sea-going and tropical variants.

SM-13

This experimental WIG vehicle was created for the purpose of studying the basic layout of a bigger design, the Raketa-2 *ekranoplan* boat, for which it served as a kind of scaled-down (one quarter scale) model. The SM-13 had rectangular wings of low aspect ratio with endplate floats at the tips. Sitting atop the low-set wings was the hull with a passenger compartment and a T-tail. The powerplant consisted of three piston engines, two of which were placed on both sides of the nose and one was mounted on the fin approximately half-way up. They were fitted with two-blade propellers. The machine successfully passed its test programme.

Raketa-2 (Rocket II)

In 1990 the Central Hydrofoil Design Bureau prepared on the basis of the Volga-2 layout the project of a bigger DAC ship called Raketa-2. This river-going vehicle was intended for transporting 90 passengers at a cruising speed of 120-130 km/h (75-81 mph) to a distance of up to 800 km (500 miles), the maximum speed being 150-180 km/h (93-112 mph). Its powerplant comprises three Klimov TV7-117 turboprops delivering 2,500 ehp (1,785 kW) each; two of them are mounted on the forward fuselage sides and serve as booster engines for take-off, while the third engine (for cruise) is mounted on the fin leading edge. The vehicle is capable of negotiating a gently sloping bank for the purpose of taking on and disgorging passengers or undergoing maintenance, which considerably simplifies it operation. Its maximum all-up weight is 33 t (72,770 lb).

Due to lack of funding this project remains on the drawing board to this day.

Raketa 2.2 (?)

This designation found in some Western publications purports to refer to a three-engined 90-passenger version of the vehicle as distinct from an original two-engine 50-seat version. Neither the twin-engined version nor the 'Raketa-2.2' designation are mentioned in available Russian sources which refer to the 90-seat vehicle simply as 'Raketa-2'.

Meteor-2, Kometa-2

These projects of river-going DAC ships have been only briefly mentioned in Russian sources. According to some Western publications, the Meteor-2 is a vehicle intended to transport 120 passengers at a speed of 170 km/h (106 mph) to a distance of 800 km (500 miles), while the Kometa-2 can carry 150 passengers at a speed of 185 km (115 mph) to a distance of 930 km (578 mph).

Vikhr'-2 (Whirlwind II)

This is a project of a large sea-going Type A WIG vehicle, about which little is known, apart from its general appearance (see drawing). According to a Western source, it has a seating capacity for 250 passengers, a speed of 280 km/h (174 mph) and a range of 1,500 km (930 miles).

UT-1 Trainer and Strizh Family of Light WIG Vehicles

The Central Hydrofoil Design Bureau has developed and, in part, brought to the hardware stage a number of projects of light WIG vehicles intended for various duties which carry the common designation Strizh (Swift, the bird) with varying sequence numbers. Their forerunner was the UT-1 two-seat training *ekranoplan* designed and built in 1968.

UT-1

The UT-1 (*oochebno-trenirovochnyy* – training, used attributively) was intended for familiarising pilots with the special features of WIG vehicle control and for providing instruction and training in all operational modes: during the take-off run and unstick, cruise flight in surface effect and alighting on water or a snow-covered even surface.

This machine with a wing span of 9.8 m (32 ft 2 in) used the aircraft layout with a T-tail and was powered by a single Walter M-332 six-cylinder in-line engine delivering 120-140 hp. It was Alexeyev's first machine to feature a water-ski impact-absorbing device. The UT-1 was used not only for training flights but also for investigating the out-of-surface-effect flight mode ('aircraft mode'). The results of these experiments were incorporated in the design of the Strizh.

Strizh

This WIG vehicle (chief designer V. Boolanov) was created in 1990 to meet the needs of training the crews for the military WIG vehicles taken on strength by the Navy. (According to one source, it also had the designation Project 19500). The machine can also be used for patrolling, liaison and business flying. The Strizh has two cockpits in a stepped-tandem arrangement with dual controls and identical sets of instruments. Thanks to a special aero- and hydrodynamic layout it has proved possible to ensure stable movement close to the supporting surface without making use of

Above: An artist's impression of the 90-seat Raketa-2 passenger dynamic air cushion vehicle travelling along one of the inland waterways.

Above: This idyllic scene shows how a river port would have looked, had WIG craft operations reached the intended scale. The type of craft is unknown (it is similar to, but obviously smaller than, the Raketa-2).

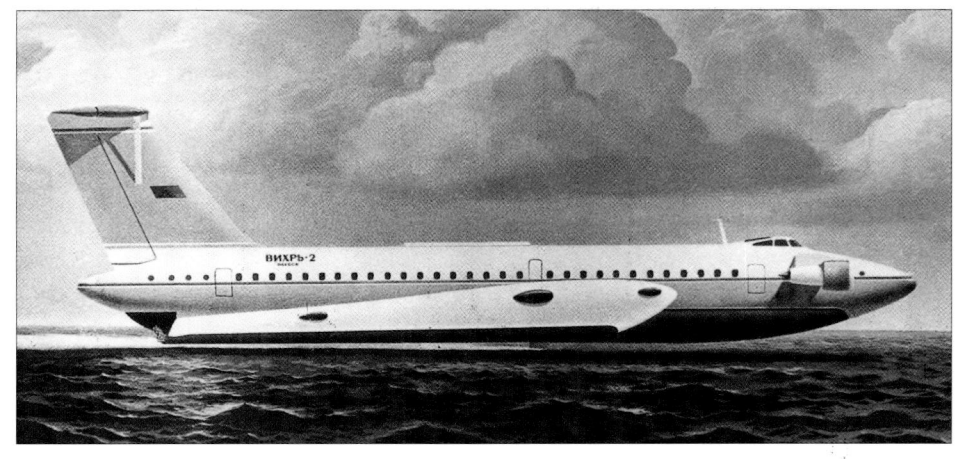

An artist's impression of the 250-seat Vikhr'-2 sea-going DACV.

Above: The tiny UT-1 WIG vehicle which served for training pilots in operational procedures. It is seen here flying over a frozen river.

Above: The UT-1 was the first Alexeyev design to feature a hydroski, which is clearly visible in this view as the craft soars.

The Strizh two-seat trainer shared the powerplant arrangement of the Volga-2, except for the shrouded propellers with movable vanes. The fairing aft of the rear cockpit is a flight data recorder housing.

automation. The Strizh possesses good manoeuvrability and controllability.

Here are some specifications of the Strizh. It is powered by two 160-hp VAZ-4133 water-cooled Wankel-type engines mounted on the wings. The five-bladed fixed-pitch propellers have a diameter of 1.1 m (3 ft 7 in); they are driven by shafts with universal joints via a single-stage reduction gear and an automatic coupling. With an all-up weight of 1,630 kg (3,600 lb) the machine has a maximum speed of 200 km/h (124 mph) and a cruising speed of 175 km/h (109 mph). Range with a passenger is 500 km (310 miles), the ferrying range is 800 km (500 miles). Flight altitude in ground effect is 0.3-1.0 m (1-3 ft). Take-off and landing can be performed with a wave height up to 0.5 m (1 ft 8 in).

A production version designated **Strizh-M** is powered by Voyager-300 engines delivering 220 hp apiece or by 175-200-hp Bakanov M-17 flat-four engines of the Voronezh Engine Design Bureau (VOKBM).

The basic layout and main design features of the Strizh were used in developing a family of small WIG vehicles for civil purposes with a flight weight ranging from 1.6 to 5 t (3,530 to 11,000 lb). It includes the following machines.

Strizh-3 (aka Kulik – Snipe)
The vehicle is powered by two 300-hp Zoche Munich aircraft diesels or two identically-rated VOKBM M-16 eight-cylinder petrol engines.

Strizh-4 (aka Baklan – Cormorant)
This machine is powered by two Lycoming TIGO-541E aircraft piston engines of 450 hp each or two TDA-450 engines.

Strizh-5
The type is powered by two Merlin aircraft diesel engines of 650 hp apiece.

Strizh-6
This is a project, currently under development, of a small sea-going WIG vehicle intended to carry 20 persons.

TAP
Since 1989 the design bureau had worked on a range of vehicles designated TAP (*trahnsportno-amfibeeynaya platforma* – transport amphibious platform). They utilise a gas dynamic cushion effect obtained by directing the efflux of forward-mounted jet engines under the flat bottom of the craft flanked by skegs. Unlike traditional WIG vehicles, the TAP remains in contact with the water or ice at all times and belongs to the ship class. Such craft displacing up to 800 t (1,763,600 lb) are intended for both civil and military uses. (See also the ATT company, Chapter 6.)

Chapter 2

Bartini: Bold Ideas

Italian-born Designer's Projects

Robert Bartini is a well-known aircraft designer of Italian descent who worked in the Soviet Union. He designed the Stal'-6 ('Steel-6'), Stal'-7, Stal'-8 and DAR aircraft which were built in prototype form; the Stal'-7 passenger aircraft served as a starting point for the Yermolayev Yer-2 bomber. Bartini authored a whole range of bold and unorthodox transport and combat aircraft projects, many of which were far ahead of their time. In addition to practical design work, he devoted much attention to scientific work in the aeronautical field, in which he achieved noteworthy results. At the final stage of his creative work Bartini devoted much attention to aerial vehicles making use of ground effect; he studied and evolved the theoretical basis for this new kind of means of transportation. It was Bartini who introduced into the Russian aeronautical terminology the term *ekranolyot* – a vehicle capable of flight not only in ground effect but also at considerable altitude over ground or water. The word *ekranoplan* was from the outset regarded as referring to vehicles flying at close proximity to a supporting surface. Bartini designed a number of flying vehicles which can be classed either as WIG vehicles proper (*ekranoplans* and *ekranolyots*), or as aircraft possessing certain features of WIG vehicles. This part of his design work, as well as his work in designing traditional aircraft, was to a large extent geared to military applications.

VVA-14 and 14M1P

In 1965 Bartini came up with the idea of building a VTOL amphibious ASW aircraft designated VVA-14 (*verti**kahl**'no vzle**ta**yuschaya am**fibi**ya* – vertical take-off amphibious aircraft; 14 was the number of engines). He envisaged the VVA-14 as *'having take-off and landing devices enabling it to operate without dependence on airfields, including operation from water and snow-covered surfaces, and permitting it to stay afloat for an unlimited time with the engines shut off, because drifting objects can be more easily camouflaged and are more difficult to detect'.* In accordance with the official specification laid down in directive No. 935-325 of the Soviet Council of Ministers and the Central Committee of the Communist Party dated 11th November 1965, he was to create an aircraft with two 8,700-kgp (19,180-lb st) Solov'yov D-30M turbofan cruise engines fitted with devices for thrust vectoring in the vertical plane, and a number of Kolesov RD36-35PR lift engines fitted with turbofan attachments. The vehicle was to possess a cruising speed of 650-750 km/h (404-466 mph) and a service ceiling of 10-12 km (32,810-39,370 ft). The practical range with a weapon load of 2,000 kg (4,410 lb) was to be within 4,000-4,500 km (2,490-2800 miles).

One of the specification points stipulated that the flying vehicle was to be capable of movement in ground effect for the purpose of achieving both greater range and greater concealment. This places the VVA-14 into the modern category of Type C WIG vehicles (*ekranolyots*), although Bartini did not use this term with reference to the VVA-14, and the aircraft mode was its main operating mode.

A model of the MVA-62 maritime VTOL amphibian which was the immediate precursor of the VVA-14. The aircraft has a similar general arrangement but is smaller and has swept wings and one cruise engine.

Above and below: A model of the second project configuration of the VVA-14 which looked almost like the actual aircraft. Note the shape of the nose with a conventional stepped windscreen and the floats which are mounted on telescopic struts.

Bartini and his associates chose for the VVA-14 a layout which differed very much from the aircraft layout adopted by the Alexeyev Design Bureau. Using modern terminology, one might call Bartini's layout the composite wing layout. The wing comprised a centre section of large thickness and chord (low aspect ratio) coupled with high aspect ratio outer wing panels placed outside the ground effect height. The wing centre section was flanked by sponsons which housed the take-off and landing device – inflatable pontoons giving the aircraft buoyancy. Thus, the water-based aircraft resembled a catamaran vehicle. The designer visualised his creation as capable of performing a prolonged flight with a high lift/drag ratio in ground effect and a flight with an acceptable lift/drag ratio at high altitude.

The VVA-14 was designed as a vehicle requiring no airfields for take-off. For this purpose it was to be fitted with twelve RD36-35PR lift engines, then under development in the Rybinsk Engine Design Bureau (RKBM) led by Pyotr A. Kolesov. The exhaust gases of these engines not only created vertical thrust but also formed an air cushion in the space beneath the wing centre section. The use of the air cushion effect made it possible to limit the thrust required for vertical take-off and landing to a value less than 1 in relation to the take-off weight.

Bartini's design bureau had no production facility of its own, therefore construction of the machine took place at the experimental production facility of Gheorgiy M. Beriev's design bureau in Taganrog. Construction of

Above: The first VVA-14, CCCP-19172 (airframe 1M), on wheels at Taganrog; a second example was also built but never flown.

two machines was initiated (only one of them was eventually completed). The RD36-35PR lift engines were not available at the stipulated time, nor were the floats; in consequence, a decision was taken to conduct testing without these engines and on a wheeled undercarriage (the machine was fitted with a bicycle undercarriage with outrigger struts). Registered CCCP-19172, the VVA-14 performed its maiden flight from a concrete runway on 14th September 1972. In the maiden flight the machine displayed satisfactory stability and controllability. Not until 1974 were the inflatable pontoons finally fitted, allowing the machine to be tested afloat. By mid-1975 the VVA-14 had made no less than 107 flights, but the lift engines were still unavailable. Finally, Bartini decided to relinquish the engines of the Kolesov design bureau, installing instead two Solov'yov D-30V booster engines flanking the forward fuselage of the 1M machine (the first of the two under construction), the way it was done in R. Alexeyev's WIG vehicles. This required stretching the fuselage by

The first flights of the VVA-14 were performed without the inflatable floats and lift engines. Note the smooth nose not unlike that of the Boeing B-29.

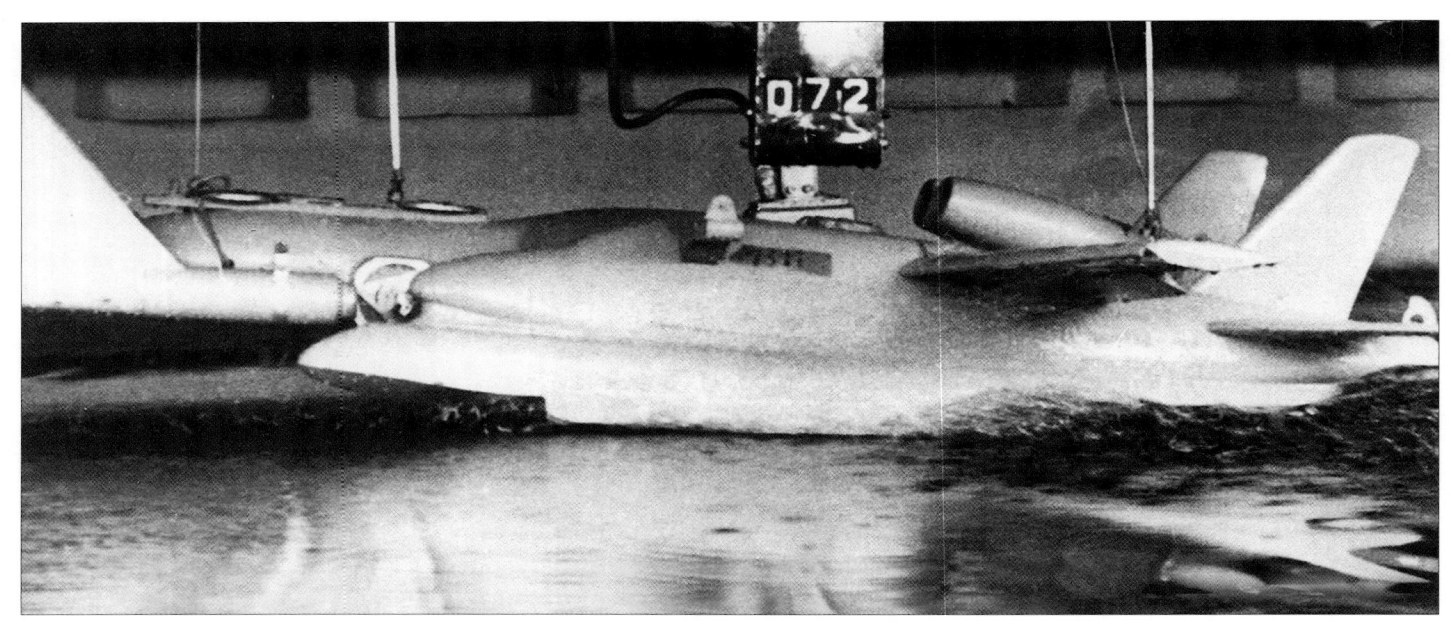

Above: A model of the 14M1P in the hydrodynamic towing basin of tsAGI, showing the floats and the nose-mounted booster engines.

inserting a cylindrical 'plug' immediately aft of the cockpit. The inflatable floats were replaced by rigid ones. The trailing edge of the wing centre section was fitted with flaps which, together with the wing centre section and the sponsons, formed a kind of 'scoop' in which the efflux of the booster turbojets created an air cushion. To enhance the effectiveness of the take-off and landing device, half-submerged skegs were mounted on the floats. The original bicycle undercarriage was replaced by a tricycle undercarriage with fixed main units mounted on the floats.

All these modifications were effected in 1976 after R. Bartini's death. The modified aircraft was no longer a VTOL machine, and the letters VVA were deleted from its designation; now it was called 14M1P. It was, in effect, a WIG vehicle in its own right.

Testing of the new machine started as pure frustration. The aircraft stubbornly refused to leave the ground during attempts to take off from a concrete runway. Trials on water proved unsuccessful as well. Successive modifications to remedy the situation proved to be a protracted affair, and the testing yielded no results that could satisfy the customer (the Soviet Navy) and the Ministry of Aircraft Industry. Gradually, the machine ceased to attract interest and work on it was abandoned.

Project T

This was the designation of a WIG vehicle design which was evolved by R. Bartini after the commencement of testing of the VVA-14. Project T was created on the basis of research associated with developing an aerodynamic layout of a future sea-going *ekranoplan*. Two

Another view of the 14M1P undergoing tests in TsAGI's towing basin. Note the measurement instrument on top of the forward fuselage.

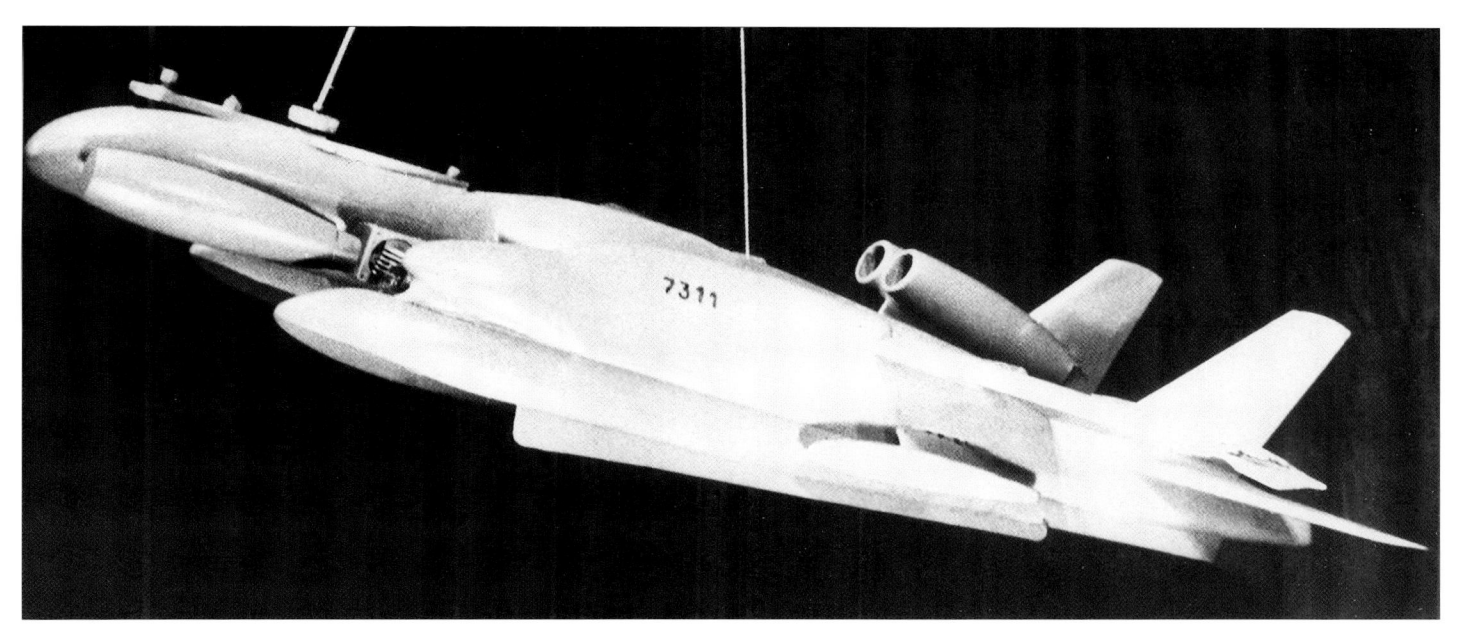

Above: A wind tunnel model of the 14M1P. The number 7311 does not mean '1973, experiment No. 11', since the 14M1P was developed in 1975.

versions of models were tested in the towing basin of TsAGI. Work was in full swing on both a military and a civil version. In the latter version the passenger compartments were placed at a good distance from the engines and accommodated in the wing centre section and in the two boat-like hulls flanking it; these provided buoyancy for the machine when afloat and helped form the air cushion for fuller ground effect. As can be seen on the available drawing, the Project T *ekranoplan* was a vehicle of catamaran layout with composite wings comprising a thick, low aspect ratio centre section coupled with outer wing panels of usual aircraft proportions possessing moderate sweepback. The outer wing panels featured leading edge root extensions. Four booster engines were mounted in pairs on pylons ahead of the centre section leading edge on both sides of the centrally mounted crew cockpit. Two turbojet cruise engines were placed on a pylon above the rear part of the wing centre section (the layout had obviously much in common with that of the VVA-14). Attached on the outside of the aft ends of the hulls were twin tail surfaces comprising horizontal tails and endplate fins and rudders.

The machine's basic specifications are as follows: wing span, 30.5 m (100 ft); length, 48 m (157 ft); all-up weight, 50 t (110,000 lb); payload, 20 t (44,100 lb); maximum speed, 550-650 km/h (342-404 mph), cruising speed, 370 km/h (230 mph). Bartini's death in December 1974 prevented the work on this machine, as well as on several other designs, from being completed.

Bartini considered WIG vehicles to be a very promising kind of aerial vehicles for use

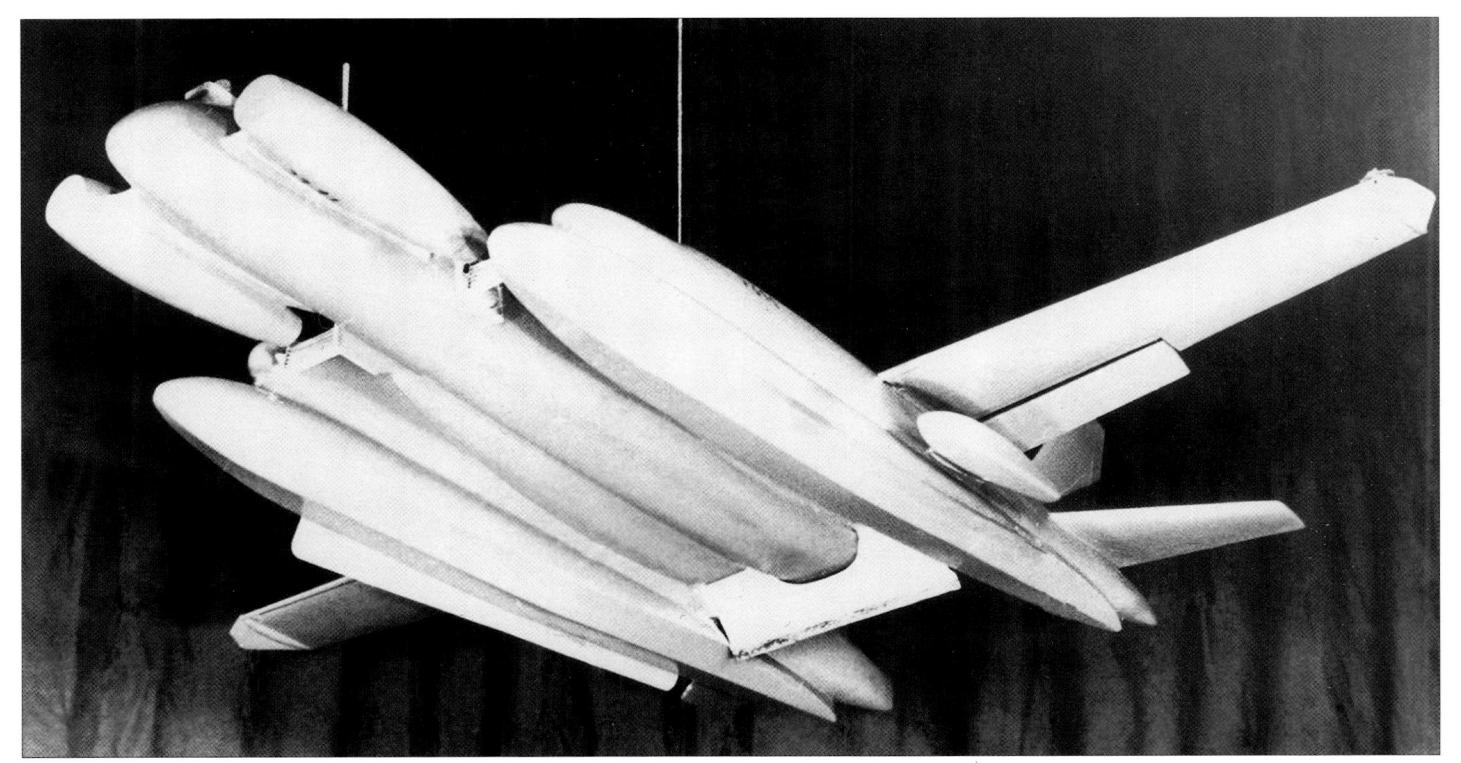

A lower view of the same wind tunnel model, showing the large flap between the floats/sponsons and the outward-canted strakes on the floats.

47

Above: The VVA-14 undergoes taxying tests on a grass strip in 1974. Note the rubberised fabric pontoons which are in deflated and retracted condition.
Below: The VVA-14 enters the water from the slipway in Taganrog with the pontoons inflated. Interestingly, the engine intakes are blanked off.

Above: Head-on view of the VVA-14 resting on the inflatable pontoons with the landing gear retracted. The aircraft appears particularly bizarre in this view.
Below: The aircraft in reverse configuration, standing on its wheels with the pontoons retracted. The undernose fairing may be provisions for a gun turret.

These stills from a cine film showing the VVA-14 in flight with the pontoons inflated (top) and deflated illustrate well the aircraft's unconventional lines. Note that the flaps are extended in the lower picture.

The VVA-14 afloat: taxying (above) and at rest (below). Note the circular escape hatch in the lower photo.

Above: Head-on view of CCCP-19172 in its ultimate form as the 14M1P *ekranoplan*, showing the new rigid floats and nose-mounted booster engines.

over the expanses of seas and oceans. Ghennadiy S. Panatov, the present leader of the former Beriyev Design Bureau (TANTK named after Beriev) noted in his report at a symposium dedicated to the 100th anniversary of Bartini's birthday: *'Bartini worked with enthusiasm on projects of giant ekranoplans and ekranolyots weighing several thousand tonnes and featuring the same basic layout as the VVA-14, on such projects as the OVA-62, PVA-70, SONA, OVA-120, on contact-free take-off and landing vehicles* (ie, vehicles with an air cushion undercarriage – Author) *– the T-2000, T-500, T-14, T-6, AER, EKhO-50 and others'*.

Concerning the T-500 and T-2000 we have the following evidence: *'In the course of the rapid development of design and construction of combat* ekranoplans *in our country in the 1960s and 1970s the concept of composite wing coupled with the use of booster engines found its worthy realisation (the 14M1P* ekranolyot *was designed and built, a contest was won for the creation of the T-500 and T-2000 heavy* ekranoplans*), and only Bartini's death and the subsequent perestroika and reforms in our country prevented these large-scale projects from being implemented'* (an excerpt from an article by V. Kolganov, a former associate of Bartini's, in the May 2000 issue of the *Kryl'ya Rodiny* (Wings of the Motherland) magazine).

Here is some information on some of Bartini's abovementioned projects involving the use of ground effect (sometimes in combination with an air cushion undercarriage):

T-6

T-6 was an agricultural aircraft powered by one Izotov TV3-117 turboshaft delivering 2,200 shp. The vehicle is similar to the VVA-14 in having composite wings with a wide-chord centre section and narrow-chord outer panels. The centre section housed six big fans enabling the vehicle to take off with a zero run: the T-6 was to lift off thanks to a static air cushion and then accelerate without contact with the ground, the take-off distance being 120-138 m (390-450 ft). The machine measuring 22 m (72 ft) in wing span and 14.2 m (46 ft 7 in) in length had a design all-up weight of 6,500-7,500 kg (14,300-16,500 lb) and a payload of 2,700-3700 kg (5,950-8,160 lb). The service ceiling was to be 3,000 m (9,840 ft). Presumably, when being operated for crop spraying it could make use of ground effect.

T-14

T-14 was a project of a cargo/passenger aircraft powered by three 1,500-kgp (3,306-lb st) Ivchenko AI-25T turbofans. Its layout was basically that of a WIG vehicle, featuring composite wings with a wide-chord centre section,

Rear view of the 14M1P, showing the rear end of the cruise engine nacelle. This makes an interesting comparison with the photo on page 55.

Above: The 14M1P makes a high-speed run in an attempt to get airborne from water. Note the boarding ladder attached to the nacelle of the starboard booster.
Below: The craft caught by the camera just as it starts accelerating, the cruise engines kicking up a plume of spray.

Above and below: The 14M1P is towed out to deep water. Note the absence of the teardrop fairings into which the outrigger struts retracted on the VVA-14; the pylons left over from these fairings serve as attachment points for beaching gear (the nose and main units are still there).

Above: A rear view of the 14M1P as it enters the water. Note that the cruise engines have been retrofitted with cascade-type thrust reversers.
Below: Another shot of the same craft on water.

Above: The object under the port wingtip of the 14M1P in this view may be a cine camera pod.
Below: Head-on view of the 14M1P under tow.

Above: A model of the single-fuselage version of the *izdeliye* T transport *ekranoplan* in TsAGI's towing basin.
Below: A model of another Bartini WIG projects making use of a static air cushion for take-off and landing; note the four large fans creating this cushion.

the lower surface of which, together with a pair of 'skegs', forms a kind of scoop for an air cushion created by blowing from two nose-mounted engines and then by forward movement of the aircraft. The third engine (a cruise engine) is mounted above the aft fuselage between the surfaces of the 'butterfly' tail unit. The cruise altitude is 6,000 m (19,700 ft), but ground effect mode is used for take-off and landing. The aircraft was supposed to lift off with a zero run and then accelerate at a distance of 500 m. The all-up weight was 15,000 kg (33,000 lb).

EKV-600

EKV-600 was a 'ground-effect speedboat' (presumably for sports use). Judging by the available drawing, this single-seat machine had a wing set of low aspect ratio with a straight leading edges and forward sweep on trailing edges. Two floats were attached to wingtips and protruded ahead of the leading edge. The noses of the floats were connected by a foreplane. Attached to the main wing centre section were outer wing panels featuring marked dihedral. The hull had a fin at its aft end. Flaps were presumably mounted at the trailing edges of the main wings. The available drawing gives no clue as to the type of the powerplant.

EKhO-50

EKhO-50 was described – presumably by Bartini himself – as 'ekrano*khod*', which can be broadly translated as a vehicle for movement (*khod*) in ground effect (*ekrahn* – supporting surface). The vehicle features a 'flying wing' layout (in the sense of this term as applied to WIG craft), ie, a rectangular platform possessing an airfoil section is flanked with endplate floats. The front part of the platform houses the crew compartment, the aft part carries a tail unit comprising two surfaces inclined at an angle of 45°. The vehicle is powered by four Izotov TV3-117 turboshafts delivering 2,200 shp each (no propellers are visible in the available drawing).

Basic specifications include: overall length, 36.0 m (118 ft); overall width, 21 m (69 ft); air cushion area, 330 m² (3,550 sq ft); all-up weight, 50 t (110,250 lb); payload, 29 t (64,000 lb); draught when afloat, 1.25 m (4 ft); height above the surface at cruising speed, 0.165 m (6.5 in); cruising speed, 130 km/h (80 mph); maximum speed, 150 km/h (93 mph); endurance, 8 hours; crew, 8 persons.

The results of the pioneering work conducted by Bartini in the field of WIG vehicles were 'inherited' by the Beriyev Design Bureau (currently TANTK named after G. M. Beriyev) under the auspices of which he worked during the last years of his life. His ideas are being followed up by this design bureau (see next chapter).

Above: A desktop model of *izdeliye* T in single-fuselage form, showing the shape of the floats.
Below: Possibly another configuration of *izdeliye* T featuring foreplanes and a butterfly tail.

Below: An artist's impression of another Bartini WIG project using three turbofan engines for blowing/cruise and possibly small lift jets for creating a static air cushion.

Chapter 3

Beriyev's Activities

Hydroplane versus *Ekranoplan*

Gheorgiy Mikhaïlovich Beriyev's design bureau, later transformed into the TANTK (*Taganrogskiy aviatsionnyy naoochno-tekhnicheskiy kompleks* – Taganrog Aviation Scientific and Technical Complex) named after G. M. Beriyev, is well known for its predominant role in the design of Soviet and Russian hydroplanes (mainly flying boats). This design bureau initiated its work on WIG vehicles in the early 1960s. This work comprised both scientific research in this field and practical design work. The latter included the development of several projects of ultra-heavy WIG vehicles and a project of an aircraft-carrier based on the use of ground effect (*ekranoplan* aircraft-carrier). These projects were evolved under the direction of A. G. Bogatyryov. Interestingly, the aircraft-carrier project, as well as several other WIG designs of this OKB, envisaged a combination of ground effect achieved on an airfoil wing with the use of hydrofoils. Enlisting assistance from TsAGI, the OKB studied a catamaran (twin-hulled) layout with hydrofoils for this aircraft-carrier project. One of the project versions envisaged the installation of five booster (power augmentation) turbojet engines ahead of the wing leading edge (for this purpose one of the two boats had an elongated forward part with a small foreplane which served as a beam for the attachment of the booster engines).

In the OKB parlance, a vehicle combining in its cruise flight mode the use of aerodynamic lift and ground effect on an airfoil wing with the lift created by hydrofoils was called **ghidroekranoplahn** (hydro-WIG vehicle). In the case of the twin-hulled (catamaran) layout the hydrofoils were located according to the so-called four-point arrangement (each of the boats had a pair of hydrofoils – one in the forward part and one in the aft part). The forward hydrofoils were located ahead of the centre of gravity and the aft ones behind it.

In cruise flight mode the *ghidroekranoplan* was supposed to be supported by the forward-mounted hydrofoils and the airfoil wings, while the aft-mounted hydrofoils left the water and became airborne. One of the stages in the investigation of this layout envisaged the testing of a self-propelled model of the ekranoplan aircraft-carrier; the purpose of this testing was to evaluate the adopted layout of hydrofoils, as well as the controllability, stability and seaworthiness of the craft.

G. M. Beriyev was entrusted with the construction of the self-propelled model, while TsAGI undertook the studies involving the use of towed models in the towing basin. In Beriyev's OKB the piloted model was officially designated Be-1 and was more commonly known as Ghidrolyot (*ghidro* = hydro, *lyot* = flyer).

Be-1 ('Ghidrolyot')

Sometimes referred to as GL-1 or G-1, this machine can be described as a WIG vehicle of a catamaran layout. When afloat, the vehicle was supported by two floats; these supported low aspect ratio wings comprising a centre section and small outer panels with endplates. The outer panels had smaller thickness than the centre section. The cockpit was installed at the leading edge of the centre section. The vehicle was provided with hydrofoils attached to the floats in a four-point arrangement. The hydrofoils' angle of incidence was 4° for the forward pair and 0° for the aft ones. The aft hydrofoils were mounted

The Be-1 (aka GL-1) experimental wing-in-ground effect vehicle skims the sea, clearly showing the hydrofoils. That was all it could do; the Be-1 was underpowered and never became truly airborne.

Above: The Be-1 on its beaching gear, clearly showing the float design and the endplate fins. Interestingly, a cockpit canopy is fitted in this case

The Be-1 floats off the Black Sea coast at Taganrog where Beriyev have their flight test facility.

60

higher up relative to the forward ones and were expected to be lifted out of the water during cruise. The tail unit comprised twin fins, the role of the horizontal tail being performed by flaps installed on the wing centre section and outer wing panel trailing edges. The vehicle was of predominantly wooden construction; it was powered by a Walter M701C-250 centrifugal-flow turbojet (imported from Czechoslovakia) mounted on a pylon above the wing centre section.

In the course of testing the vehicle put to sea twelve times. It made eight runs in the displacement mode, forty runs in the hydrofoil mode and another forty in the airfoil-supported mode with flaps set at 20-25°. To reduce the gap between the wing trailing edge and the water surface, the chord of the flap mounted on the centre section was doubled, which resulted in a marked increase of the wing-generated lift. According to the designers' calculations, the thrust of the engine was presumed to be sufficient to accelerate the Be-1 into a flight in ground effect when the hydrofoils would become inoperative. However, the testing failed to produce this result, and the vehicle moved in all cases with the hydrofoils submerged, though the floats were lifted out of the water.

Be-11

This was a project of a 100-seat passenger *ghidroekranoplan*, the work on which was conducted in the Beriyev OKB on the basis of the results of the work on the Be-1. The powerplant in one of the versions was to comprise two AI-20 turboprops driving AV-68 four-bladed propellers (well-known for their use on the Il'yushin IL-18 airliner and the Antonov An-12 and An-32 transports).

P-2

A project of the Beriyev OKB bearing this designation is known from a photo of a model published in a collection of reports from a symposium held at the Ghelendzhik-98 hydro aviation show. It is described as amphibious aircraft. The photograph (unfortunately too poor to be reproduced) shows a large vehicle with four turbojets mounted in the nose part of the fuselage in a fashion similar to Alexeyev's ekranoplans. The machine has wings with a wide-chord centre section and outer wing panels of greater aspect ratio. Placed on the underside of the wings, at the junction of the centre section and the outer wing panels, are vertical walls (a kind of skegs) obviously intended to create a chamber under the centre section for building up an air cushion with the help of blowing from the nose-mounted engines.

A-70, A-2500

These two designations accompanied one photo of a towing-basin model of an 'ultra-heavy amphibious aircraft' published in the same source as above. The configuration of the model corresponds to that of the Be-2500 project with aft-mounted engines (see below). Apparently, the A-2500 and the Be-2500 are two designations of the same project. The same goes for the A-70 (the Be-70 designation is mentioned in one source). The relation between the A-70 (Be-70) and the A-2500 (Be-2500) is not clear (these may be projects sharing a common layout but differing in dimensions).

Be-1200, Be-2000

This is a project of an amphibious flying boat which was presented in model form by the TANTK at the Ghelendzhik hydro aviation show in 1996 as Be-1200; at Ghelendzhik-98 the same model bore the designation Be-2000. The layout of this gigantic machine powered by six powerful jet engines clearly places it in the category of Type C WIG vehicles, or *ekranolyots*, in Russian parlance. In its general configuration it comes close to a flying wing, though it features an empennage in the shape of two wing-mounted vertical tail surfaces topped by separate horizontal stabilizers. The wings have considerable sweepback; a thick, wide-chord centre section with a straight trailing edge blends into the fuselage. Outer wing panels of smaller thickness are attached to the centre section, producing what is known as composite wings. Large pylons acting as stabilising floats are

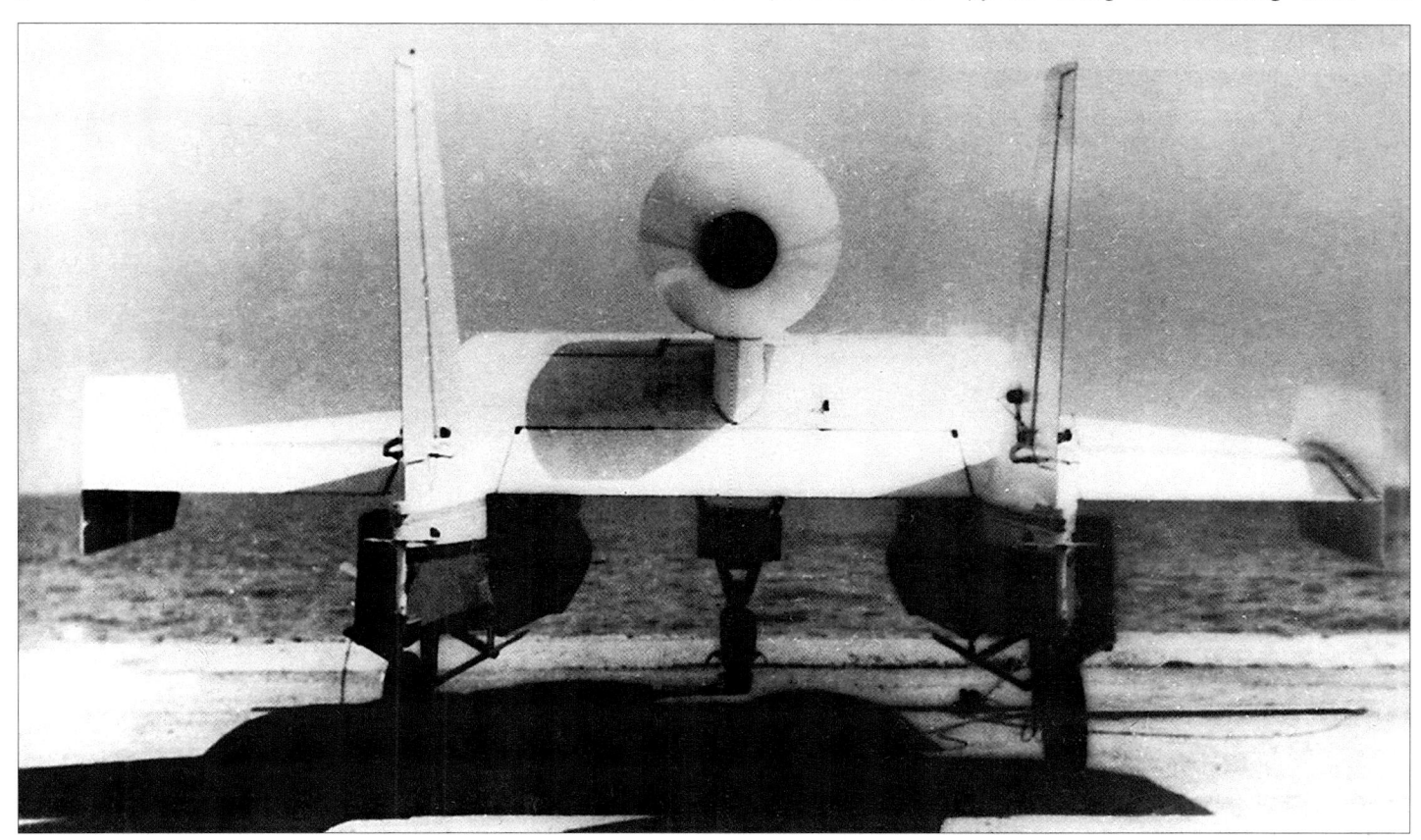

Rear view of the Be-1, showing the flaps, wing endplates and V-shaped rear hydrofoils.

Above: An artist's impression of the Be-11 sea-going passenger WIG. The centrally placed crew cockpit and the shrouded propellers are noteworthy.

attached to the underside of the wings at the junction of the centre section and the outer panels; they also act as walls forming a closed space under the wing into which the exhaust of the four nose-mounted engines is directed at take-off, in the same fashion as of Alexeyev's KM and Loon' vehicles. In cruise flight they presumably supplement the thrust of two cruise engines placed on pylons above the aft part of the wing centre section inboard of the fins.

Be-2500

Information on this project was presented by the TANTK at the Hydro Aviation Show 2000 in Ghelendzhik in September 2000. This huge machine weighing 2,500 t (5,500,000 lb) at take-off is a further development of the Be-1200 (Be-2000) layout. It combines the properties of a traditional seaplane (flying boat) and a WIG vehicle, being capable of flying both in ground effect and at a high altitude. The vehicle features a 'flying wing' layout, the wings blending smoothly into the fuselage (integral layout). During take-off the mutual position of the boat-type fuselage and the wings with a large-area centre section enables the aircraft to perform hydroplaning with the step of its hull and the trailing edge of the wing centre section touching the water surface. As with the Be-1200 (Be-2000), the empennage consists of two separate T-tails.

The machine has been designed in two versions: Be-2500 and Be-2500P, which differ

A model of the Be-1200 ultra-heavy *ekranolyot* amphibian unveiled at the 1996 Hydro Aviation Show in Ghelendzhik, showing the unusual aerodynamic layout with twin T-tails and the booster engines mounted on canard foreplanes.

Above: As can be seen here, the wing centre section of the Be-1200 is thick enough to accommodate auxiliary cargo bays. The main freight hold in the fuselage is spacious enough to accommodate bulky vehicles – even a Kamov helicopter with a co-axial layout and hence a tall rotor mast.

This view shows clearly the wing planform and the extreme sweepback of the vertical tails. In 1998 this very model was displayed at Ghelendzhiik under a new designation, Be-2000.

in their aerohydrodynamic layout. In the case of the Be-2500 'with no suffix' all six engines are aft-mounted (two of them are installed above the fuselage and the other four in pairs on both sides of the two fins. This means there is no provision for using the engine exhaust as a means of building up an air cushion under the wing during take-off. The outer wing panels are blended smoothly into the wing centre section, the chord and thickness increasing gradually from tip to root. As for the Be-2500P, its layout is almost identical to that of the Be-1200 (Be-2000), the only difference being the shape of the wing centre section trailing edge (which has sweepback instead of being straight) and the location of aft-mounted engines which are placed outboard of the fins, not inboard. Thus the Be-2500P, unlike the Be-2500, can use its nose-mounted engines for power-augmented take-off, directing their exhaust under the wing.

The Be-2500 is to be provided with a retractable undercarriage designed to sustain only the minimum take-off weight. It is intended to be used only when ferrying the machine to factory airfields for repairs, and for beaching the machine. The nose gear comprises two independent units side by side, each with a four-wheel bogie, while the four main units are equipped with 12-wheel bogies having three rows of four wheels, the outer units being mounted further aft.

The basic specifications of the Be-2500 are as follows. Powerplant: six Kuznetsov NK-116 turbofans; maximum payload, 1,000 t (2,200,000 lb); cruising speed in high-altitude flight (H = 10 km/32,810 ft), 700 km/h (435 mph), in ground-effect mode, 450 km/h (280 mph); ferrying range in high-altitude flight, 17,000 km (10,600 miles).

In the Be-2500P version the wing area is reduced from 3,428 to 3,184 m² (36,860 to 34,236 sq. ft), the payload in ground-effect mode is increased from 450 to 630 t (990,000 to 1,390,000 lb), the ferrying range is reduced 15,800 km (9,810 miles), safe take-off speed is reduced from 420 to 360 km/h (260 to 224 mph), the take-off run is reduced from 15,000m (49,200 ft) to 9,300 m (31,500 ft).

This project is a long-term prospective design not intended to be implemented in the immediate future. It is presumed that such ultra-heavy aerial vehicles may be used for transportation on transatlantic and transpacific routes.

Be-2500 as part of a maritime space complex

The unique potential of the TANTK named after G. M. Beriyev with regard to designing and producing hydroplanes in any weight category and for any duties (including WIG vehicles) called forth a very unorthodox idea of creating a maritime space complex (MSC)

Specifications of the Be-2500 and Be-2500P

Characteristics	Be-2500		Be-2500P	
All-up weight, t (lb)	2,500 (5,500,000)		2,500 (5,500,000)	
Wing area, m² (sq ft)	3,428 (36,900)		3,184 (34,275)	
Engine type	Kuznetsov NK-116 turbofan		Kuznetsov NK-116 turbofan	
Take-off thrust, kgp (lb st)	6 x 105,000 = 630,000		6 x 105,000 = 630,000	
	(6 x 231,500 = 1,389,000)		(6 x 231,500 = 1,389,000)	
Maximum payload, t (lb)	1,000 (2,200,000)		1,000 (2,200,000)	
Cruise flight mode	High altitude	In ground effect	High altitude	In ground effect
	(H = 10 km/ 32,810 ft)		(H = 10 km/ 32,810 ft)	
Cruising speed, km/h (mph)	800 (497)*	450 (280)	800 (497)	450 (280)
Payload, t (lb), at stage length of:				
7,000 km (miles).	700	450	700	630
	(1,540,000)	(990,000)	(1,540,000)	(1,390,000)
10,000 km (miles)	480	80	460	300
	(1,060,000)	(177,000)	(1,014,000)	(660,000)
Ferrying range, km (miles)	17,000	10,700(	15,800	12,700
	(10,600)	6,650)	(9,800)	(7,900)
Safe take-off speed, km/h (mph)	420 (260)	420 (260)	360 (224)	360 (224)
Take-off run, m (ft)	15,000 (49,200)	15,000 (49,200)	9,300 (31,500)	9,300 (31,500)

*700 km/h (435 mph) in another source

designed to tackle a wide range of tasks of global scope. This complex would make it possible to launch any space objects and manned space vehicles in a wide range of latitudes and trajectories and bring them back into the required point of the world's oceans which cover 71 per cent of the globe's surface. One of the projected versions of the MSC, called MSC-2500 and intended for launching payloads of more than 20 t (44,000 lb) to low orbits around the Earth envisages the use of a Be-2500 ultra-heavy amphibious carrier aircraft and an air/space vehicle (ASV, shuttle orbiter) capable of performing descent and landing in stages. The idea is based on the assumption that the Be-2500, by virtue of its enormous cargo-carrying capacity (1,000 t/ 2,204,000lb) will be able to carry the heavy ASV and a maximum fuel load, using large water areas as its base, and the ASV will comprise a manned module in the shape of an amphibious vehicle capable of performing take-offs and landings on water, land or the deck of a receiving vehicle.

Be-1500
A Russian reference book on aircraft industry published in 1996 claimed that the TANTK named after Beriyev was working on an *ekranolyot* bearing this designation. There has been no confirmation from other sources (it may well be a misprint for Be-2500).

Prospective designs
Drawings have appeared in Russian and Western aeronautical publications of two design studies made in the TANTK and representing ultra-heavy hydroplanes (presumably with *ekranoplan* properties). One of these drawings was published in the materials of a Ghelendzhik symposium on hydro aviation. It shows a vehicle of the flying wing layout with wings featuring double sweepback on the leading edges blending smoothly into a boat-type fuselage (integral layout). It is powered by three turboprops mounted on pylons above the fuselage. The other drawing (from a Western source) shows a twin-fuselage vehicle with composite wings (a centre section of low aspect ratio and outer wing panels of greater aspect ratio). The two main fuselages are of a boat hull type; a third fuselage is placed on the centre line, obviously above the water. The three fuselages are linked by what looks like a foreplane. The location of the engines is not shown. The two drawings are presumably strictly preliminary studies, not detail designs.

As may well be seen, the TANTK named after G. M. Beriyev, following up the traditions laid down by Robert Bartini during the years of his work in this design bureau, continues serious research in the direction of creating large-size water-based WIG vehicles intended for transcontinental transportation. Hopefully these efforts will bear fruit in due course. At present the emphasis is placed on traditional hydroplanes (flying boats), but, as noted by A. K. Konstantinov, one of the Design Bureau leaders, in a report in Ghelendzhik, further development of hydro aviation will also comprise the creation of WIG craft – bearing in mind, among other things, the military aspect.

Chapter 4

Sukhoi Diversifies

WIG Vehicles on the Agenda

The Sukhoi Design Bureau, or OKB (at present officially known as Aviation Scientific and Technical Complex named after Pavel Osipovich Sukhoi) is world-renowned for its designs of fighters, fighter-bombers and attack aircraft. In the mid-1980s it also embarked on work associated with WIG vehicles. From 1985 onwards it has been co-operating in these matters with the Central Design Bureau of Hydrofoils named after R. Alexeyev and with such organisations as TsLST (Central Laboratory for Research on Rescue Equipment) and the Krylov Central Shipbuilding Research Institute in St. Petersburg.

In 1989 the Sukhoi OKB began working on a programme to define the concept and configuration of a WIG vehicle. The following configurations were considered:
- single and twin fuselages;
- wings of various sweep, aspect ratios and dihedral angles;
- different types of vertical tail surfaces (single-and twin-finned, a V-tail, with and without a horizontal tail);
- wing centre sections of different planform and shapes, and different means of air flow under the bottom surface of the vehicle;
- with different numbers and types of engines, as well as different powerplant arrangements;
- configurations of various dimensions.

By early 1992 the layouts of Sukhoi's S-90-8 and S-90-200 WIG vehicles had been frozen as the basic designs for further investigation. (For the outsider, Sukhoi confuse the picture by using the S-90 designation for a number of very different designs; in these designations '90' means the 1990s and '-8' and '-200' refer to the seating capacity, so that each of them may cover several designs.)

By 2000 ten versions of vehicles of varying dimensions were under consideration. They represented variations of the composite wing concept developed by Bartini together with TsAGI and SibNIA (Siberian Aviation Research Institute in Novosibirsk) and used in his VVA-14 vehicle. Here follows the description of Sukhoi WIG vehicle projects, some of which have been presented to the public at various aviation events at home and abroad.

S-90-8

This is a small WIG vehicle intended for carrying eight passengers over water on short-haul routes. It is powered by a Czech-built series-produced Walter (Motorlet) M-601 turboprop engine optimised for the occasion. The S-90-8 features a twin-fuselage layout with a centre wing section arranged between the fuselages. The fuselages of a moderate fineness ratio are oval cross-section structures which have segmented rubberised fabric shells on their bottom surfaces. The nose section of each fuselage accommodates an avionics bay followed by a passenger cabin. There are a pilot's station and three passenger seats in the port fuselage and four passenger seats in the starboard one. The large glazing area of the bubble canopies affords a good view in all directions.

Flanked by the fuselages is a thick-profiled wing centre section with a cutout at the

A model of the eight-seat S-90-8 light passenger ekranoplan. Note the cutout in the wing centre section for directing part of the prop wash under the craft.

65

Above: This 40-seat passenger ekranoplan utilising an aircraft layout was designated simply S-90 (with no suffixes). The wings featuring a kinked leading edge and reverse sweep on the trailing edge are noteworthy, as is the cruise engine placement inspired by the Orlyonok.

Oddly enough, this twin-hull WIG developed by Sukhoi has been billed as an S-90-200, though the size of the vehicle suggests a considerably smaller capacity. It is not clear whether the objects on the foreplane are simulated turboprop engines or fuel tanks.

front to pass the propeller wash under the wings for creating a static air cushion. The wings, with an aspect ratio of 5, are slightly swept forward at the leading edges, the sweep angle being –1°. The wings are fitted with ailerons for lateral control. Dihedral is 10°. The tail sections of the fuselages mount a Vee tail unit, the panels of which are canted 45° outboard; each tail unit panel has a control surface.

An engine nacelle housing a Walter M-601 turboprop with a four-bladed variable pitch propeller is mounted on a pylon located along the line of symmetry of the centre wing section in its forward part. The engine is rated at 740 hp (551 kW).

Here are some specifications and performance figures of the machine: length, 11.7 m (38 ft 4½ in); wing span, 15.1 m (49 ft 6½ in); tailplane span, 9.3 m (30 ft 6 in); wing area with centre section, 48.2 m² (518.78 sq. ft); take-off gross weight, 3,700 kg (8,155 lb); maximum speed, 300 km/h (186 mph); cruising speed, 200 km/h (124 mph); maximum range, 640 km (397 miles); range with maximum payload, 440 km (273 miles); ground effect altitude, 1.5-2 m (4.9-6.6 ft).

S-90-200

This project of an amphibious passenger/cargo WIG vehicle was developed by the Sukhoi OKB on the basis of a preliminary agreement with the Aero Marine Singapore PTE Ltd. It is intended for carrying passengers and cargoes on medium- to long-haul maritime routes with poorly equipped hydro-airports. The S-90-200 is a twin-fuselage (catamaran) WIG vehicle accommodating 210-220 passengers in a two-deck layout.

The fuselages are oval cross-section structures provided with inflatable rubberised fabric shells installed on their bottom surfaces. The front fuselages accommodate crew workstations. The main fuselage space is occupied by a two-deck passenger cabin. The upper-deck section of each fuselage is divided into a compartment for 39 first class passengers and a compartment for 54 business (tourist) class passengers. The lower deck houses eight one- or two-passenger state rooms. The vehicle has a crew of 14.

The fuselages are interconnected by a thick airfoil-shaped centre section, ie, a wing of low aspect ratio. The centre section is supplemented by outer wing panels of greater aspect ratio which enable the vehicle to move out of ground effect if necessary to avoid obstacles or overfly areas with intensive shipping. The wings with an aspect ratio of 5.0 are slightly swept forward at the leading edges, the sweep angle is –1°. Each outer wing panel is fitted with three-section flaperons. The vehicle has a Vee tail unit with one panel installed on each fuselage. The panels are canted 45°

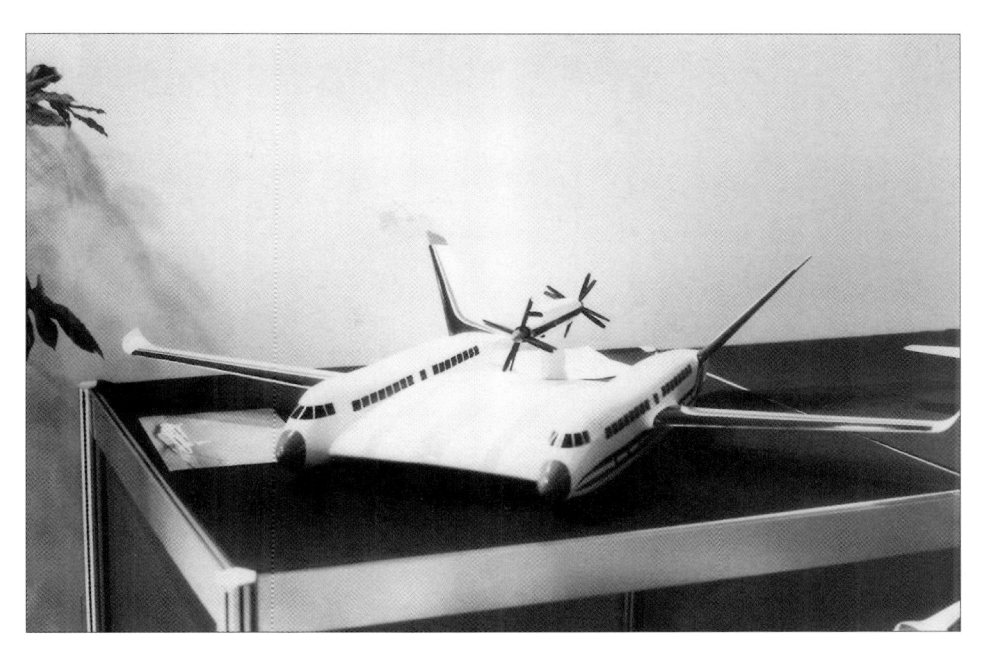

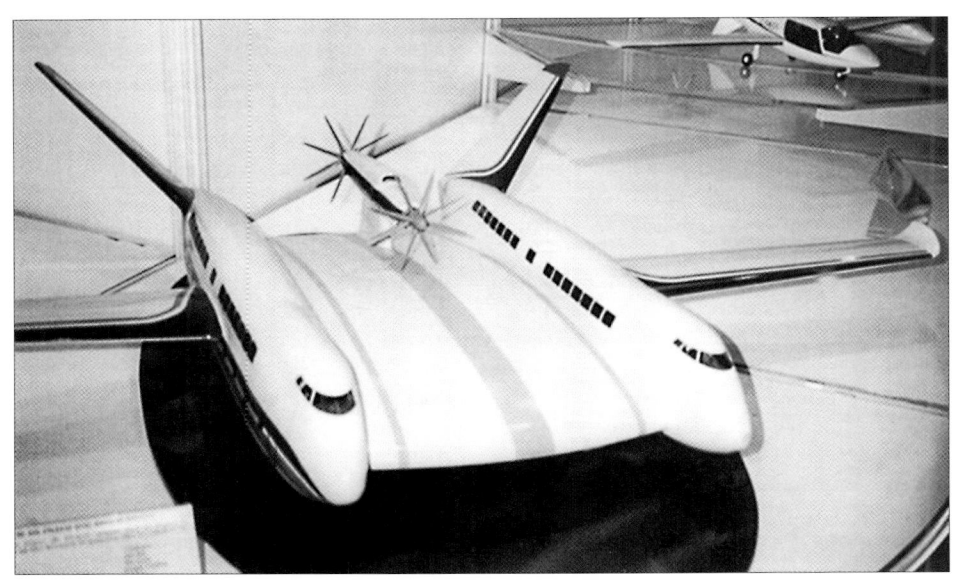

Two models of another WIG vehicle designated S-90-200 displayed at various airshows.

Another view of a model of the S-90-200 project – the one which lives up to its designation. The double-deck layout with the widely-spaced windows of the individual staterooms on the lower deck is well visible in this view.

outwards. Each panel is provided with a control surface.

The powerplant comprises two 15,000-ehp Kuznetsov NK-12MK turboprops driving eight-blade contra-rotating propellers. The engines are installed in tandem in a pylon-mounted nacelle on the rear part of the wing centre section. During take-off and landing the propeller wash is ingested by a special device and directed through a system of air passages to be discharged under the bottom surface of the wing centre section. Thereby a static air cushion is created, supplementing the dynamic air cushion produced by ram air during cruise flight. There is a provision for a flexible skirt which is retracted in the process of transition from the static to the dynamic air cushion; the longitudinal segmented components of the skirt act as shock absorbers during landing.

Here are some basic specifications: length, 40 m (131 ft 2.8 in); wing span, 60.92 m (199 ft 10.42 in); take-off gross weight, 132,000 kg (291,000 lb); payload, 20 t (44,080 lb); maximum speed, 470 km/h (292 mph); cruising speed, 380 km/h (236 mph);* maximum range with 220 passengers, 8,000 km (5,000 miles); maximum flight altitude, 1,500 m (4,920 ft);* ground effect altitude, 2.0-5.5 m (6.6-18 ft).

*Note: An advertising leaflet cites the cruising speed as 470 km/h (292 mph) and the service ceiling as 2,500 m (8,200 ft).

S-90-200 (another project with this designation)

Pictures have been published of a model representing another twin-fuselage WIG vehicle project from the Sukhoi Design Bureau. It is basically similar to the S-90-200 described above, but is obviously scaled down to possess maybe half the seating capacity (which makes the use of the same designation – S-90-200 – somewhat surprising). Other differences include a different powerplant arrangement: the vehicle had a pylon mounted turbojet as a cruise engine and possibly two booster engines ahead of the wing centre section leading edge (two streamlined bodies on the model may well simulate the engines for a wind tunnel test).

S-90

In 1997 the OKB started work on the S-90 project which featured a layout considerably differing from the two projects described above. This time it was a version of the 'Bartini layout' featuring an integral fuselage and an air cushion undercarriage provided with a special fan and a separate power unit. It is intended for passenger and cargo transportation both in aircraft mode at high altitude and in ground effect mode. In the latter case it can fly over water surface in sea states up to 2 and over flat areas on the ground with hummocks up to 0.5 m (1.6 ft) high. Initially the designers studied a layout featuring a hydrodynamically shaped displacing hull with planing steps on the bottom and endplates at the wingtips; it was to have booster engines placed ahead of the centre section leading edge and injecting an air stream under the wing (Alexeyev's layout).

However, as the work progressed, the engineers decided to abandon the hydrodynamic take-off; instead, they adopted a layout featuring an air-cushion undercarriage with retractable skirts fore and aft and with streamlined inflatable pontoons instead of rigid endplates incorporating steps on the underside. The use of a special fan for building up the pressure in the static air cushion made it possible to reduce by half the planform area of the wing centre section and accordingly the planform area of the machine as a whole, while retaining the same all-up weight. In addition, the smaller size of the wing centre section and reduction in the airframe weight made it possible to increase the seating capacity and to switch over from a traditional lifting wing centre section to an integral lifting fuselage which is shaped as a low fineness-ratio structure formed by high-thickness airfoils with an ogival forward portion. The aerodynamic layout of the S-90 features composite wings comprising a low aspect ratio fuselage/wing centre section which is intended for creating lift in ground-effect flight mode and for accommodating the payload, and aircraft-type outer wing panels (with a high aspect ratio). A 350-shp Allison 250C-20R turboshaft engine (which powers the Kamov Ka-226 helicopter) is used for driving the air cushion fan; it also doubles as an APU. The cruise powerplant comprises two 960-ehp PZL-10S (Glushenkov TVD-10B) turboprops mounted on the fins which serve as pylons. The fins are topped by the 'bench-shaped' tailplane

Research has shown that the flight altitude in ground-effect mode should not exceed 0.5 m (1.6 ft) and that flights at this height should be performed over an ideally flat surface (the surface of rivers and lakes in calm weather). According to some calculations, flights of this kind will make up not more than 5-10 per cent of the total flight time in the course of, say, a year. Therefore a view is held that the S-90 can be constructed and operated as a Type C WIG vehicle (*ekranolyot*), or an aircraft operating independently of airfields, with the 'aircraft' flight mode as the principal one, while the flight in ground effect is reserved as a supplementary function for short-distance flights or for carrying out special tasks.

S-90 (another project with this designation)

This 40-seat passenger WIG vehicle powered by three turbojets (or, more likely, turbofans) is intended for medium-haul routes over sea and ocean areas. It differs from those described above in being based on a single-fuselage 'aircraft' layout reminiscent of Alexeyev's designs, featuring a single cruise engine at the top of the fin and two booster engines in nacelles flanking the forward fuselage. The machine has a cruising speed of 400 km/h (248 mph) and a range of 2,000 km (1,240 miles).

Chapter 5

Enthusiasts

Make Their Contribution

Research in the field of ground effect and practical design of WIG vehicles in the USSR were not the exclusive domain of big design bureaux tasked by the government. Enthusiastic individuals, both specialists and amateur designers, were also engaged in this work, as were enthusiast design teams set up in various institutions of higher learning (student design bureaux, or SKB – *stoodencheskoye konstrooktorskoye biuro*). In addition, a number of scientific institutions did theoretical studies in this field, sometimes supplemented by practical design work. This chapter contains a brief review of the designs created by such enthusiasts. It covers the designs related to the whole of the Soviet Union including those republics (the Ukraine, Lithuania) which later, after the break-up of the USSR, became independent states.

TsLST and Educational Institutions

TsLST
A prominent place in the work under review belongs to the TsLST OSVOD RSFSR (*Tsentrahl'naya laboratoriya spasahtel'noy tekhniki Obschchestva spaseniya na vodakh* – Central Laboratory of New Types of Rescue Equipment under the Nautical Rescue Agency of the Russian Federation). Enlisting the support of several SKBs and young designers, this organisation produced a whole range of designs of light WIG vehicles in the 1970s and 1980s.

ES-1
This machine of wooden construction was developed in 1971 as *ekranolyotnyy stend* (ekranolyot test vehicle), hence the ES. It was intended for studying the stability and controllability of a wing of circular planform during movement close to the supporting surface, as well as for investigating the possibilities of using an ultralight *ekranoplan* for rescue purposes. The test vehicle was designed by Yu. V. Makarov. The ES-1 had a water-displacing hull in the shape of a boat with small chines and a flat bottom. The outer rim of the wing was made flexible. The rigid central part of the wing was surrounded by a flexible ring-shaped surface made of sheet polyethylene 0.5 m (1 ft 7¾ in) wide; it increased the diameter of the wing to 3.6m (11 ft 9¾ in).

Above: The ESKA-1 rescue WIG on display at the NTTM-74 exhibition at the VDNKh fairground in Moscow. The digits 0673 are the first flight date (June 1973). Note the cowled engine and the propeller spinner.

The ESKA-1 (with uncowled engine and no spinner) in flight, showing the angled wingtip aerodynamic surfaces.

The rigid part of the wing had an incidence of 10°, while its flexible leading edge had zero incidence. Thus, the rigid wing with an elastic rim had a concave profile. At the wingtips the elastic rim was bent downwards at an angle of 30°, producing the effect of endplates.

The *ekranolyot* had a T-tail unit featuring a slab stabilizer. There being no ailerons, the rudder was used as the means for lateral control. Placed behind the cockpit was an M-107 two-stroke motorcycle engine with a pusher propeller. The ES-1 was tested on the Moskva River.

ESKA-1
This *ekranolyot* (Type B WIG vehicle) based on the Lippisch configuration was designed and constructed in the TsLST by a group of young designers under the guidance of A. V. Gremiatskiy who was chief designer of the project. Yu. S. Gorbenko, Yu. V. Makarov and Yevgeniy P. Groonin (the latter is referred to in several sources as the author of the ESKA-1 design) also participated actively in the design and construction work.

The ESKA-1 was designed as a rescue vehicle intended for rendering urgent aid at a

The ES-2M WIG vehicle on show at the NTTM-76 exhibition; its L-13 Blanik origins are patently obvious.

distance of up to 50 km (31 miles) from a coastal rescue station. It was a two-seat machine of wooden construction. Simple and easily available materials were used, such as pinewood, aviation plywood, Styrofoam and fibreglass.

The reversed delta wing with anhedral on the leading edges created a dome-shaped cavity enhancing the ground effect. The wing trailing edge was slightly submerged when afloat and acted as a step during the take-off run. The airfoil section of the delta wings with a flat undersurface ensured high longitudinal static stability. Lateral stability and control were ensured by small detachable aerodynamic surfaces fitted with ailerons and attached at an angle to the tips of the main wing. The strut-braced tailplane was mounted at the top of the swept fin. The vehicle was powered by a 32-hp M-63 flat-twin motorcycle engine with reduction gear driving a wooden fixed-pitch propeller of 1.6 m (5 ft 3 in) in diameter; the engine was mounted above the hull on a cabane made of steel tubes. The all-up weight of the machine was 450 kg (992 lb), the payload being 220 kg (485 lb).

The first flights took place in the summer of 1973. All flight modes were tested: hydroplaning, flight in ground effect and free flight at an altitude of more that 2 m (6.5 ft). The most effective height of flight in ground effect was between 0.3 and 1.5 m (1 and 5 ft). With a 50 per cent payload the ESKA could soar to 50 m (164 ft) to surmount obstacles. In ground effect mode with a full payload the ekranoplan could work up a maximum speed of 122 km/h (75 mph). Range with full fuel tanks was 300-350 km (186-217 miles). The single example built was used as a shuttle transport on the Volga river for more than ten years.

Further developments of the ESKA-1 proposed by Ye. P. Groonin were designed in the TsLST. They included:

ESKA-4
This is a four-seat *ekranolyot* of the Lippisch configuration powered by one engine with a tractor propeller mounted of the leading edge of the fin.

T-301
A similar machine differing in having two engines with pusher propellers mounted on pylons above the fuselage.

LP-901
This is also a Lippisch-style machine, but a twin-fuselage design with twin fins, powered by an engine with a pusher propeller mounted on a pylon above the wing centre section.

T-503
T-503 was a WIG vehicle with twin floats and a dome-shaped (anhedral) wing topped by the crew cockpit.

ES-2 (1974)
This was yet another *ekranoplan* test vehicle intended for investigating the properties of a flexible wing and for studying its stability and controllability during flight in ground effect. It was produced by converting a Czechoslovak-built Let L-13 Blanik sailplane. The control system, undercarriage and equipment of the sailplane were retained. An M-63 motorcycle engine was installed above the fuselage. The original wings were removed and replaced by new ones featuring a rigid profiled leading edge and a flexible lifting surface made of two layers of rubberised fabric. The ES-2 had large 'armpits' between the wings and the fuselage, the spars and supporting struts were in the air flow.

Tests conducted in Liubertsy just outside the Moscow city limits revealed satisfactory stability and controllability. The aerodynamic characteristics obtained could also be regarded as sufficiently high.

ES-2M
In 1975 a further development of the vehicle described above resulted in the ES-2M which was built in the SKB of MVTU (Moscow Higher Technical College named after Nikolay E. Baumann) jointly with the TsLST. The main design and construction work was performed by V. A. Akinin, Yu. V. Makarov, A. B. Sobolev and Yu. S. Gorbenko. The ES-2M based on the L-13 sailplane had an all-metal construction. The fuselage and the tail unit were strengthened by installing two additional frames designed to carry the engine mount and attachment points for two wing spars. The central unit of the control system was completely reworked and considerably simplified. The ES-2M was powered by a 32-hp M-63 engine with a propeller of 1.6 m (5 ft 3 in) diameter.

For operations from water, the *ekranolyot* was provided with a detachable boat hull which was attached to the fuselage at four points. In that case the undercarriage monowheel was enclosed in a vertical niche placed along the axis of the boat. When extended, the wheel enabled the vehicle to go out onto a gently sloping bank, taxy and perform a take-off from land while being fitted with the flotation gear.

Thanks to the thin airfoil section of insignificant curvature, the clean wings and slender fuselage this *ekranolyot* had better aerodynamic characteristics, improved stability and easier handling compared to the original ES-2.

After testing conducted in the summer of 1976 the ES-2M was shown at the Exhibition of Scientific & Technical Achievements of Young Enthusiasts (NTTM-76 – Na**ooch**no-tekh**nich**eskoye **tvor**chestvo molo**dyo**zhi) in Moscow where it earned a gold medal.

An-2E
This WIG vehicle project based on the An-2V floatplane version of the well-known An-2 biplane was prepared in the TsLST in 1973 by a group of young specialists under the direction of Yevgeniy P. Groonin. The new machine inherited from the An-2 the forward fuselage, the cabin and the 1,000-hp Shvetsov ASh-62IR engine with an AV-2 four-blade variable-pitch propeller.

These elements of the airframe were coupled with a new low-set wing of the reverse-delta type having a marked anhedral and fitted with floats at wingtips; attached to the floats at an angle were small wing outer panels with ailerons.

The vehicle was also given a new T-shaped tail unit. The An-2E was to be provided with a retractable wheel undercarriage which would enable it to operate from land, as well as from the surface of lakes, rivers and coastal sea areas.

An-2V conversion with a flexible wing

Another project of an *ekranoplan* based on the An-2V was proposed by a group of young designers in the TsLST. As distinct from the An-2E described above, this project retained virtually the whole of the floatplane aircraft with the exception of the biplane wing set which was replaced by a flexible fabric lifting surface of reversed-delta planform. The rigid leading edges were formed by special outrigger structures attached to both sides of the fuselage and also carrying small surfaces with ailerons, like those used in vehicles of the Lippisch layout.

A WIG vehicle with a Rogallo wing

Yevgeniy Groonin, one of the designers of the ESKA-1 vehicle, came up with the idea of making use of Rogallo type flexible wings on WIG vehicles. In co-operation with S. Cherniavskiy and N. Ivanov he fitted a flexible wing to the fuselage of a Czechoslovak-built L-13J Blanik powered glider provided with a 42-hp Java M-150 motorcycle engine. The engine was mounted on a metal cabane behind the cockpit. Tests yielded satisfactory results.

A TsLST project of a two-seat WIG vehicle

This project is designated R-1001 Manta in some sources. In 1974 a group of young specialists in the TsLST developed a two-seat *ekranoplan* intended for liaison with the Soviet fishing fleet. The machine's configuration was reminiscent of some designs of Dr. A. Lippisch. That was seen, among other things, in the asymmetrical location of the cockpit which was placed on the left side of the airfoil-shaped body. The outer wing panels followed the well-known Lippisch layout, the tail unit had twin fins and a horizontal tail placed on top of them. The 210-hp Walter Minor VI six-cylinder in-line engine was mounted above the body. The vehicle had an all-up weight of 1,460 kg (3,218 lb). The project did not progress further than the drawing board.

E-120

Built in 1971, that was one of the experimental WIG vehicles designed in the TsLST. This single-seat machine distinguished itself with its wing of circular planform. Such a wing possesses some unique qualities, including the ability to preserve the lift without stalling at very high angles of attack right up to 45°. Such a wing is also capable of efficiently using the ground effect for lift increase and may prove promising for WIG vehicles, provided the questions of controllability are solved successfully.

ESKA EA-6A

This is a project of an improved four-seat version of the ESKA-1. In its contours it is nearly identical with its forerunner, featuring a wider cabin with a curved panoramic windshield and a slightly raised aft fuselage. A scaled-strength model of the EA-6A to 1/4 scale was tested in September 1973. It had a span of 1.75 m (5 ft 9 in) and was powered by a 1.8-hp two-cylinder engine driving a propeller of 300 mm (11.8 in) in diameter.

Parawing

This WIG vehicle was designed at the initiative of Yevgeniy Groonin. The machine featured an unusual configuration with two wings of triangular planform, shaped like a semi-circle when viewed from the front. The wings' planform, coupled with the floats at wingtips and the aileron-carrying surfaces attached to the floats, is reminiscent of the Lippisch machines. Originality consists both in the semi-circular front-view shape of the leading edges and in the fact that each of the wings is attached to the fuselage only at the front, while the aft portions of the wings serve as a kind of booms carrying the twin fins topped by horizontal tail. The vehicle is powered by a 42-hp Java M-150 engine with a propeller of 1.1 m (3 ft 7¼ in) diameter.

TsLST projects for converting aircraft into WIG vehicles

After the successful tests of the ES-2M the TsLST turned its attention to studying the possibility of converting some aircraft types about to be phased out from Aeroflot service (Yakovlev Yak-12, Lisunov Li-2) into WIG vehicles. These studies also involved the An-2 and the Be-12 ASW amphibian. It was presumed that the Be-12 powered by less powerful and, consequently, less thirsty piston engines (as compared to the turboprop-powered baseline aircraft) could find wide use in the national economy. A project designated Be-12E is described elsewhere in this chapter. There was even a project for transforming the Yak-40 jet airliner into a WIG vehicle!

The ELA-01 WIG vehicle on its ground handling dolly. Note the three-bladed propeller (see next page!).

Moscow Aviation Institute (MAI)

ELA-01

The student design bureau (SKB) of this institute jointly with the SKB of the Riga Institute of Civil Aviation Engineers (RIIGA, later RKIIGA) designed and built an experimental vehicle designated ELA-01; ELA presumably stood for *eksperimentahl'nyy letahtel'nyy apparaht* – experimental aerial vehicle. The ELA-01 can be placed in the WIG vehicle category, although it is sometimes described as a 'light rescue hydroplane'. The vehicle has a wing centre section resting directly upon two floats. These floats, together with the underside of the wing centre section, form an air chamber so characteristic of WIG vehicles. Attached to the leading edge of the wing centre section is a cockpit nacelle; behind it, a Walter Minor air-cooled in-line engine with a tractor propeller is installed. The vehicle was designed under the direction of A. A. Badiagin and V. Z. Shestakov and built at the experimental sports aviation factory in Prienai (the then Lithuanian Soviet Republic). The vehicle successfully passed flight testing, making its first flight on 4th November 1978.

Grach-2 and Grach-3

In 1980 the students of MAI under the direction of A. A. Badiagin were working on the design of several agricultural aircraft making use of ground effect during crop dusting. Two layouts were considered: a 'flying wing' and a low-wing monoplane with a T-tail. The wings of the agricultural aircraft had a broad-chord centre section of low aspect ratio and wing outer panels of greater aspect ratio which, in addition to improving the lift-to-drag ratio, increased the width of the strip covered by chemicals (the wings had a span of 22 m/ 72 ft 2 in). The projects dubbed Grach-2 and Grach-3 (Rook) were based on the An-2R agricultural aircraft and made use of its fuse-

Above: The ELA-01 afloat during trials, clearly showing the 'aerodynamic chamber' formed by the floats and the wing centre section. Interestingly, the craft is equipped with a two-bladed propeller in this view.

lage, undercarriage, engine and agricultural equipment. The Grach-2 and Grach-3 carried a load of chemicals 200 kg (440 lb) greater than the An-2; they promised a lower cost of agricultural work per hectare and a better payload-to-weight ratio at a lower all-up weight (5,300 kg/11,684 lb). Models of the Grach-2 and Grach-3 aircraft were demonstrated at the NTTM-82 exhibition of technical achievements of young specialists in 1982 and were awarded medals and diplomas.

WIG vehicle of a twin-fuselage flying-wing layout

This project was proposed by MAI students; in 1968 it was demonstrated in model form at the All-Union Exhibition of Economic Achievements fairground (VDNKh – *Vystavka dostizheniy narodnovo khoziaistva*). In this machine two fuselages flanked a thick wing of a very low aspect ratio. The wing housed a rotor (fan) designed to provide the vehicle with a vertical take-off capability. In cruising flight the rotor was switched off and faired over by deflectable vanes forming a smooth wing surface. In forward flight the wing created lift augmented by ground effect. The model was intended for research of aerodynamics and structural layouts of aircraft.

Be-12E

This design was offered in 1979 at MAI by Yu. V. Makarov, a well-known designer of ultra-light aircraft and a participant in the development of several WIG vehicles in the TsLST. The Be-12E (*ekranoplan*) was a WIG vehicle based on the conversion of the Beriyev Be-12 ASW amphibious flying boat; it was to be fitted with two ASh-62IR piston engines delivering 1,000 hp each. The gull-shaped wings of the amphibian gave way to a reversed-delta wing of low aspect ratio. The tail unit of the Be-12 and its control system were retained. The transformation of the Be-12 into a WIG vehicle reduced its empty weight to 14,000 kg (30,860 lb) and the all-up weight to 23,500 kg (51,810 lb). Therefore the 2,000 hp delivered by the ASh-62IR engines were quite sufficient for overcoming the 'drag hump' during acceleration at take-off and for ensuring a rate of climb of 0.5-0.7 m/sec (98-137 ft/min) required for making the vehicle capable of manoeuvres over the supporting surface at altitudes up to 50-100 m (164-330 ft). The designer regarded the project as possessing good fuel efficiency, but difficulties with providing gasoline for piston engines led him to the idea of making use of diesel engines in WIG vehicles.

Moscow Aviation Technical School named after Godovikov

EMA-1

In 1967 the students of this technical school designed and built an ultralight WIG vehicle designated EMA-1 and featuring a canard layout. The project was prepared by Yu. V. Makarov. The vehicle had a three-spar wing of circular planform. Placed ahead of the wing was a lifting stabiliser, also of circular planform, fitted with large-area elevons. The engine delivering a mere 4 hp was placed behind the pilot's cockpit. The EMA-1 featured a wooden construction with fabric skinning, an enclosed cockpit and a three-unit undercarriage with a tail skid. The vehicle, described as an *ekranolyot*, was tested at the Khodynka airfield in Moscow in 1968-1969. It showed good stability and controllability and accelerated to 50 km/h (31 mph) but failed to enter the ground effect flight mode due to being underpowered.

WIG vehicle designed by Skvortsov and Gorshunov

In 1995 two young designers, Konstantin Skvortsov and Yevgeniy Gorshunov, designed at the MATI (Moscow Aviation Technology Institute) a passenger WIG vehicle intended for use over land. The vehicle had two fuselages flanking a wing of large dimensions. It was to be equipped with a highly unorthodox powerplant in the shape of a huge flywheel placed in the wing. The flywheel actuated two propelling devices fitted with conventional airscrews. It was to be spun up by current from a ground-based power source and was expected to rotate for several hours, ensuring a flight speed of no less than 300 km/h (186 mph) at the height of 1.5 to 3 m (5-10 ft). The vehicle was to make a halt every 200-300 km (124-186 miles) in order to give a booster charge to the flywheel with the help of compressed air. The vehicle with its twin-deck fuselages was expected to carry as many passengers as a usual train. In 1996-97 work on the project was still going on.

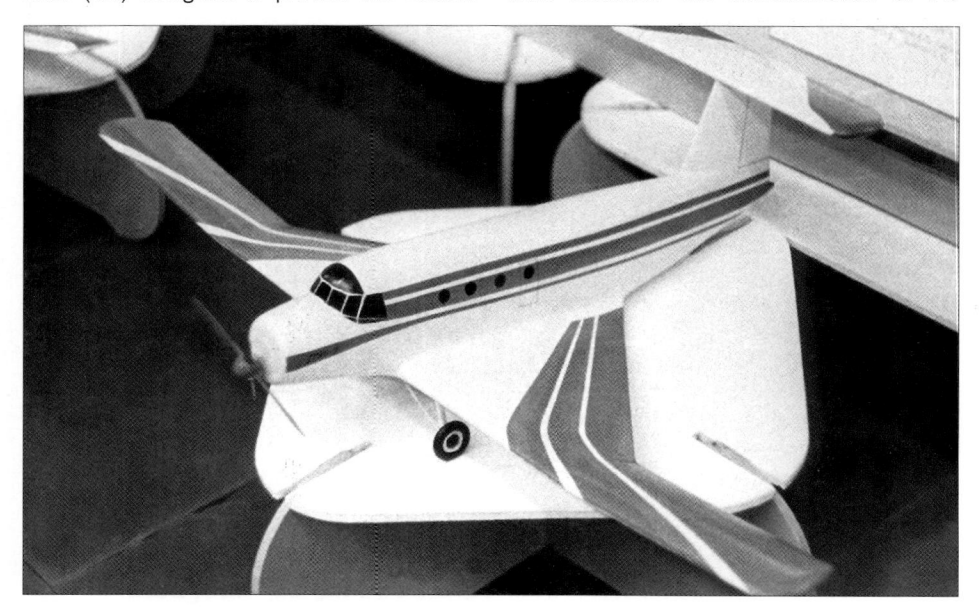

A model of the Grach-2 agricultural WIG craft displayed at the NTTM-82 exhibition, clearly showing the craft's An-2 origins.

MVTU (Moscow Higher Technical College named after Nikolai E. Bauman)

Magnus-2

Apart from the above-mentioned work on the ES-2M (jointly with the TsLST), MVTU students designed and built the Magnus-2 WIG vehicle which was actually a 'speedboat with aerodynamic off-loading'. A standard lightboat hull was fitted with stub wings, tail surfaces and a piston engine with a shrouded propeller placed behind the open driver's seat. In 1982 the vehicle was demonstrated at the exhibition of technical achievements of young specialists in Moscow (NTTM-82).

OIIMF (Odessa Institute of Marine Fleet Engineers)

In 1963-1966 a group of students of this institute (OIIMF – *Odesskiy institoot inzhenerov morskovo flota*) working under the direction of Yu. A. Boodnitskiy designed and built the OIIMF-1 WIG vehicle and its subsequent versions – the OIIMF-2 and OIIMF-3. All of them featured a 'flying wing' layout with two wing sets spaced apart both longitudinally and in height. The wing chord was 1 m (3 ft 3½ in) on the front wings and 3 m (9 ft 10 in) on the rear wings. They were attached to end-plate floats (skegs). The single-seat open cockpit was placed on top of the main wings. The first of the vehicles was powered by one 18-hp Izh-60K motorcycle engine, the second model had two such engines mounted on the leading edge of the main (aft) wings. Their propellers drove the air under the main wings, thus creating an air cushion retained with the help of flaps hinged at the wings' trailing edge. At a speed of 35-40 km/h (22-25 mph) the lift, including that produced by ram air pressure, reached 80% of the vehicle's weight. The power of the two engines proved insufficient for reaching the design speed of 100-120 km/h (62-75 mph), and the OIIMF-3 model received two K-750 engines of 26 hp each. The airframe was lightened and the front wings were fitted with flaps. Testing was planned for the summer of 1967 but failed to take place due to some technical problems.

KnAPI

KnAPI – Komsomol'sk-on-Amur Polytechnical Institute (*Komsomol'skiy-na-Amoore politekhnicheskiy institoot*).

ELA-7 Albatross

In 1968-1971 the participants of the student design bureau of the Polytechnical Institute in Komsomol'sk-on-Amur created an experimental flying vehicle dubbed ELA-7 Albatross. This was a 'hydroplane with a lifting fuselage' – actually a WIG vehicle. It had a wing centre section of rectangular planform and substantial area, supplemented in its rear part by small outer wing panels fitted with ailerons. The wing centre section was flanked with two floats which each had a keel surface at the bottom centreline. A 32-hp MT-8 flat-twin engine from a Dnepr motorcycle driving a tractor propeller was mounted on the leading edge of the wing centre section. The engine cowling blended into a fairing of the open cockpit. A flap attached to the trailing edge of the centre section, together with the floats, formed a cavity for an air cushion under the wing. The ELA-7 was provided with Vee tail surfaces attached to tail booms.

The airstream produced by the propeller served in part for injecting the air under the wing. A small steerable foreplane mounted behind the propeller on the leading edge of the wing centre section deflected the air flow increasing the area of the airstream directed under the wing.

The ELA-7 was tested in the summer of 1971 on a lake near Komsomol'sk-on-Amur. Due to insufficient propeller thrust the vehicle developed a speed of a mere 36 km/h. The testing was concentrated mainly on investigating the effect of off-loading the wing by means of injecting (blowing) the air under its surface. The off-loading amounted to 100 kg (220 lb) at the propeller's maximum static thrust. The designers of the vehicle came to the conclusion that the chosen layout was quite satisfactory as far as the aerodynamic off-loading was concerned.

ELA-8

This was a further development of the ELA-7 featuring changes in aerodynamic layout. These included installation of a single-fin empennage and refinement of the hydrodynamic shape of the floats. The horizontal empennage of the ELA-8 was installed in the front part of the floats and had no dihedral. The outer wing panels mounted on the aft sections of the floats were attached at an angle of 5°. Thus, the hydroplane featured a tandem-wing aerodynamic layout with a lifting fuselage. The forward set of wings was fitted with elevators, while the aft set of wings, as distinct from the ELA-7, had no control surfaces and was fitted with small endplates. To increase the air blowing effect the axis of the propeller was moved downward, closer to the leading edge of the wing centre section. The foreplane directing the airstream downward was shaped as a multi-slot deflector. The flap installed on the trailing edge of wing centre section received spring loading and was deflected automatically as the pressure under the wing decreased.

The all-up weight of the vehicle powered by the same 32-hp MT-8 engine was brought down to 380 kg (838 lb).

The ELA-8 was tested on a lake near Komsomol'sk-on-Amur in summer 1974. Several runs were made, the speed reaching 50 km/h (31 mph). The blowing produced an aerodynamic off-loading effect up to 280 kg (617 lb).

ELA-13

This WIG vehicle built in the SKB of the KnAPI in 1977-1978 was, in effect, a research vehicle for investigating the influence of the proximity of the water surface on the take-off and landing performance of hydroplanes. It had a lifting fuselage, an open cockpit, a T-tail and was powered by a 32-hp MT-8 engine with a pusher propeller of 1.6 m (5 ft 3 in) in diameter. Two floats were attached to the sides of the fuselage. Attached to the centre part of the fuselage were two outer wing panels with ailerons. The ailerons doubled as flaps, their deflection being geared to the movement of

The Magnus-2 WIG vehicle designed by MVTU students, seen here at the NTTM-82 exhibition in 1982.

Above: The KnAPI ELA-7 Albatross WIG vehicle on a lake near Komsomol'sk-on-Amur during tests. The tail unit design is well visible.

Above: The refined ELA-8, showing the repositioned engine driving the propeller via an extension shaft, the redesigned fuselage and tail surfaces.

The ELA-13 research vehicle. The apparent boxy shape is due to the sidewalls flanking a 'lifting body'.

the elevator. This ensured the functioning of a direct wing lift control system which performed well in the course of the ELA-13's flight tests. Endplates installed at the tips of the outer wing panels helped cut induced drag.

The vehicle's all-up weight was 250 kg (551 lb), markedly less than that of the ELA-7 and ELA-8.

During the tests which commenced on the Amur river in July 1978 the vehicle suffered a crash after pitching-up on take-off. Repairs made in the winter of 1978 were accompanied by modifications which included increasing the floats' displacement in their nose sections, shifting the centre of gravity forward and selecting a propeller with a static thrust increased to 100 kg (220 lb). The modified vehicle was designated **ELA-13M**. During the testing conducted on the Amur river in July 1979 the *ekranolyot* made 32 successful flights, displaying good stability and controllability in different flight modes both in and out of ground effect. The maximum flight speed was in excess of 90 km/h (56 mph). The flight altitude out of ground effect reached 10-12 m (33-40 ft). The vehicle won the first prize at the All-Union contest of scientific work performed by students, held in Leningrad in 1981.

Komsomol'sk-on-Amur State Technical University (former KnAPI)

In 1996 design work was conducted there aimed at creating a dual-purpose transport means. It was envisaged as combining the features of a hydrocycle and a light WIG vehicle, the one being easily transformed into the other. It was to be a WIG vehicle of Type A, requiring no aircraft-type certification.

RKIIGA (formerly RIIGA)

Riga Red Banner Institute of Civil Aviation Engineers (now Riga Aviation University).

Apart from the ELA-01 (a joint project with MAI, see above), the SKB of this educational institution developed a project of the ELA-3 *ekranolyot*. Its scale model was presented at the Exhibition of scientific and technical work of young specialists in Moscow in 1984 (NTTM-84); further details of the vehicle are not available. Students of the RKIIGA prepared a number of graduation designs of WIG vehicles of various categories. These included some projects prepared at the initiative of the TsLST (as mentioned above) on the basis of the An-2, Yak-12 and Yak-40 aircraft. In all cases the reversed-delta wing layout was used. Interestingly, a project based on the An-2 envisaged converting the machine into a WIG vehicle by fitting it with rigid monoplane low aspect ratio wings while retaining the floats of the An-2V hydroplane. The conver-

Irkutsk Polytechnical Institute (IPI)

In 1982-1983 a group of students and engineers under the direction of S. V. Trunov working in the SKB of the aviation faculty of this institute developed a design of the EVP-1 WIG vehicle. The machine featured aircraft layout with a T-shaped tail unit and slab stabiliser. The wings of trapezoidal planform had anhedral on the leading edges. The trailing edge section of the wing behind the rearmost spar was made elastic. The 18-hp Izh-P3 cruise engine (from an Izh Planeta motorcycle) with a pusher propeller was installed on a pylon ahead of the fin. The EVP-1 was also fitted with a 2-hp Sh-52 lift engine which drove a fan producing a static air cushion. The wings with a total area of 5 m² (53 sq. ft) and a span of 4.5 m (14 ft 9 in) ensured aerodynamic off-loading of the vehicle amounting to 90% of its all-up weight at speeds of 65-70 km/h (40-43 mph). The *ekranoplan* had an empty weight of 100 kg (220 lb) and an all-up weight of 180 kg (397 lb). In the course of testing conducted at the Irkutsk water reservoir in 1983 the EVP-1 displayed excellent manoeuvrability and stability in all flight modes in ground effect.

M-6

This light *ekranoplan* was built under the auspices of the IPI in the NPS Scientific Development and Production Centre in mid-1990s. The machine featured a canard layout with a foreplane that was diamond-shaped in planform. The foreplane was split into two halves, their edges forming a 'reverse slot'; the designers claimed that this layout helped ensure stability in ground-effect flight mode through auto-stabilisation without resorting to an automatic control system. The vehicle was powered by a Rotax engine, the air flow being directed under the wings during take-off.

MIIGA (Moscow Institute of Civil Aviation Engineers)

This institute provided the framework for the activities of a group of young enthusiasts who created the T-501 WIG vehicle. This two-seat machine was designed and built in 1976-1983 by a group of young aircraft designers led by Yevgeniy Groonin who started their work at a Youth Technical Club in Kaliningrad (now Korolyov) near Moscow. The airframe was produced by adapting the Czechoslovak L-13 Blanik sailplane. Its fuselage was modified to feature the hydrodynamic contours of a planing speedboat with a step on the bottom. The tail unit was T-shaped. The wings of wooden construction featured a reversed-delta planform (Lippisch layout) and anhedral on the leading edge. Two modified Neptoon-23 (Neptune) outboard engines with a total output of 46 hp were mounted on a horizontal beam above the fuselage.

MIIGA students took an active part in the design work, and in 1980 the group fully transferred its activities to the MIIGA. Testing conducted in 1982 showed that the power of the two Neptoon-23 engines was insufficient. In consequence, this powerplant was replaced by a Lyul'ka TS-21 gas turbine engine (designed as a jet fuel starter for the AL-21 military turbofan), initially driving a two-blade wooden propeller. The TS-21 mounted on a cabane above the fuselage developed a static thrust of 240 kg. However, this engine, too, could not enable the T-501 to reach its design objective – flight in ground effect mode. The reason was traced to the unsatisfactory hydrodynamic shape of the boat hull.

Above: This unorthodox vehicle is one of the projected configurations of the M-6 passenger ekranoplan created in Irkutsk in the mid-1990s. The model shown here was displayed at the MAKS-95 airshow.

Kazan' State Technical University

In August 1999 the Kazan' State Technical University named after Andrey N. Tupolev (formerly KAI – the Kazan' Aviation Institute) presented at the MAKS-99 airshow a project for a light cargo/passenger WIG vehicle intended to transport 400 kg (1,310 lb) of cargo or five passengers and pilot. The vehicle copied in miniature the 'aircraft layout' of Alexeyev's big *ekranoplans* (albeit without separate booster engines), featuring a boat-type hull, low-aspect-ratio wings of rectangular planform, a T-tail. The powerplant was a 165-hp horizontally opposed piston engine (presumably of Western origin) with a pusher propeller on a pylon above the fuselage. The vehicle has an all-up weight of 1,500 kg (3,300 lb) and a design cruising speed of 150 km/h (93 mph). It is intended for operation over water surfaces and coastal areas, as well as above ice- and snow-covered expanses. Possible uses include river-going taxi, transportation of small cargoes, patrol duties and rescue work.

An artist's impression of a light WIG vehicle developed by the Kazan' State Technical University.

Above: The MS-04 speedboat with dynamic offloading designed at the Krylov Central Shipbuilding Institute. Note the unusual all-movable tail unit hinged at the fin root.

Work on WIG Vehicles Conducted by Scientific Institutions

WIG designs of the Krylov Central Shipbuilding Research Institute

The St. Petersburg-based Central Scientific Research Institute of Shipbuilding named after Academician A. N. Krylov (known by its Russian abbreviation of TsNII) has long been engaged in work associated with WIG vehicles. Emphasis is placed on theoretical studies, but some attention is devoted also to practical design. Several small machines designed by Ye. A. Kramaryov are known to have reached the hardware stage. One of these is a light WIG vehicle, pictures of which were circulated by the TASS News Agency in 1990. This single-seat vehicle designated **MS-04** features an 'aircraft layout' with low-set stub wings and a T-tail. The boat-shaped hull accommodates an open cabin in its front part. The wings of trapezoidal planform, fitted with endplate floats, have prominent root fillets. Attached to the aft end of the hull under the tail unit is an outboard boat engine with a water propeller. The vehicle is thus a speedboat with aerodynamic off-loading. It is presumably this vehicle that is referred to in the text to the TASS pictures, where mention is made of a TsNII-designed WIG vehicle with a 350-cc engine produced by König GmbH (West Germany), capable of developing a speed of 160 km/h (99 mph).

The same TASS text mentioned a TsNII-developed project of a WIG vehicle bearing a superficial resemblance to a modern airliner and 'powered by engines with propellers' (presumably turboprops). The project had been demonstrated at international exhibitions in New York, Tokyo and Munich and patented in 15 countries.

SSS

The Krylov Shipbuilding Institute has also prepared an advanced design project for a heavy WIG vehicle weighing some 750 t (1,653,440 lb) and intended to be a part of a global rescue system. (Presumably it is the twin-hull vehicle referred to in some sources as the SSS). It was mentioned in the materials of a symposium held in 1997 to commemorate Robert Bartini's 100th anniversary. The vehicle is capable of taking off and alighting in sea states up to 5 inclusive, staying afloat and drifting for a long time and reaching a port of refuge at low speed if it is prevented from normal flight for some reason. The WIG vehicle can reach speeds of 400-500 km/h (249-311 mph) and operate within a radius of 3,000-4,000 km (1,865-2,490 miles) from a port. The *ekranoplan*-ship can deliver to the scene of an accident a large number of rescue means ranging from life rafts and self-propelled boats to special boats for setting up floating barriers (used for containing oil spills), a diving vehicle and a helicopter. On board the WIG vehicle the survivors are provided with the necessary medical aid without waiting for arrival at a port. The safety of operation of such a WIG vehicle in sea conditions is far superior to various types of aircraft-based means.

To substantiate the project, the Krylov Institute (TsNII) has conducted a vast amount of design studies and experimental research in wind tunnels, towing basins, on test rigs and on the open water surface. The design of the heavy WIG vehicle has been developed on the basis of using available engines, construction materials, onboard equipment and with due regard to the present level of technology and production methods in the construction of high-speed ships and aircraft. Further development of the project, construction and operation of the rescue WIG vehicles and of the system as a whole can be put into effect by an international consortium of shipbuilding and aircraft companies with financial support from nations having an interest in maritime rescue operations.

The SSS WIG vehicle developed by the TsNII (Krylov Central Shipbuilding Research Institute) is a catamaran vehicle with two boat hulls and a composite wing layout. Placed between the hulls is a wing centre section of large chord and relative thickness; outboard of the hulls it is supplemented by outer wing panels of greater aspect ratio and lesser relative thickness. The twin-fin tail unit includes a horizontal tail resting on top of the fins. The crew stations are housed in a nacelle attached to the leading edge of the wing cen-

A model of the SSS twin-hull WIG vehicle. The meaning of the SSS acronym remains unknown.

tre section and two foreplanes joining the nacelle and the hulls. Suspended under the foreplanes are four turbojets which act both as booster engines for take-off and as cruise engines. For slow-speed movement when afloat the vehicle is fitted with diesel engines driving water propellers in the aft parts of the hulls. The vehicle can carry a Kamov Ka-27PS SAR helicopter on top of its wing centre section.

Krylov Institute Branch in Nizhniy Novgorod

This organisation has developed a project for a passenger WIG vehicle designated KEP-6 (KEP-6A; KEP = *kah*ter-ekrano*plahn* – WIG speedboat) designed to carry four to six persons. Its wings have a composite configuration in planform and consist of a centre section and outer wing panels with endplates. According to some sources, the KEP-6A has a twin-fin tail unit and a powerplant with two propellers that can change their plane of rotation. The project was presented at the 'Ekranoplan-96' international conference. The KEP-8 has been mentioned in some sources. The branch has also prepared a technical proposal for a series of business-class light amphibious WIG vehicles powered by indigenous automobile engines from the VAZ and ZMZ enterprises and by the series-produced 360-hp Vedeneyev M-14P aircraft radial engine. Their feature an 'aircraft layout' (like that of the SM-6). The programme includes such vehicles as the RT-2, RT-2M, RT-4, RT-5, RT-6MA, also presented at the 'Ekranoplan-96' conference. The branch has developed also some projects for sea-going WIG-vehicles (*morskiye ekranoplahny*, ME), including the ME-50.

Recent information indicates that the branch has been taken over by another owner, which makes the fate of the projects described above uncertain.

Hydromechanics Institute of the Academy of Sciences of the Ukrainian SSR

In the 1960s several WIG vehicles bearing the common designation ADP (*appa*raht *na dina*micheskoy [*voz*dooshnoy] *po*doosh*ke*, dynamic air cushion vehicle) were built in the abovementioned research institution in Kiev under the direction of A. N. Panchenkov. Theoretical research and experimenting led him to the conviction that the required stability of flight in ground effect could be achieved in a WIG vehicle featuring a canard layout. In consequence, the ADP vehicles had an elongated fuselage with a stabiliser mounted in its front part. The first such vehicle was the ADP-1 built in 1965. It had a K-750 motorcycle engine with a pusher propeller placed behind the cockpit. The main wings were fitted with flaperons and endplates; placed on top of the wings, in the propeller wash, was the fin and rudder assembly. Hydrofoils were mounted on the forward fuselage. During trials the vehicle showed a maximum speed of 110 km/h (68 mph) in flight at the height of 0.25 m (10 in). Stabilisation of the flight altitude over the surface was ensured by the lifting stabiliser mounted on the forward fuselage. Increasing the stabiliser's angle of attack caused it to lose its lift due to stalling at supercritical angles, and the vehicle lowered the nose, restoring the working AOA of the stabiliser.

In 1965-1966 the WIG vehicle was fitted with a tricycle wheeled undercarriage; the main wing endplates were deleted. The two-blade propeller was replaced by a four-blade one. The fuselage acquired streamlined contours and was fitted with a windshield. The airframe weight rose to 380 kg (838 lb). In this guise the vehicle was redesignated ADP-2. Tests were conducted at an airfield near Kiev. The ADP-2's design performance included a flight altitude of 0.25 m (10 in) and a maximum speed of 150 km/h (93 mph).

In the subsequent years Panchenkov designed several more machines. At a certain stage he parted company with the Kiev Institut and moved to Irkutsk, where he continued designing WIG vehicles, the highest project number being 10.

Irkutsk State University with IAPO (Irkutsk Aviation Production Association)

In 1993 a laboratory of complex studies of this university headed by B. S. Berkovskiy conducted research and design work in the framework of a programme named *Skaht* (ray, the marine animal). It envisaged the design of WIG vehicles with an all-up weight ranging from 1 t to 1000 t (2,200 to 2,205,000 lb) featuring an air cushion undercarriage. It was presumed that, given the required funding, these vehicles could be developed to the hardware stage. In 1993 design studies evolved by the laboratory were presented at the MAKS-93 airshow; a model was shown of a 'flying wing' WIG vehicle with an air cushion undercarriage. The vehicle was envisaged as a means of solving transport problems in Siberia and the Far North. Such vehicles require no roads or prepared airfields and can be used all the year round over any flat surface which promises a good economic effect.

The WIG vehicle can be built in two basic layouts. One of them features wings of triangular planform with a thick S-shaped airfoil and is intended for medium-haul (2,000-km/1,240-mile) cargo transportation; the second one is a flying wing shaped as a flat platform and is intended for short-haul (1,500-2,000km/930-1,240-mile) cargo routes.

In addition to passenger and cargo transportation, such WIG vehicles were considered to be suitable for other duties, such as fighting forest fires. The results of the laboratory's work were demonstrated at international exhibitions in Seattle (USA), Hannover (Germany) and Moscow.

Development of these projects was conducted with the participation of the Irkutsk-based Stela commercial aviation company having a research division.

Some of the projects (illustrated by the photos on these pages) bore the designations M-5-1, M-5-01, M-5-2

Andrey N. Tupolev

The well-respected Tupolev Design Bureau is mentioned here, among scientific institutions, entirely because WIG vehicles did not occupy any place of importance in its activities and do not merit a separate chapter. Actually, the only project from this design bureau that can be classed as a WIG vehicle is the project of

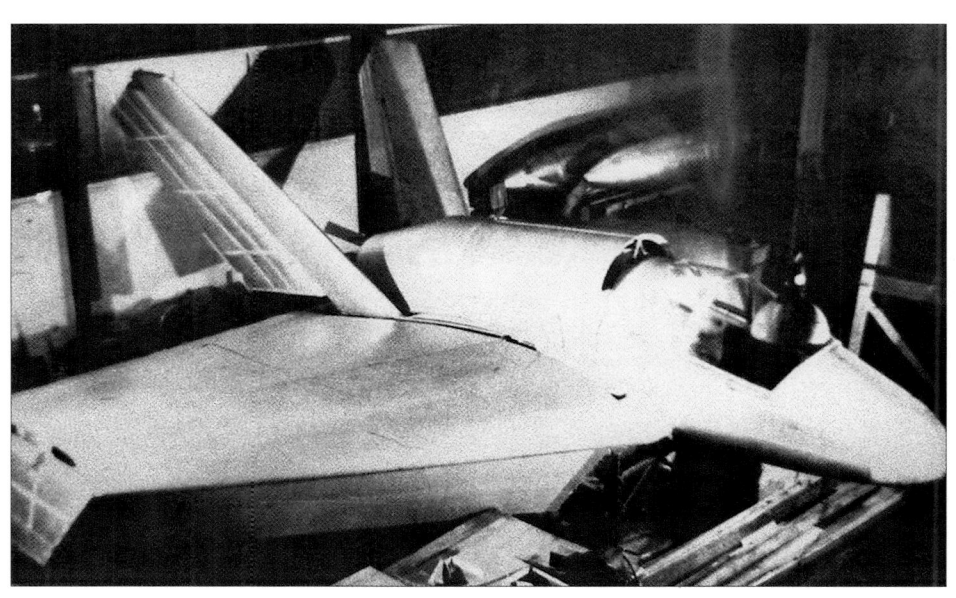

The M-5-1 subscale WIG vehicle nearing completion. Note the dorsal air intake and the hinged flaps under the wing leading edge.

Above: A wind tunnel model of the M-5-01 heavy WIG vehicle utilising the flying wing layout. This model does not feature the six turbofan engines to be mounted on the upper surface near the trailing edge.

an aerosleigh with a TsAGI-developed wing system. Information on this project appeared in the Russian aeronautical magazine *Kryl'ya Rodiny* in 1994. Judging by the published photo of a model, the aerosleigh has a boat-shaped hull and is powered by an engine with a pusher propeller installed above the aft part of the hull. The vehicle is provided with high-set wings of normal 'aircraft' aspect ratio; two booms attached to the wings carry the tail surfaces. The wings working in ground effect are presumably intended to only partially off-load the vehicle, reducing the pressure on the snow or other supporting surface (water or marshland). There is no evidence of a prototype ever being built.

A vague reference to 'A. Tupolev's *ekranoplan*' can be found in another source where it is put into the category of vehicles intended for 'crawling on the ground' (more precisely, for moving over water, ice, snow and marshes). Presumably, it is a reference to the vehicle described above.

It is worth noting that as far back as the 1960s the Tupolev Design Bureau designed and built an aerosleigh of an unusual configuration. It had a boat-shaped hull which enabled the vehicle to move on water, snow and marshland. It may be presumed that the weight of the vehicle was partially off-loaded by the pressure of the ram air on the front undersurface of the hull in cruise. In the 1990s the Tupolev OKB designed and built yet another aerosleigh – the AS-2 – again with a boat-hull body. It was exhibited at the MAKS-97 and MAKS-99 airshows in Zhukovskiy.

WIG Vehicles Designed by Individuals

R. Adomaitis

In 1982 an amphibious ekranolyot was built under the direction of A. Adomaitis in the then Soviet Lithuania. It was built by members of the Kaunas aviation sports club in the village of Pacunai. The vehicle, powered by a 105-hp Walter Minor engine, had a low-aspect-ratio wing of triangular planform. It underwent testing at the airfield of the Kaunas club with Adomaitis at the controls.

E. A. Aframeyev

This is the author of an article in the April 2001 issue of the Russian aeronautical magazine *Ves'nik Aviahtsiï i Kosmonahvtiki* (Aviation and Space Herald) presenting a project for a WIG vehicle intended to be a part of the WIG Sea Launch system and designed to serve for the launch and retrieval of space shuttle vehicles. The description contained no reference to the actual originator of the design.

The whole concept is based on the assumption that the use of a WIG vehicle in procedures associated with the launch and retrieval of space shuttles will make it possible to perform an aircraft-type horizontal landing of the shuttle, just like a landing on a conventional airstrip (which is singularly difficult to find in equatorial latitudes). As pointed out by Aframeyev, such projects are usually based on the use of huge WIG vehicles with an AUW of 1,500-2,000 tons (3,300,000 to 4,400,000 lb) and space shuttles weighing 600-800 t (1,320,000 to 1,760,000 lb) but their emergence is a matter of a remote future. However, there is no need to wait that long, says he. The problem of horizontal launch from an ocean surface and landing on it can be solved much earlier if WIG vehicles weighing up to 750 t (1,650,000 lb) and space shuttles weighing up to 300 t (660,000 lb) are used.

The system is supposed to function as follows. Immediately prior to launch the shuttle orbiter is loaded onto the WIG vehicle and both of them are refuelled. Then the WIG vehicle with the shuttle on board takes off. When the required speed is reached, the shuttle ignites its engines and separates from the carrier vehicle. In the case when a two-stage shuttle vehicle is used, separation of the stages takes place at the altitude of some 30,000m (98,400 ft) and the stage which has fulfilled its mission makes a landing on the airborne WIG vehicle and is then re-loaded onto the delivery ship. The same procedure is repeated by the shuttle orbiter upon its return, after which it can be re-used.

The M-5-2 (evolved from the M-5-1) at MosAeroShow'92 minus tail section, showing the RU19-300 turbojet in cloth wraps. It carries the logo of the Stela Aviation Company which assisted in funding the programme.

The WIG vehicle, as presented in the published drawing, is a gigantic machine with a wingspan of some 80 m (260 ft), featuring a twin-fuselage layout with a wide-chord thick wing centre section and wing outer panels of trapezoidal platform. The two boat hulls each carry their own set of tail surfaces. Placed on a crosspiece connecting the front parts of the boats are six turbojets performing the double function of boost (blowing) engines (during take-off) and cruise engines. The shuttle orbiter is placed above the wing centre section. The WIG vehicle is provided with retractable diesel-driven water propellers for slow-speed manoeuvring when afloat. The front parts of the boat hulls incorporate flight decks and compartments for the transported personnel.

Here are some basic specifications. The full take-off weight with the space shuttle on board is 750 t (1,650,000 lb), the main powerplant comprises six turbojets rated at 30,000-35,000 kgp (66,000 to 77,000 lb st) apiece, the powerplant for slow movement on water comprises two high-rpm diesel engines. Cruise flight speed is 550 to 600 km/h (342 to 373 mph), slow speed for manouevring when afloat is 25 km/h (16 mph).

Yu. S. Bakanov

This enthusiast designer, assisted by his friends, designed and built a two-seat flying boat/WIG vehicle designated SABAK-1M (SABAK stands for *soodno amortizeerovannoye Bakahnova* – Bakanov's shock-absorbing vessel). It has a configuration of a normal light hydroplane powered by a single Walter M-332 piston engine with a pusher propeller installed above the fuselage. A special feature of the vehicle is its boat fuselage featuring chines shaped like skis, the space between them forming a sort of tunnel. The aircraft entered flight test on 12th January 1991 but crashed in its fifth flight, suffering serious damage, after which it was not repaired. Actual performance, including behaviour in ground effect, was not recorded, the design speed being 140 km/h (87 mph).

Blinov

In 1965 one Blinov, an employee of the Moscow Aviation Institute, evolved a concept of a cargo transport vehicle called 'Flying wing'. The amphibious design with a wingspan of 125 m (410 ft) was intended to transport a cargo of 550 t (1,200,000 lb) at a cruising speed of 400 km/h (249 mph) to a distance of 5,000 km (3,100 miles) at an altitude of 2,000 m (6,560 ft). Actually this was a hydroplane making use of ground effect for take-off. Blinov noted that 'pockets' placed at the wingtips produced the surface effect, reducing the take-off distance and the required engine power. To check the concept, several radio-controlled models were built and flight-tested.

I. Vorontsov.

In 1977-1978 in the city of Perm' a group led by I. I. Vorontsov designed and built an ekranolyot named Elektron. It was of wooden construction and had a configuration similar to that of the TsLST ESKA-1. The vehicle was powered by a 32-hp engine from a Ural motorcycle driving a wooden propeller of 1.7 m (5 ft 7 in) in diameter through reduction gear. Initially it was powered by an engine from a Czech-built CZ motorcycle (pronounced '*chezet*'), but its output proved insufficient for a vehicle weighing 400 kg (880 lb).

In March 1979 the ekranolyot was flight-tested, making take-offs and landings on snow. The tests demonstrated good stability.

R. N. Kolokol'tsev

In the 1980s this enthusiast designer, a resident of Leningrad (now Saint-Petersburg), designed, built and tested two single-seat WIG craft (see photos).

A. I. P'yetsukh

In 1967 A. I. P'yetsukh, a former test pilot and a combat pilot during the war, designed and built the **PAI-67** WIG vehicle. The machine had two sets of wings arranged in tandem, the main wings having a diamond-shaped planform. The lifting surfaces were spaced in height and featured anhedral. The vehicle was powered by a 20-hp Vikhr' (Whirlwind) outboard engine retaining its water propeller. To reduce the unstick speed at take-off, the vehicle was provided with hydrofoils which in cruise flight were lifted to a height of 10 cm (4 in) above the

Above: A model of the WIG Sea Launch space system proposed by E. A. Aframeyev, showing the bizarre WIG launch/retrieval vehicle and the space shuttle mounted piggy-back.

The SABAK-1M homebuilt aircraft with WIG properties. The wings could be detached, turning it into an aerosleigh. What looks right flies right, they say; unfortunately the SABAK-1M crashed on its fifth flight.

Above: The MKh-2 *Bahbochka* (Butterfly) homebuilt WIG vehicle designed and built by R. N. Kolokol'tsev. A curious aspect of the design is the inverted-Vee ('butterfly') tail which probably accounts for the name.

Another one of Kolokol'tsev's WIG endeavours – the MBB. Note the skid landing gear which is due to the fact that the vehicle was tested from the frozen surface of the Gulf of Finland.

water. Directional control was effected by water rudders mounted on the pylons of the rear hydrofoil. A large-area lifting steerable stabiliser was fitted. Roll control was effected by differential deflection of the port and starboard elevators. The water displacing hull housed an enclosed cockpit in its centre section and tapered off aft of the cockpit into a fin and a large-sized rudder. A. I. P'yetsukh himself tested the PAI-67 at the Khimki Reservoir north of Moscow. The vehicle lifted itself out of the water in 12 to 15 seconds and developed a speed of 60 km/h (37 mph), far superior to the speed of boats with the same engine.

N. I. Stoyano
In 1975-1980 N. I. Stoyano, a resident of the town of Mytischi (Moscow Region), designed and built an ekranolyot called Ayans-86 (the meaning of the name remains obscure). The vehicle had two sets of wings arranged in tandem and measuring 3.6 m (11 ft 10 in) in span. The wings were joined together by floats at their tips. The 140-hp Walter Minor engine with a pusher propeller was placed behind a two-seat enclosed cockpit. The tail unit comprised a fin-and-rudder assembly and a stabiliser with an elevator. The vehicle was tested in 1985. When flown from the water it failed to reach the design speed due to the unsatisfactory hydrodynamic shape of the floats. In tests on snow with a ski undercarriage it showed a top speed of 150 km/h (93 mph). The all-up weight of the rather heavy machine was 1,100 kg (2,425 lb).

'Ekranolyot' from the Far East
In 1974 enthusiast aircraft designers from the Oogol'nyy township in the Far-Eastern Primor'ye region built an ultra-light single-seat WIG vehicle dubbed '*Ekranolyot*' (a proper name, in this case). This was a typical 'homebuilt' job, no aviation materials, good production facilities or a really suitable engine being available. The vehicle of wooden construction featured the Lippisch configuration. Ailerons were carried by winglets set at an angle to the main wing. The T-tail featured strut-braced stabilisers. The bare airframe (less canvas skinning) weighed 350 kg (771 lb). The vehicle was powered by a 10-hp PD-10 two-stroke engine normally used as a starter for heavy tractor diesels. During tests in 1975 the machine proved to be sensitive at the controls, which was detrimental to stability in flight.

P. Tsymbalyuk
A group of enthusiasts in Arkhangelsk headed by P.Tsymbalyuk designed and built a vehicle called '*Ekranolyot*' (again!). In this case, too, the Lippisch layout was used, with a reversed-delta wing having anhedral on the leading edges and supplemented with aileron-carrying winglets. The tail unit included all-movable strut-braced stabilisers placed atop the fin. Floats were attached under the wingtips. A 105-hp M-332 engine was mounted on a truss cabane above the wing centre section; it drove a standard propeller but with cropped blades, which resulted in a substantial loss of thrust. The boat hull was strengthened with glassfibre. The vehicle was tested in 1977, reaching a speed of more than 60 km/h (37 mph) on water and up to 80 km/h (50 mph) on ice.

P. P. Yablonskiy
In 1985 a student of the Zhukovskiy Military Engineering Air Academy P. P. Yablonskiy submitted a graduation project of a transport WIG vehicle. It had two fuselages joined together by a low-aspect-ratio wing centre section. To reduce the outward air flow from beneath the wing centre section, strakes were fitted to the underside of the fuselages in the area of the wings. A high-set horizontal tail was used. Wind-tunnel tests simulating the ground effect were conducted with models. Test results corroborated the design characteristics of the WIG vehicle.

N. V. Yakubovich
A design belonging to Nikolay V. Yakubovich is mentioned in his article *Between two elements* published in the July 1998 issue of the *Kryl'ya Rodiny* magazine: '*In 1975 this author submitted a project of a transport WIG vehicle intended for transporting cargoes of up to 365 t to a distance of up to 9,000 km [5,590 miles] at a cruising speed of 410 km/h [254 mph]. It featured a wing centre section with an aspect ratio of 0.5, flanked by boats of a planoconvex shape. /.../ When the vehicle was loaded, special elastic floats were inflated on the sides. /.../ To create an air cushion, a stream of air from turbofan installations was pumped into the cavity formed by the underside of the wing centre section, and the front and rear flaps. As the cruise engines accelerated the vehicle, the front flap was retracted and a transition from the static to the dynamic air cushion took place. The powerplant consisted of several tandem pairs of high-output NK-12 turboprops*'.

Chapter 6

Free Enterprise

Enter New Firms

The beginning of the 1990s was marked by the break-up of the Soviet Union. It gave place to the Russian Federation and new independent states, former Soviet Republics which, together with Russia, formed the Commonwealth of Independent States (CIS). The construction of WIG vehicles as a branch remained virtually 100 per cent within the boundaries of the Russian Federation (apart from Russia, only the Ukraine could boast some scientific work in this field during the Soviet period).

Sweeping market reforms giving full rein to private enterprise in the Russian economy had their effect on the situation also in the aircraft industry and associated branches.

The early 1990s saw the emergence of a large number of private companies (design bureaux) which declared their intention to engage in the design of aircraft. Among these there were several firms whose plans encompassed the design and construction of WIG vehicles. These were small enterprises which, as a rule, had no production facilities of their own and possessed very limited financial resources. Their activities only rarely resulted in producing real hardware even in prototype form, to say nothing of series production. However, they produced a number of 'paper designs' which merit some attention because of their innovative spirit.

Among the new companies engaged in the design of WIG vehicles only two can boast construction of prototypes intended for series production. These are the Amphibious Transport Technologies Joint-Stock Company (JSC) – initially known as Technology and Transport – and the KOMETEL JSC. It stands to reason that the following review of designs produced by new firms should start with these two enterprises.

Amphibious Transport Technologies (ATT, Joint Stock Company)

This company was founded in 1992 in Nizhniy Novgorod as Technology and Transport (TET) JSC. It was formed by some 130 engineers who, until then, had worked in the Central Hydrofoil Design Bureau named after R. Alexeyev. The new company was headed by D. N. Sinitsyn, his deputy was A. M. Maskalik. The company declared its intention to pursue the design of WIG vehicles for civil duties. The newly formed design team embarked on the design of a small WIG boat named Passat (Tradewind); in 1996 it was renamed Amphistar.

Amphistar

The Amphistar belongs to the category of small Type A WIG vehicles – high-speed craft intended for operation only within the height of ground effect, powered by an engine of more than 55 kW, carrying not more than 12 passengers, operated only in daytime within 20 miles from the coast and within 100 miles from a place of refuge, and having an all-up weight of not more than 10 t (22,045 lb). The five-seat Amphistar is intended for maritime pleasure rides and tourism. It is a dynamic air cushion speedboat with an enclosed cabin, featuring a forward location of the engine.

One of the ten pre-production Amphistar vehicles comes out onto the shore at high speed; note the tubular guard connecting the skegs and the upward tilt of the propellers. The emblem on the rear fuselage refers to the craft's marketing name in the USA, Xtreme Xplorer.

An Amphistar in cruise mode (left) and at rest on the shore. Apart from the twin fins and powerplant arrangement, the vehicle is similar to the larger Volga-2.

Here are the main specifications and performance figures of the machine: overall length, 10.44 m (34 ft 3 in), overall width (wingspan), 5.9 m (19 ft 4¼ in); overall height, 3.35 m (11 ft); maximum all-up weight, 2,720 kg (6,000 lb); operating empty weight, 2,200 kg (4,850 lb); crew and equipment weight, 117 kg (258 lb); payload, 300 kg (660 lb); fuel load, 100 kg (220 lb). Range with 100 kg of fuel is 350-400 km (217-248 miles) depending on the weather (wind force, wave height). The vehicle is amphibious – it can negotiate shallow places, come out onto an unprepared bank with a gradient of up to 5°, move on the ground at speeds of 10-15 km/h (6.2-9.3 mph) and go back to the water. The airframe of the Amphistar is made of corrosion-proof composite materials.

The Amphistar's wing set of rectangular planform and low aspect ratio is fitted with flaps and provided with endplates in the shape of inflatable pontoons which ensure the vehicle's stability when afloat and form the sidewalls of the 'scoop' in which the air cushion is created (there is also a retractable inflatable support pontoon on the centreline). A compartment placed amidships in the hull accommodates four passengers and a driver. The aft bay of the hull houses equipment, while the forward part of the hull is occupied by a 300-hp Mercedes-Benz engine which transmits its torque through a central gearbox and two side gearboxes to two AV-110 tractor propellers with ground-adjustable pitch. The propellers can swivel their plane of rotation and direct the air stream under the wings for take-off.

The tail unit comprises twin fins and rudders mounted of the aft fuselage and slightly canted outwards, with the horizontal tail placed atop the fins. Directional control is effected by two rudders during movement in ground effect and by a retractable water rudder when afloat.

The Amphistar vehicle was built to a specification issued by the Taiwanese company Seagull Decor Co. Ltd which, however, later backed away from supporting the project. In 1997 the Amphistar was certified in the Russian Shipping Register in accordance with IMO rules (adopted somewhat later) for type A vehicles designed for flying only in ground effect and regarded as boats for certification purposes. The ATT company prides itself on having obtained this certificate which had

Another view of the Amphistar as it comes out on the shore, showing the air intakes of the engine buried in the fuselage nose and the propeller drive shafts.

Two views of the prototype Aquaglide-5, an updated version of the Amphistar, showing the additional roof pillars and the lack of the 'bumper' at the front.

required a lot of effort and entailed considerable expenses.

In all, 11 machines of the Passat/Amphistar type were built between 1992 and 1997. This machine was demonstrated in Düsseldorf in 1996 and 1997. At that time a Russian company called Pacific Technique Development handled the marketing of the machine.

Efforts were undertaken to promote sales of the Amphistar in North America. For this purpose a company named Amphistar USA Ltd was formed in 1998. This company began marketing the machine in the USA under a new name, Xtreme Xplorer. Yet another company, Amphistar Bahamas Ltd, was established in 1999 to promote the vehicle in the Bahamas. Trial operation and demonstration flights of the Xtreme Xplorer were undertaken both in the USA and in the Bahamas.

However, in April 2000 the project was closed down at the insistence of the US partner due to some financial disagreements. The Amphistar vehicles were withdrawn from operation and placed in storage. The Amphistar USA Ltd still formally exists but has ceased all activities.

Three years before that, in 1997, the Technology and Transport company had entered into co-operation with the Russian company named ATTK (*Arkticheskaya torgovo-trahnsportnaya kompahniya* – Arctic Trade & Transport Co.) which is engaged in transportation of goods into regions of the Russian Far North. The ATTK undertook the marketing of TET designs and funding of the design team's work. Practically, since 2000 the ATTK has been sponsoring this design team based at Nizhniy Novgorod which in that year changed its name to Amphibious Transport Technologies JSC (ATT).

Aquaglide

The ATT company turned a new page by introducing the Aquaglide programme replacing the defunct Amphistar programme. The new programme includes the Aquaglide 5 WIG speedboat and a project of a multi-seat passenger WIG craft designated Aquaglide 50 (the two machines have a seating capacity of 5 and 48 passengers respectively). There are also other designs in this series.

The Aquaglide 5 is a somewhat reworked Amphistar. The changes include introducing four smaller windows instead of two big windows on each side of the passenger cabin (which makes the hull more rigid). The forward parts of the pontoons have been shortened, and a protective bar ahead of the propellers deleted. One example of the Aquaglide 5 has been built and a second is under construction; the machine is ready for series production which depends on finding a customer that would be prepared to contribute to financing the project.

The specifications of the Aquaglide 5 and Aquaglide 50 are given at the foot of the page.

TAP

In addition to the Aquaglide series of passenger craft, since 1997 the ATT company has been working on a series of vehicles of various sizes under the common designation TAP (*trahnsportno-amfibeeynaya platforma* – transport amphibious platform) which are intended for carrying cargo in the regions of the Far North.

TAP vehicles look like elongated flat platforms flanked along the whole of their length by endplate floats. Placed in the front part of the platform is the enclosed crew workstation (cockpit). Most of the flat upper surface of the platform is used for open carriage of various cargoes. Since the upper surface of the platform is not shaped like an airfoil section, the lift during cruise is created solely by the dynamic air cushion created by ram air in the cavity which is formed by the bottom of the platform and the floats. The powerplant of some of the TAP vehicles comprises four turbojets arranged in tandem pairs in each float.

While the aft-positioned engines act as cruise engines only, the forward engines can deflect their jet exhaust and discharge it through special ducts beneath the bottom of the platform, thus creating a static air cushion during take-off and landing. The platforms are amenable to producing derivatives with enclosed accommodation for the carriage of cargo or passengers – they have simply to be 'crowned' with a suitably shaped superstructure.

As an example, the specifications and performance figures for two designs in the TAP range are given on page 84.

MPE model range

The MPE acronym stands for *morskoy passazheerskiy ekranoplahn* – sea-going passenger WIG vehicle. This was a common designation for a series of projects of passenger ekranoplans evolved originally in the Central Design Bureau and taken over for further development by the TET (later ATT) company when it separated from the mother organisation. This series includes machines of different weight, ranging from the 10-ton (22,045-lb) MPE-10 to the 470-ton (1,036,155-lb) MPE-400, with a seating capacity from 20 to 500 passengers. Their Alexeyev lineage is reflected in their general configuration similar to that of the Orlyonok, Loon' etc., with booster engines on the front fuselage and cruise engines placed high on the tail unit. A distinctive feature of these designs is the use of composite wings with high aspect ratio outer wing panels added to the main wings outboard of the wingtip endplate floats. Equally characteristic is the tail unit and engine arrangement. The tail unit consists of two fins and rudders

Type	Aquaglide 5	Aquaglide 50
Length, m (ft)	10.7 (35)	30.0 (98)
Width, m (ft)	5.9 (19)	15.0 (49)
Height, m (ft)	3.4 (11)	8.0 (26)
Displacement, t (lb)	2.4 (5,290)	24.0 (52,900)
Seating capacity, persons	5	48
Cruising speed, km/h (mph)	150 (93)	200 (124)
Range, km (miles)	up to 400 (248)	up to 1,000 (620)
Seaworthiness, wave height m (ft)	0.35 (1)	1.0 (3)

Aquaglide-50

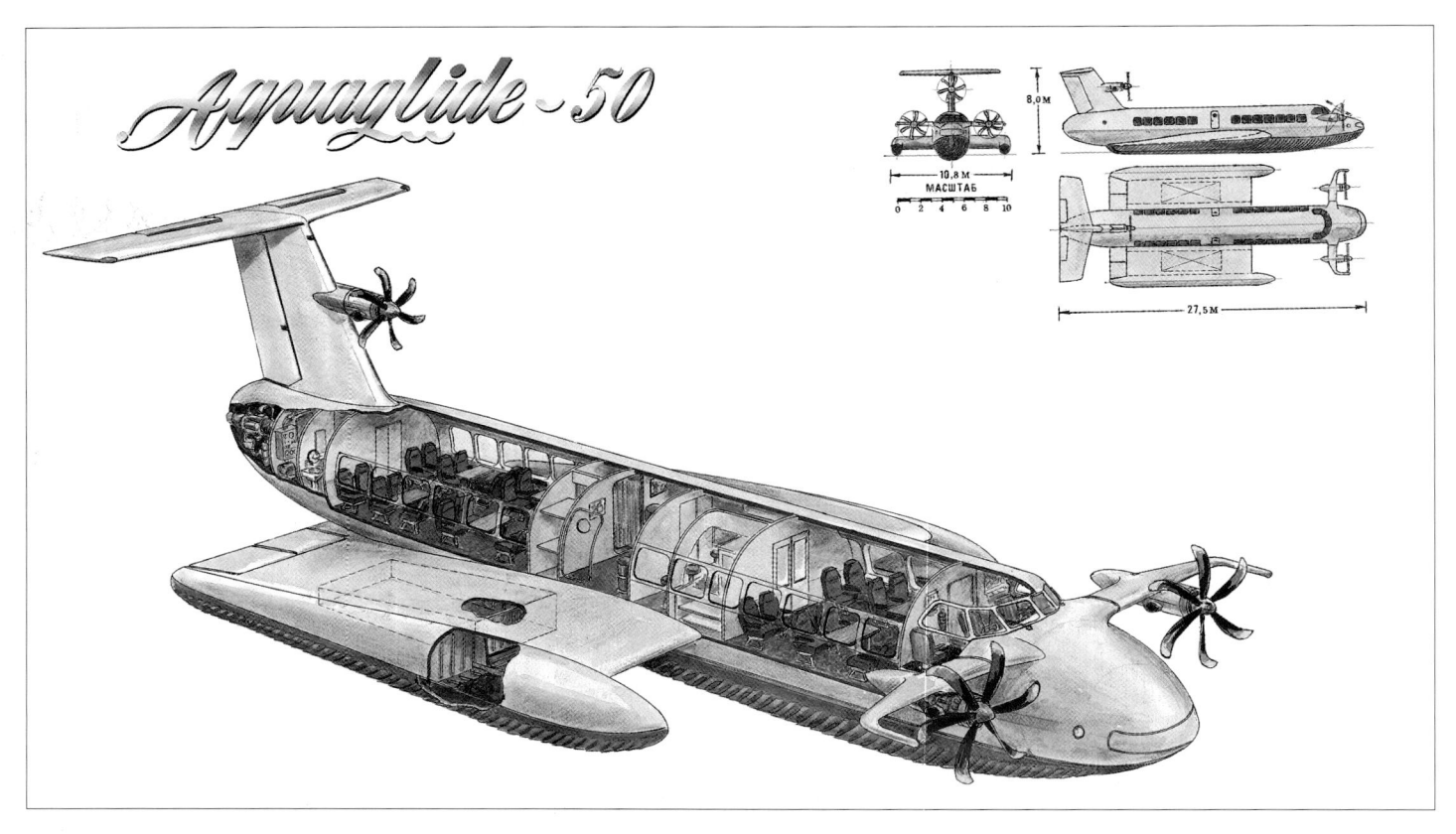

TAP Specifications

Length, m (ft)	23 (75)	43 (141)
Width, m (ft)	9.5 (31)	16 (52)
Height, m (ft)	6 (20)	9.5 (31)
Displacement, t (lb)	24 (52,900)	100 (220,000)
Seating (cargo) capacity, persons/t (lb)	60 persons, 10 t (22,000 lb)	200 persons, 35 t (77,200 lb)
Seaworthiness, wave height m (ft)	up to 1.25 (4)	up to 1.5 (5)
Cruising speed, km/h (mph)		
over calm water	120 (75)	150 (93)
over rough seas	90 (56)	110 (68)
over ice and snow	120 (75)	120 (75)
Range, km (miles)	up to 200 (124)	up to 1,000 (620)
Cargo deck dimensions, m (ft)	12 x 4 (39 x 13)	n.a.

Above: A three-view and a cutaway drawing of the projected 48-seat Aquaglide-50. As can be seen, the powerplant combines the features of Alexeyev's Orlyonok (the fin-mounted cruise engine) and the Amphistar-turned-Aquaglide-5 (the forward engines can swivel together with the pylons to direct the airflow under or above the wings, depending on the flight mode).

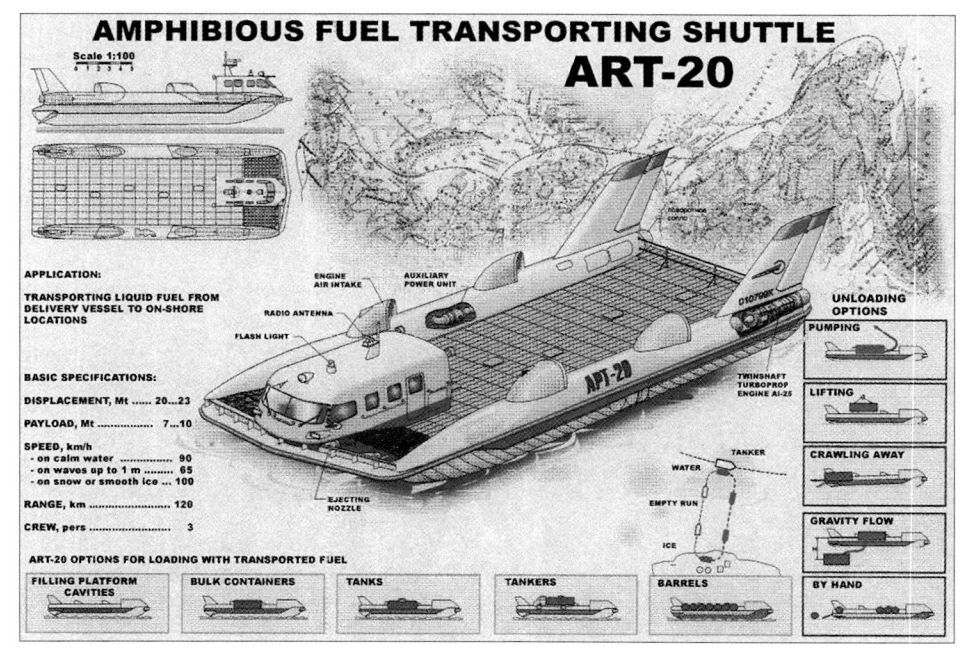

AMPHIBIOUS FUEL TRANSPORTING SHUTTLE ART-20

Scale 1:100

APPLICATION:
TRANSPORTING LIQUID FUEL FROM DELIVERY VESSEL TO ON-SHORE LOCATIONS

BASIC SPECIFICATIONS:
DISPLACEMENT, Mt .... 20...23
PAYLOAD, Mt .... 7...10
SPEED, km/h
 - on calm water 90
 - on waves up to 1 m 65
 - on snow or smooth ice ... 100
RANGE, km 120
CREW, pers 3

ART-20 OPTIONS FOR LOADING WITH TRANSPORTED FUEL:
FILLING PLATFORM CAVITIES | BULK CONTAINERS | TANKS | TANKERS | BARRELS | BY HAND

UNLOADING OPTIONS: PUMPING | LIFTING | CRAWLING AWAY | GRAVITY FLOW | BY HAND

Left: An artist's impression of the ART-20, a WIG cargo carrier platform from the TAP family developed by the ATT company (the ART designation may denote 'Arctic Regional Transport'). The accompanying inset pictures detail possible payload options and alternative liquid fuel loading and unloading operations.

An artist's impression of the 200-seat MPE-200. Its Alexeyev origins are obvious – apart from the tail, the MPE-200 is very similar to the Orlyonok.

canted slightly outwards, with the horizontal tail placed on top of the fins; two turboprop engines are placed at the fin/tailplane junctions. An example of this configuration is the MPE-200 project. The table at the foot of this page provides information on some designs in the MPE range.

Not included in this table are projects of MPE vehicles with an all-up weight of 25 t (55,114 lb) and 60 t (132,275 lb) currently under development in the ATT company.

Wing-in-Ground-Effect Vehicles Designed by the KOMETEL Company (TREK concern)

In 1996 the community of Russian firms and organisations engaged in design and manufacture of ekranoplans was joined by the KOMETEL JSC set up in Moscow. Under the guidance of its director and chief designer Viacheslav Kolganov it developed several projects of WIG vehicles which, in the firm's advertising materials, were classed as ekranoplans and ekranolyots (ie, Type A and Type B vehicles).

EL-7 Ivolga (Golden Oriole)

This is the first design of this company that has been developed as far as the hardware stage. It is a Type B vehicle intended for the transportation of 8 to 11 passengers or small cargoes. The EL-7 features a composite wing aerodynamic layout well suited for a vehicle intended to be operated both in and out of ground effect. The wings comprise a centre section of high relative thickness and low aspect ratio with a straight leading edge and negative sweep on the trailing edge, and folding outer wing panels of greater aspect ratio (borrowed from the Yak-18T cabin monoplane) attached to it. The wing centre section has a dome-shaped configuration in front view and rests upon large floats, producing a kind of catamaran with the fuselage (passenger cabin) placed on the centreline atop the wings. The wing centre section is equipped with front and rear flaps which, together with the floats, form a cavity in which an air cushion is created; the cavity assists the machine's take-off and can be used as a thrust reverser to shorten the landing run.

The powerplant comprises two car engines installed separately, each in its own bay in the centre section. Other types of engines, including diesels and aircraft engines, can be installed.

The engines transmit their power through cardan shafts to two propellers in annular shrouds installed on each side of the forward fuselage. The shrouds enhance the propellers' thrust at low speeds, protect them from foreign objects, serve as a safety device for people coming close to the propellers and reduce the noise level. Depending on the flight mode, the propellers can alter the direction of their thrust. In take-off mode the air flow created by the propellers is directed under the wing centre section, during cruise flight it is directed above it. The EL-7 makes use of air injection from propellers into the cavity formed by the wing centre section, the aft flap

Type	Displacement, t (lb)	Cruising speed, km/h (mph)	Seating capacity	Range, km (miles)	Max wave height on take-off, m (ft)
MPE-10	10 (22,045)	250	18	1,00	1.0
MPE-100	90 198,412)	320	150	1,800	1.5
MPE-200	210 (462,962)	400	250	3,000	2.0
MPE-300	300 (661,375)	450	340	4,500	2.5
MPE-400	470 (1,036,155)	500	460	6,000	3.0

Above: A model of the EL-7 unveiled at the MAKS-99 airshow in Moscow. Note the six-bladed propellers.

and the floats. The propellers are deflected in concert with flap deflection, but in other flight modes they can be deflected independently of each other.

The static air cushion thus created enables the vehicle to move without contact with the underlying surface at heights up to 0.3 m (1 ft) at a speed of up to 80 km/h (50 mph). During further acceleration the ram air pressure makes it possible to change the direction of the propellers' thrust and enter the dynamic air cushion (ground effect) mode.

The EL-7 is an amphibious craft capable of coming out onto a gently sloping bank under its own power and returning to the water surface. When taxying on water, differential use of the front centre section flaps enables the machine to make a full turn literally on the spot.

The vehicle has a T-tail. Its control system comprises a rudder, an elevator, ailerons, controls for the devices governing the air cushion (devices for rotating the axles of propellers and deflecting the wing centre section flaps). Directional control can be effected not only by the rudder but also by using differential thrust through changing the propeller speed, switching off one propeller by means of a clutch or changing the propellers' pitch.

Testing of the EL-7 was initiated in Moscow in September 1998; it started with checking out the control system during taxying on water, including the air injection ('blowing') mode. In January 1999 the WIG vehicle was tested in Irkutsk under the conditions of the harsh Siberian winter. The first flight in air injection mode was effected at the Irkutsk water reservoir on 16th February. Four days later V. V. Kolganov, General Director of the KOMETEL company and of the TREK concern, performed a flight on the EL-7 powered by 150-hp ZMZ-4062 piston engines of the Zavolzhskiy engine factory (as fitted to the GAZ-3110 Volga saloon car) and tested the surface effect mode in cruise configuration (with flaps retracted and propellers in the cruise position), at speeds of 80-110 km/h (49-68 mph).

With two ZMZ-4062-10 engines the EL-7 proved to be underpowered when flying with a full payload. There were plans to re-engine

The as-yet unpainted prototype of the EL-7 Ivolga in flight during initial flight tests.

Above: The EL-7 prototype during water handling trials.
Below: This view shows how the outer wings are folded for manoeuvring beside the pier and docking. Note the four-bladed propellers of the real thing.

Painted in a smart orange and white colour scheme, the BMW-powered EL-7S had its public debut at the MAKS-2001 airshow in August 2002. The Cyrillic VLRP titles on the tail are the name of the launch customer (Upper Lena River Shipping Company) whose financial support enabled the project to go ahead.

the EL-7 with turbocharged ZMZ-4064-10 engines delivering 210 hp apiece, but they were not available in time, and the machine had to be equipped with 286-hp BMW S38 engines as fitted to the BMW 5 Series saloon (in this version the machine was designated EL-7S). In August 1999 V. V. Kolganov, flying the machine equipped with these engines, demonstrated the vehicle descending from the bank to the water surface, flying in ground effect in a cruise configuration and coming out to the bank again. In December 1999 another pilot, D. G. Shchebliakov, demonstrated a flight at the height of 4 m (13 ft), including changes of flight direction. Somewhat later the vehicle rose to a height of more than 15 m (50 ft) and demonstrated its ability to fly out of ground effect. In February 2000 the first long-distance flight took place. In the autumn of 2000 the vehicle confidently made a lift-off and alighted on waves more than 1 m (3 ft) high.

The EL-7 proved to be simple in handling, forgiving even serious piloting errors. 'Aircraft' flight modes were successfully tried out. Banking turns in the proximity of the water surface were performed with a bank angle of 15° at heights beginning with 3 m (10 ft) and up to the altitude where the vehicle left the ground effect zone (above 10 m/33 ft); turns above the ground effect zone were performed with bank angles of 30-50°.

During flight close to the supporting surface the lift/drag ratio of the EL-7 Ivolga WIG vehicle reached 25, which is more than twice the corresponding figure for aircraft of a comparable category. When operation is limited to heights of up to 3 m (10 ft), the EL-7 is certified in the Registers for River-going and Sea-going Ships. When equipped with aircraft engines, avionics and piloting and navigation systems, the vehicle can also be certified in the Aviation Register, including 'aircraft' flight modes. In these, the vehicle will have a performance comparable to that of aircraft of the same dimensions. It will retain the ability to operate from unprepared dirt airstrips, ice, deep snow and water, including swamp areas.

In its baseline version the EL-7 WIG vehicle has a passenger cabin with easily removable folding seats making it possible to transform the cabin into a cargo compartment or a mixed cargo/passenger cabin. The *ekranolyot* can be supplied to customers in one of the following versions: cargo/passenger version, a version for tourism and excursions, border guard version, patrol version for use by law enforcement and nature protection agencies, SAR, fire-fighting, ecological monitoring, VIP/executive and other versions to cater for the customer's special needs.

For the purpose of production and operation of WIG vehicles the design bureau – the KOMETEL company – and the launch customer, the Upper Lena River Shipping Company (VLRP – **Verkh**ne-**Len**skoye rechnoye paro**khod**stvo), as well as some other organisations, have formed a consortium named TREK Joint-Stock Company (the acronym TREK stands for **trahns**port eko**logi**cheskiy – environmentally friendly transport). At the end of 2001 it was reported that the concern had already launched production of the 14-seat EK-12 WIG vehicle similar to the Ivolga and incorporating refinements based on the testing of the original model. At the same time preparations were under way for the manufacture of the 27-passenger EK-25 WIG vehicles. Here follows a description of these and other designs of the KOMETEL.

EK-12

This machine is closely similar to the EL-7 and differs mainly in the design of the folding wing outer panels which have moderate sweepback and no taper and are attached to the floats via sections with an extended leading edge. The EK-12, intended for carrying 12 passengers and one or two crew, is powered by two 286-hp BMW S38 engines. The EK-12R version of somewhat smaller cargo capacity (the R refers to Russian engines) is intended to carry eight passengers and one pilot and will be powered by two 210-hp ZMZ-4064-10 engines. Interestingly, the EK-12 shares the layout and basic parameters of the EL-7 ekranolyot (Type B vehicle) but is classed as a Type A vehicle – obviously with a view to simplifying the certification procedure.

EK-20

This is a pure Type A WIG design based on a 'flying wing' layout. It has much in common with the EL-7, featuring the same twin-float configuration with a dome-shaped (inverted-V) wing topped by the cabin for the crew and passengers. Also similar is the arrangement and design of the powerplants with propellers in annular shrouds. The main difference is the absence of outer wing panels and a revised tail unit design. The tail unit comprises twin fins and rudders mounted on the aft ends of the floats and slightly canted outwards; the horizontal tailplane surfaces are attached to the tops of the fins on the outboard sides (this places the horizontal tail outside the influence of the downwash over the rear part of the wing). Powered by two 300-hp BMW M10 automobile engines, the vehicle was expected to carry a payload of 1,980 kg (4,365 lb) to a distance of 1,370 km (850 miles) when flying at 0.5 m (1.6 ft) over the surface and 1,120 km (695 miles) when flying at the height of 1 m (3 ft).

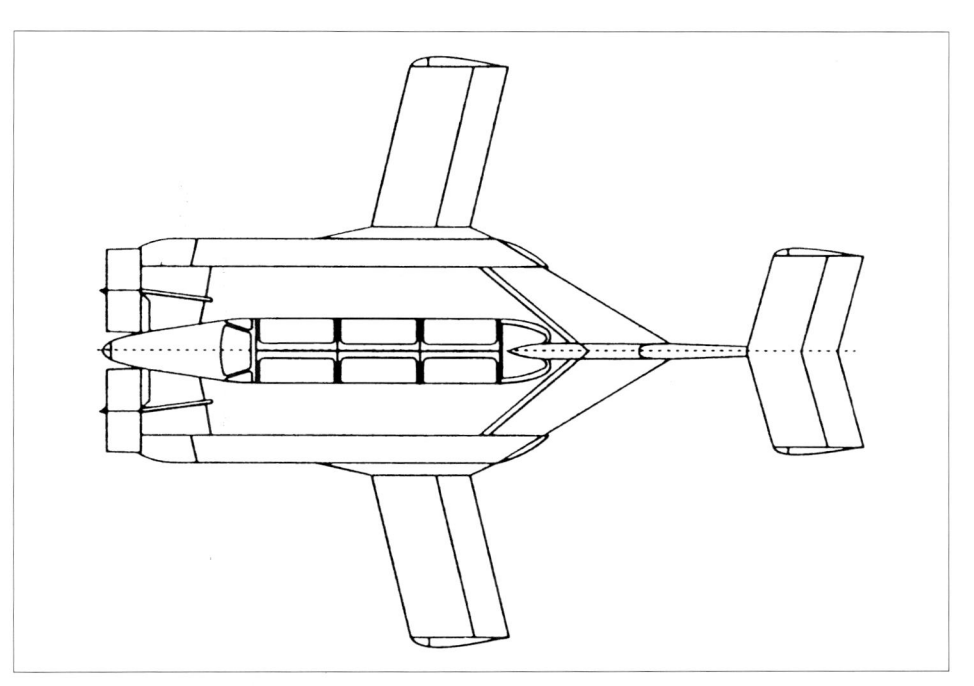

A drawing off the EK-12 passenger WIG vehicle, showing the new shorter, sweptback outer wings.

EK-25

This WIG vehicle is a scaled-up version of the EK-20 powered by two 400-hp BMW S73 automobile engines. It is intended for transporting 25 passengers and two crew at a cruising speed of 160-175 km/h (99-108 mph) to a distance of 1,120-1,370 km.

Designs by other Companies

The designs of other companies are described on the following pages in alphabetical order of the names of the relevant firms.

Type	EL-7	EL-7S	EK-12	EK-12R	EK-20	EK-25
All-up weight, kg (lb)	3,300 (7,275)	3,600 (7,936)	3,600 (7,936)	3,100 (6,834)	4,900 (10,802)	5,500 (12,125)
Crew (passengers)	1 (7)	1 (10)	1-2 (12)	1 (8)	2 (19)	2 (25)
Payload, kg (lb)	700 (1,543)	1,000 (2,204)	1,200 (2,645)	850 (1,873)	1,980 (4,365)	2,500 (5,511)
Engines	automobile	automobile	automobile	automobile	automobile	automobile
Type	ZMZ-4064.10	BMW S38	BMW S38	ZMZ-4064.10	BMW M10	BMW S73
Number/power, hp.	2x210	2x286	2x286	2x210	2x340	2x400
Fuel load, kg (lb)	160 (352)	160 (352)	250 (551)	200 (440)	300 (661)	300 (661)
Range, km (miles):						
at 0,8 m (2.6 ft)	1,150 (714)	1,210 (751)	1,210 (751)	1,150 (714)	1,120*(695)	1,120 (695)
at 0,3 m (1.6 ft)	1,480 (919)	1,520 (944)	1,520 (944)	1,480 (919)	1,370** (850)	1,370 (850)
Speed, km/h (mph):						
cruising	150-175 (93-108)	180 (111)	180 (111)	160-175 (99-108)	150-175 (93-108)	160-175 (99-108)
maximum	200 (124)	210 (130)	210 (130)	200 (124)	195 (121)	205 (127)
Sea state, Beaufort scale	3-4	3-4	3-4	3	3-4	4
Taxying height, m (ft)	n.a.	n.a.	0,1 (0.32)	0,1 (0.32)	0,1-0,2 (0.32-0.65)	0,1 (0.32)
Draught, m (ft)	0.45 (1.47)	0.45 (1.47)	0.35-0.45 (1.15-1.47)	0.35-0.45 (1.15-1.47)	0.55 (1.8)	0.55 (1.8)
Overall dimensions, m (ft)	n.a.	n.a.	15.6x12.7x3.7 (51'2.17"x41'8"x12'1.6")	15.6x12.7x3.7 (51'2.17"x41'8"x12'1.6")	n.a.	20.1x18.2x5.1 (65'11.33"x59'8.5"x16'8.78")
Dimensions with outer wings folded, m (ft)	n.a.	n.a.	15.6x4.8x4.0 (51'2.17"x15'9"x13'1.5")	15.6x4.8x4.0 (51'2.17"x15'9"x13'1.5")	n.a.	20.1x8.3x5.6 (65'11.33"x27'2.77"x18'4.5")

* at 1.0 m (3 ft) altitude; ** at 0.5 m (1.6 ft) altitude

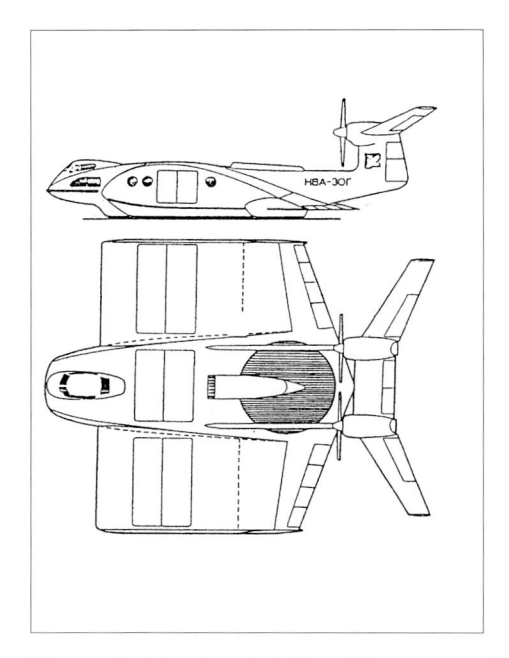

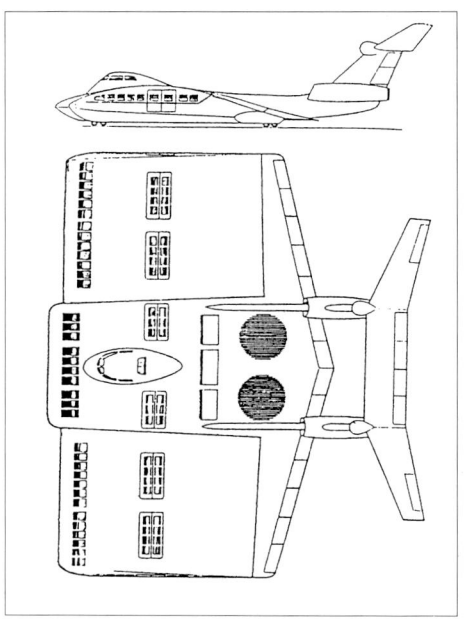

These project drawings depict two of the passenger WIGs developed by Amphicon – the NVA-30G (left) and the NVA-120P. The fans creating a static air cushion are clearly visible.

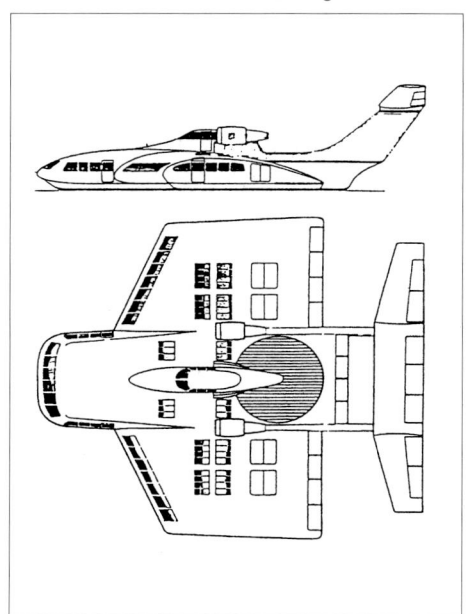

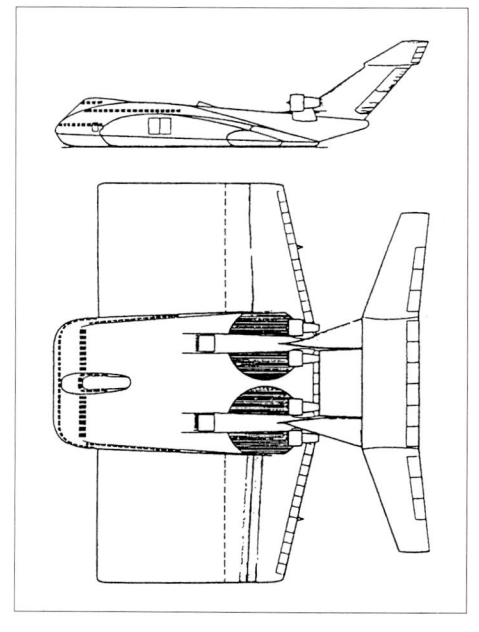

Two more Amphicon projects – the NVA-60P (left) and the NVA-600. Note the wingtip entry/cargo doors.

Amphicon

Amphicon is an abbreviation for *Amfibeeynye konstrooktsii* (amphibious designs). The full name of the company is NPF Amphicon, NPF is deciphered as *naoochno-proizvodstvennaya feerma* – Science and production firm.

This commercial enterprise was set up in Nizhniy Novgorod with N. N. Nazarov as General Director and Chief Designer. Initially, the Amphicon company had borne the name of Ecolen Science and Production Association and had been based at St. Petersburg (Ecolen is an abbreviation of *Ekologiya Lenskovo reghiona* – Ecology of the Lena River Region, indicating that the projects were to be tailored to the needs of that region).

In the early 1990s the company presented a national development programme of means of transportation in Russia based on a new generation of WIG vehicles – the so-called Ground-and-Air Amphibious Vehicles (GAAV), the Russian abbreviation being NVA (*nazemno-vozdooshnyye amfibii*). The programme covered a 15-year period up to 2008. The range of projects envisaged in the programme represents a gradual transition from a 3-tonne (6,610-lb) vehicle of 'aircraft layout' to a 'flying wing' vehicle weighing 5,000 t (11,022,930 lb). In all, by 1993 the Amphicon company had developed ten baseline projects, each in several versions. Information about them was presented in the catalogue of the MAKS-93 airshow (September 1993); every project was accompanied by the planned year of construction (between 1996 and 2008). The machine to be built in 2008 was to have an all-up weight of 5,000 t (11,022,900 lb)! Drawings of the following eight projects were published in the catalogue: NVA-1SM (1996), NVA-30P (1997), NVA-30G (1997), NVA-120P (1997), NVA-60P (1997), NVA-600 (2003). The G and P suffixes refer to cargo (*groozovaya*) and passenger (*passazheerskaya*) versions respectively. Other sources also mention such projects as the NVA-60G, NVA-120GP, NVA-600TP, NVA-900, NVA-2000, NVA-5000 (this list is not exhaustive). In English-language advertising materials the abbreviation NVA is replaced by GAAV. As witnessed by the drawings, many of the projects envisage the use of powerful fans creating a static air cushion during take-off, making these craft a combination of ACV and WIG vehicle. The company advertised such an 'important advantage' of the NVA vehicles as 'their load-carrying capacity amounting to 50% of the all-up weight'

The very ambitious programme described above could have a chance of being implemented only on the condition of a massive financial support from the Government or other sources – which was far from realistic to expect under the circumstances prevailing in Russia. To date, not a single of the listed projects progressed further than the drawing board, and the Amphicon and Ecolen firms no longer signify their presence in this field.

Delaero JSC

In 1994 this small company proposed a multi-purpose WIG vehicle named Globus-1 (Globe-1), intended for cargo and passenger transportation, as well as for ambulance, patrol and liaison duties, to be operated mainly above water. It had wings of composite layout with large-size outer wing panels, designed to ensure an adequate lift-to-drag ratio in the case of short-time out-of-ground-effect fly-overs (Type B vehicle). The machine had a retractable tricycle undercarriage. Three powerplant variants were envisaged: either two DV-4 piston engines of 130 hp apiece, or two Wankel-type engines of 140 hp each, or one MKB Granit TVD-400 turboprop delivering 400 ehp. No prototype was built.

EKIP flying vehicles

During the last decade, unusual airborne vehicles capable, among other things, of flying in ground effect, have been under development within the framework of the EKIP company (EKIP stands for *Ekologiya i Progress* – Ecology and Progress). The post of general designer of the EKIP was occupied by Dr.Sc., Professor Lev N. Shchookin until his demise in August 2001. Previously he had worked for many years in Sergey P. Korolyov's OKB-1 renowned for its leading role in the Soviet rocketry and space research programmes. It was there that he conceived his idea of creating a new flying vehicle with an air cushion undercarriage which was originally intended for ensuring the mobility of strategic missile launch systems. Such vehicles requiring no prepared airfields could, in his opinion, find useful employment on the expanses of Siberia. However, the problem of missile mobility was solved by other means (wheeled mobile launchers), and Shchookin decided to use his concept for other purposes.

Under Shchookin's guidance fundamental principles and specific design features were evolved for a radically new type of aerial vehicles which distinguish themselves by a highly unusual appearance. Their cushion-like lifting fuselage profiled like a very thick-section airfoil combines the functions of a fuselage and a wing (lifting body). It is fitted with small stub wings required for placing ailerons on them, and with aerodynamic surfaces acting as a tail unit. The powerplant of the EKIP vehicles is accommodated inside the vehicle's body and comprises turbofan cruise engines and auxiliary turboshaft engines driving fans which produce an air cushion during take-off and landing. One of such designs has two cruise engines and two auxiliary engines.

The air required for the engines is taken up through a slot on the upper side of the centre wing (fuselage) section. The efflux of the cruise engines is emitted through flat nozzles placed along the whole span of the wing centre section in the plane dividing the air streams coming from the upper and lower surfaces. Control vanes are installed in the nozzles. According to calculations, if an EKIP vehicle weighing 120 t (264,550 lb) is powered by two ZMKB (Lotarev) D-18T turbofans rated at 23,400 kgp (51,587 lb st) each the power-to-weight ratio of the vehicle will be 0.38 – 0.40, which will enable it to perform a take-off from a ground strip or water surface no more than 500 m (1,640 ft) long – which is outstanding short-field performance. EKIP vehicles with a cargo capacity of several hundred tonnes will not necessitate the construction of special airports with 5,000-m (16,400-ft) concrete runways as required, for example, for the Airbus Industrie A380 megaliner.

The air cushion take-off and landing device featuring a combined air jet and chamber layout is placed well within the contours of the body and is placed beneath the whole of the body which makes it possible to ensure a low level of pressure both on the body itself and on the underlying surface (ground, water). In addition to this static air cushion, the EKIP vehicles are capable of making use of a dynamic air cushion characteristic for WIG vehicles; there is a provision for operating these vehicles in ground effect mode in addition to the basic high-altitude ('aircraft') flight mode. In actual fact, the EKIP vehicles combine the properties of an ACV, a WIG vehicle and an aircraft. They can move in close proximity to the ground or water on an air cushion at speeds of up to 160 km/h (99 mph), perform a flight in ground effect like WIG vehicles at speeds up to 400 km/h (248 mph) and fly like aircraft at altitudes up to 10 km (32,810 ft) with a speed of up to 750 km/h (465 mph).

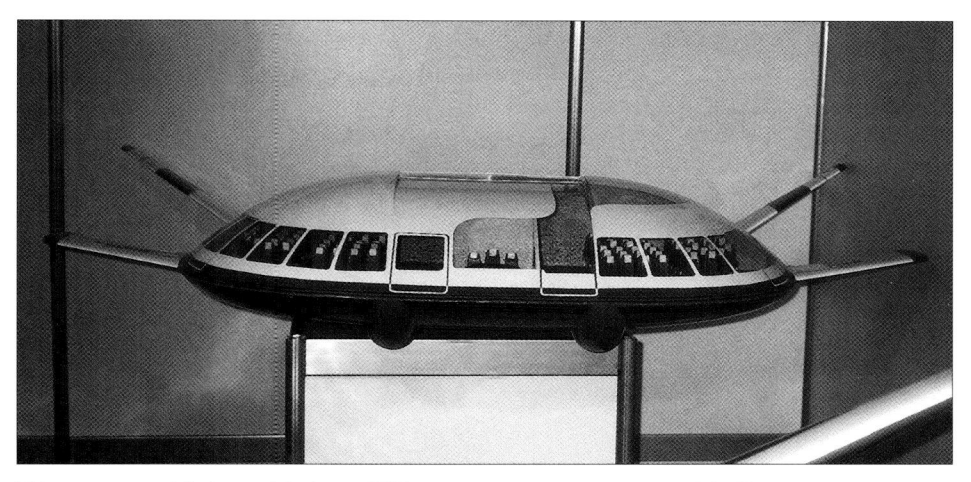

As envisioned by the author of the idea, the EKIP vehicles should possess a number of advantages over traditional aircraft. EKIP vehicles require no airfields and are designed to be able to land not only on airfields of any category, but also on unprepared ground strips and water surface. The high thickness ratio of the body affords internal volumes for the accommodation of passengers and cargoes that exceed by a factor of several times the volumes available in traditional aircraft of the same cargo lifting capacity. The weight of the EKIP vehicle's airframe in relation to the all-up weight, according to estimates of specialists, is 30% lower than that of existing aircraft, which makes it possible to increase the payload accordingly. The big volume of the body makes it easier to adapt these vehicles to the use of natural gas or hydrogen as fuel.

EKIP vehicles offer enhanced flight safety. Take-off and landing are performed at speeds which are 2-2.5 times lower than those of the present-day cargo and passenger aircraft; EKIP vehicles with an all-up weight of 300 t (661,375 lb) will have a take-off speed of not more than 140 km/h (87 mph) and a landing speed of not more than 100 km/h (62 mph). Even when three of the four engines have cut, the power of the remaining engine is sufficient to ensure a safe landing mode. Provision is made for active boundary layer control so as to ensure a smooth airflow around the thick body and reduce drag, which also enhances flight safety.

The main technical feature of the EKIP aircraft is the vortex-based boundary layer control system (BLCS) controlling the airflow at the aft-facing surface of the vehicle. Creating a multitude of consecutively placed transverse vortices, the BLCS ensures separation-free flow around the body of the vehicle and a reduction of aerodynamic drag. The system is actuated by auxiliary engines which run at an economic rating in cruise flight. Operating in the maximum rating mode during take-off, they also ensure the functioning of the air cushion undercarriage.

The company effected a large volume of experimental work involving the use of the **L-1** and **L2-3** radio-controlled flying models. Construction was initiated of the **L2-1** automatically controlled full-scale demonstrator vehicle weighing 9 t (19,840 lb), the testing of which was expected to pave the way to creating a whole range of type of such machines with an all-up weight ranging from 9 t (19,840 lb) to hundreds of tonnes. A project was prepared of an EKIP-type vehicle for fighting forest fires. Called *Lesnik* (Forester), this vehicle was to have an all-up weight of 12 tonnes (26,455 lb) and carry a 5-t (11,020-lb) load of water or fire retardant. Its performance included a maximum speed of 600 km/h (372 mph), a speed of 140-150 km/h (87-93 mph) during fire-fighting, a ceiling of 10 km (32,810 ft), a range of 2,000 km (1,240 miles) and a take-off/landing distance of less than 500 m (1,640 ft). Series production of this and other vehicles in the EKIP range was expected to be launched at the Saratov aircraft plant. There were plans to enlist the services of the Yakovlev Design Bureau for the detail design of the EKIP airframes.

By the end of 1993 the Triumph company which is a part of the EKIP concern completed design work on the 120-tonne (264,550-lb) **EKIP L-3** vehicle. Its designers hoped that by 1997 the machine would reach the stage of

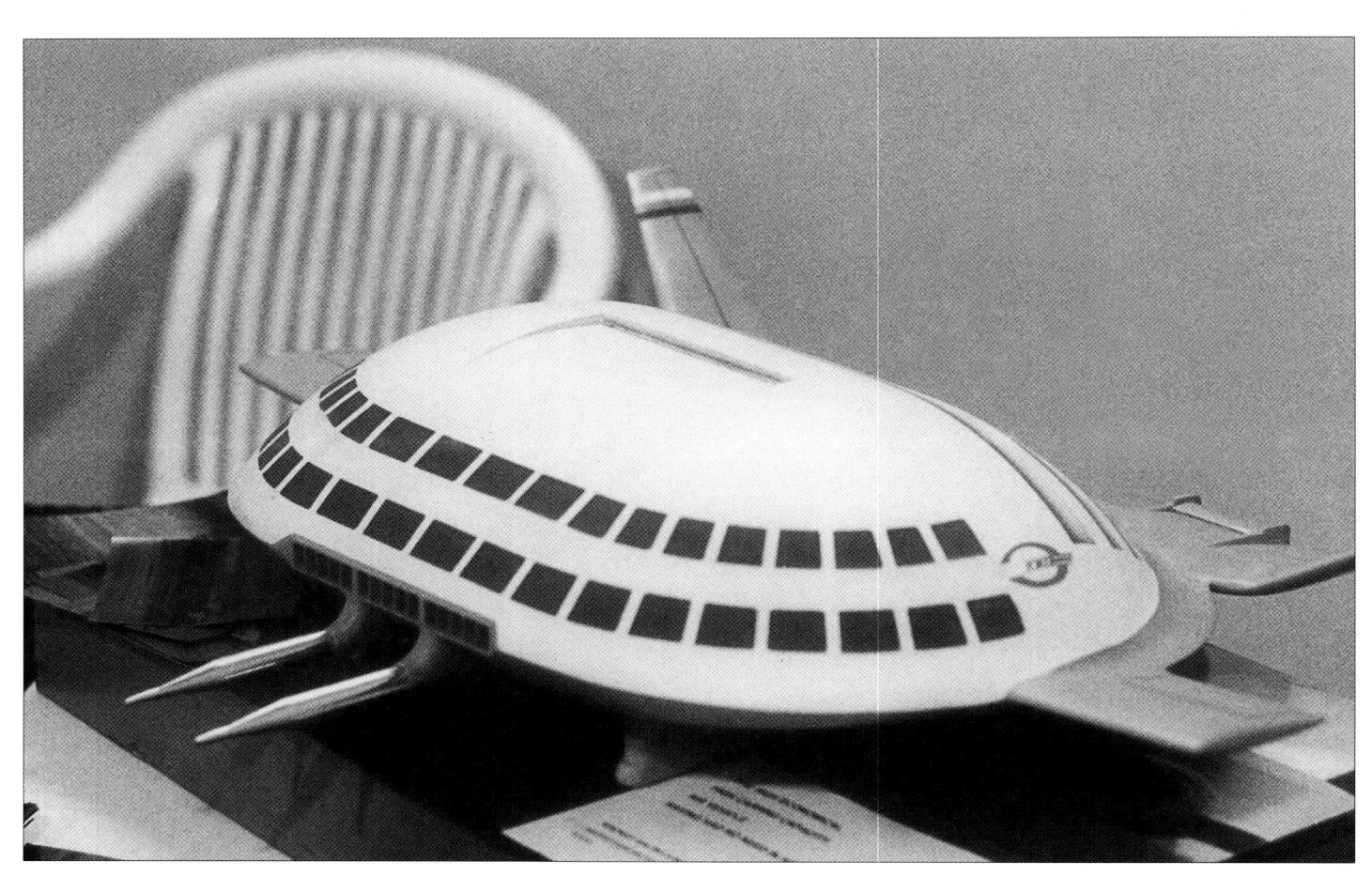

The photos on this page show two more EKIP models sharing the same UFO-like appearance. The extensive glazing is noteworthy, as is the flat dorsal air intake for the cruise engines on the model in the lower photo. The function of the long probes on the model in the upper photo is unclear.

Top: Yet another cutaway model of an EKIP displayed at the MAKS-95 airshow in Zhukovskiy, showing the flat nozzle located between the canted fins.
Above: Another MAKS-95 exhibit – the L2-3 radio-controlled model. The photos on the wall beyond show the very first L-1 RC model (featuring a T-tail) in flight.

The L2-1 automatically controlled full-scale flying demonstrator is the closest the EKIP programme has yet come to fruition. The unfinished L2-1 is seen here in the assembly shop of the Saratov aircraft factory No. 292.

series production. These hopes proved unjustified, yet in 1998 L. N. Shchookin, the leader of the project, spoke optimistically in a magazine article about the chances for a relatively speedy implementation of his concept, provided sufficient funding was forthcoming for the design and development work. It seemed that the ball was set rolling. Construction of the abovementioned automatically-controlled vehicle was proceeding at the Saratov aircraft factory No. 292. The authorities of the Saratov Region promised their support for the project; it was endorsed by the Russian Academy of Natural Sciences and by the then President Boris Yeltsin.

Unfortunately, as it often happens in the present situation in Russia with its persistent financial and economic problems and meagre financial outlays for research, the funding of the project came to a halt, it ceased to attract interest and the work all but stopped. Shchookin began to encounter all sorts of hindrances, including false promises of funding; these vicissitudes seriously affected his health.

In August 2001 Lev N Shchookin passed away. The duties of General Designer were taken over by Semyon M. Zel'vinskiy. The EKIP company is still hopeful of getting access to the necessary financial resources which would make it possible to implement the projects in hand. At present the programme of the EKIP concern includes the L-2-3, L-3-1 and L-3-2 vehicles with an all-up weight of 12, 45 and 360 t (26,455; 99,200; and 793,650 lb) respectively and a passenger seating capacity of 40, 160 and 1,200 persons respectively. All three vehicles have a speed of 700 km/h (434 mph) at altitude and a take-off run of 450-600 m (1,480-1,970 ft)

In addition to the heavy manned vehicles, the company's programme includes a development of a small unmanned vehicle – the **EKIP-AULA** (AULA stands for *avtomaticheski oopravlyayemyy letahtel'nyy apparaht* – automatically controlled aerial vehicle) with an all-up weight of 250-280 kg (551-617 lb), capable of fulfilling reconnaissance, monitoring and other similar duties.

According to some press reports, of late the Russian military displayed some interest towards L. Shchookin's invention (no comment was forthcoming from them). It may well be presumed that troop-carrier and transport versions of EKIP vehicles could be of great value for the armed forces.

LAT

LAT (**Lyoh**kaya Avia**h**tsiya Tagan**ro**ga – Light Aviation of Taganrog). This joint stock company which styles itself as Science & Production Enterprise (*na**ooch**no-proi**zvod**stvennoye predpri**yah**tiye* – NPP) is headed by Yuriy Usol'tsev. It came into existence as a result of activities of a group of young designers who, to begin with, worked within the framework of the **Krahsnyye Kryl'ya** (Red Wings) Centre of aviation enthusiast work. Later this centre transformed itself into a small private enterprise under the same name; inside this enterprise the LAT company was organised. In 1992 it became an independent structure.

Under Usol'tsev's guidance several light aircraft designs were developed first by the abovementioned Centre and then by the LAT company. These were the R-01, R-01M, R-02 and R-50 light amphibious hydroplanes which bore a common name, Robert (in honour of Robert Bartini). Owing to some special features of their design they possessed pronounced WIG vehicle properties. All of these machines have low-set wings with a wide-chord centre section which rests on the water surface when the machines are afloat, thus ensuring stability and buoyancy. During take-off and landing the ram air creates a dynamic air cushion under the wing centre section.

R-01, R-02

The R-01 aircraft weighing 350 kg (771 lb) at take-off was a single-seater with an open cockpit; its outer wing panels had pronounced forward sweep. It was successfully test-flown in 1989. The improved R-01M version powered by a 44-hp Robin-140EC piston engine had a take-off weight of 440 kg (970 lb). The R-02 differed in having an enclosed two-seat cockpit and straight wings with an extended-chord centre section. It was intended for use as an executive, patrol and trainer aircraft.

The aircraft is powered by an 80-hp Rotax 912A3 engine installed behind the cockpit and driving a pusher propeller. The R-02 is provided with a quick-action parachute safety system. Here are some basic figures for the R-02: wingspan, 10.0 m (32 ft 9.7 in); length, 6.3 m (20 ft 8 in); wing area, 12.4m² (133.3 sq ft); all-up weight, 560 kg (1,234 lb); speed, 165 km/h (103 mph).

R-50

In 1992-1994 the LAT designers prepared an advanced development project of a multi-purpose amphibian designated R-50 Robert. The baseline version was a cargo and passenger aircraft with a cabin accommodating a pilot and five passengers; the passenger seats could be easily removed for carrying cargo. The basic version could also be used for patrol and liaison duties. Other versions under development included ambulance, firefighting, agricultural, SAR, ecological survey and other versions. The baseline version was to be powered by two Czech 140-hp Motorlet (Walter) M-332AR engines which could eventually be replaced by indigenous MKB Granit TVD-400 turboprops (the definitive version is expected to deliver 500-560 ehp) or 250-hp VOKBM M-17 piston engines. Provision was made for the installation of the MIKBO-43 multi-function integrated avionics suite permitting the aircraft to fly in adverse weather conditions and at night. The R-50, like its predecessor, the R-01, has a wide-chord wing centre section creating a WIG effect during take-off and landing. In ground effect the lift/drag ratio of the wings rises to 19-20 versus 11-13 in normal cruise flight. One can also use the ground effect mode for cruising flight, but prolonged flight close to the supporting surface is possible only on condition of prior installation of an automatic pitch stability augmentation system which can be done at the customer's request.

In 1995 there were plans for creating the R-50M version with a cabin lengthened by 0.75 m (2 ft 5.5 in). Design specifications for it included a take-off weight of 2,700 kg (5,950 lb), a payload of 560 kg (1,234 lb) for a range of 600 km (370 miles) with two 210-hp engines or 650 kg (1,433 lb) for a range of 750 km (465 miles) with two 240-hp engines. Its dimensions were: wingspan, 15.40 m (50 ft 6 in); wing aspect ratio, 8.227; length, 11.40 m (37 ft 5 in); height, 4.30 m (14 ft 1 in). Series production of the R-50 was to be launched at an aircraft plant in Doobna, but financial difficulties prevented these plans from being implemented.

Roks-Aero JSC

This company was active in the light aircraft design business in the mid-1990s. It took over the design bureau previously known as RosAeroprogress, or simply Aeroprogress; later this design team headed by Yevgeniy Groonin became the aeronautical subdivision of the Khrunichev State Science and Production Centre active in the field of missile and space technology.

Among the many various designs studied by the Roks-Aero there were some WIG projects. Notably, in 1994-1995 a project for an eight-seat multi-purpose amphibious *ekranolyot* (Type B vehicle) for local routes and special duties (no designation has been published) was under development. It was a machine based on the Lippisch layout with reversed-delta wings and a T-tail; indeed, it was remarkably similar to the Lippisch X-113AM. The wings featured anhedral and had endplate floats at the tips to which small surfaces fitted with ailerons were attached at an angle of 45°. The wings were attached to a boat-shaped hull, the front part of which provided accommodation for the pilot and passengers under an extensively glazed canopy. The vehicle was powered by a 360-hp Vedeneyev M-14P nine-cylinder radial engine

Above: The LAT R-02 Robert on a ground handling dolly at the Hydro Aviation Show-2000 in Ghelendzhik. The aircraft is registered by the Aviation Enthusiasts' Federation of Russia (FLA RF) as FLA-RF 02558.

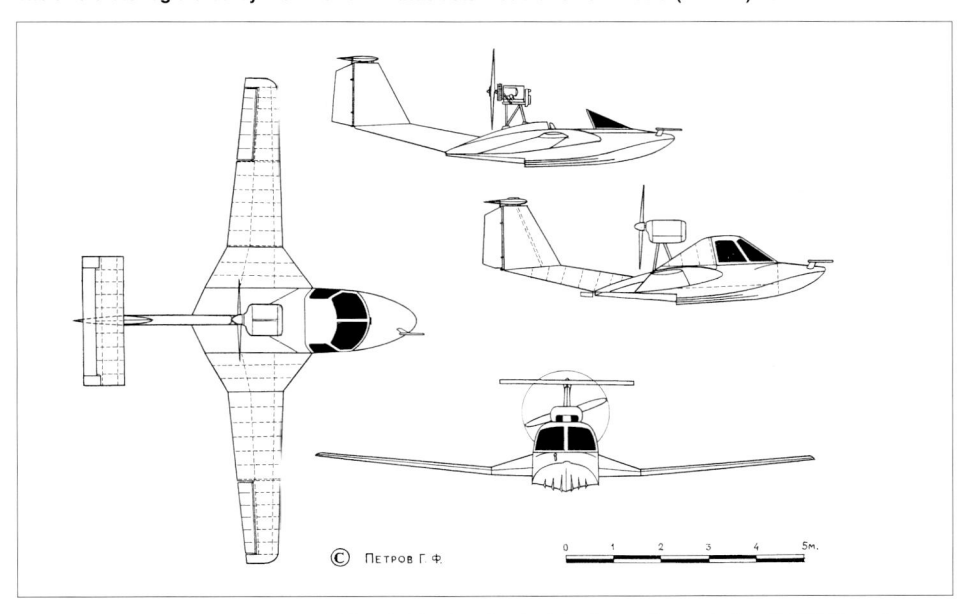

A three-view of the R-02, with an additional side view (top) of the forward-swept wing R-01M Robert.

This model seen at one of the Moscow airshows represents a projected WIG vehicle developed by the RosAeroprogress company. Judging by the shape of the engine nacelle, the vehicle (which in all other respects is strikingly similar to the Lippisch X-113AM) was to be powered by a small turboprop engine.

mounted on a pylon above the aft fuselage and driving a tractor propeller; another version featured a small turboprop engine with a six-bladed pusher propeller. A scaled-up 16-seat machine of similar layout powered by a 960-ehp Glushenkov TVD-10 turboprop was also under development. There were several more projects sharing this basic configuration and differing in dimensions, powerplant type, undercarriage and onboard equipment.

The Roks-Aero company had also some WIG vehicle projects featuring quite different configurations, including catamaran layouts.

Transal-AKS

The name of this firm set up in Nizhniy Novgorod and headed by Latyshenko is sometimes shortened to simply Transal. This is an abbreviation of the words **Trahns**port Alek**seyev**a – Alexeyev's Transport, as a tribute to Rostislav Ye. Alexeyev. Thus, the very name of the company contains a sort of pledge to pursue the development of WIG vehicles. Yet, no projects of this nature emanating from this firm have come to the public knowledge (although they may exist). The only known project associated with this company is a project of a two-seat light aircraft on an air-cushion undercarriage on which Transal has worked jointly with the Mikoyan Design Bureau; it is designated **MiG-TA-4**. This machine uses a fan to create a static air cushion and does not appear to be making use of a dynamic air cushion in any of its flight modes, so it does not qualify for being regarded as a WIG design.

It would appear that the company has abandoned work on the WIG projects for the time being. As far back as January 1996 Craig Mellow in his article *When Ships Have Wings* in the *Air & Space* magazine noted that Latyshenko '*has for the moment turned his back on the* ekranoplan'. He quoted Latyshenko as saying that '*there was no commercial application yet*' for WIG vehicles.

Wingship Airlines

The Russian company which styles itself in English in this way was founded in 1998. Its Russian name is '*Krylahtyye korablee*', literally simply 'Wingships'. Contrary to the name, it is engaged in the design, not operation, of WIG vehicles. In late 2000 the Russian magazine *Aviapanorama* informed its readers that the said company, assisted by specialists from TsAGI, was completing the design of the **PM** *ekranolyot* (Type C WIG vehicle) weighing 3.5 t (7,716 lb) at take-off. This is a project of a multi-purpose sea-going WIG vehicle intended to transport a payload of 1 t (2,204 lb), or 8 to 10 persons, to a distance of up to 2,400 km (1,490 miles). It is to be produced in **PM-1** patrol version and the **PM-2 Odyssey** passenger version.

The PM features an 'aircraft layout' with a wide fuselage, composite-type wings (in the case of the PM-2) and a tail unit of V-shaped or traditional configuration; the two configurations are currently being studied and the definitive one is to be chosen later. The dimensions of the fuselage, which is 2.8 m (9 ft 2 in) wide and 11.9 m (39 ft) long, provide comfortable accommodation for two pilots and six to eight passengers in a compartment measuring 2.5 by 5.5 m (8 ft 2½ in by 18 ft) with an average height of 1.7 m (5 ft 7 in). The PM-2 has a wing span of 11.4 m (37 ft 5 in). The maximum speed of the PM-1 and PM-2 is 350 km/h and 310 km/h (218 and 193 mph) respectively.

The vehicle is to be powered by two Soyuz R-127-300 turbojet aircraft engines (PM-1) or two German BMW S28 automobile engines (PM-2) delivering 320 hp apiece and driving two shrouded fans of 1.1 m (3 ft 7 in) in diameter; the latter are mounted on the forward fuselage or aft fuselage, depending on the project version.

The unorthodox hydrodynamic layout of the vehicle features a kind of elongated tunnel under the bottom of the fuselage into which ram air is fed. There is also a provision for an engine driven fan to create the static air cushion. Investigations conducted in the TsAGI towing basin have shown that the vehicle will be able to tackle a wave height of up to 1 m (3 ft) during take off.

By late 2000 a preliminary design project of the *ekranolyot* had been prepared and the advanced development project was nearing completion. The company has started construction of a full-scale mock-up for demonstration purposes.

A wind tunnel model of the Wing Ships PM-2 featuring composite wings and aft-mounted ducted fans.

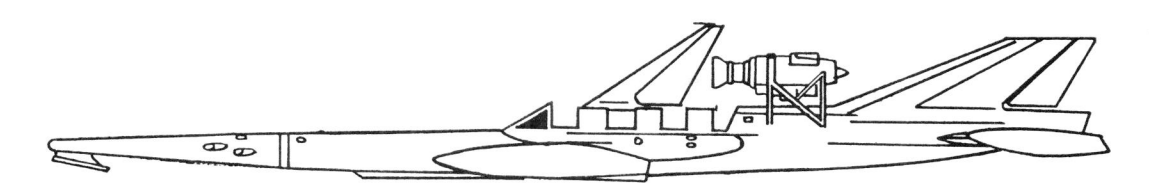

The SM-1 development WIG vehicle.

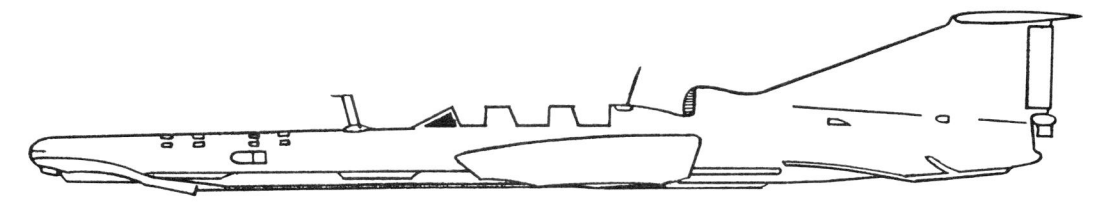

The SM-2 development vehicle as it was flown.

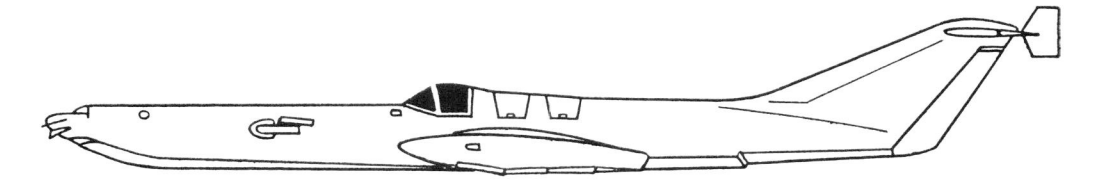

The SM-2P7 development vehicle.

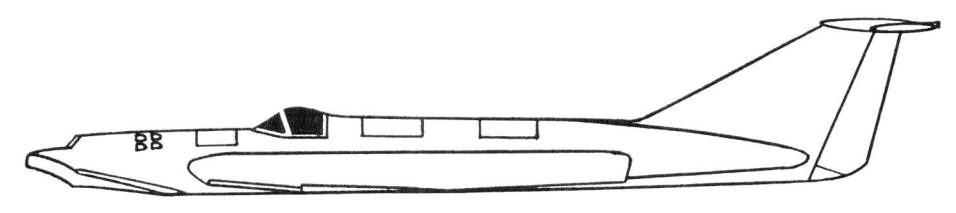

The SM-3 development vehicle.

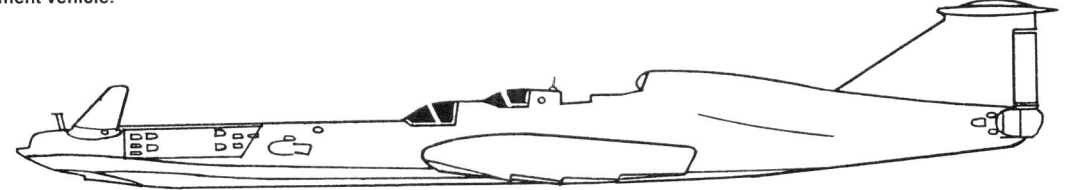

The SM-4 development vehicle.

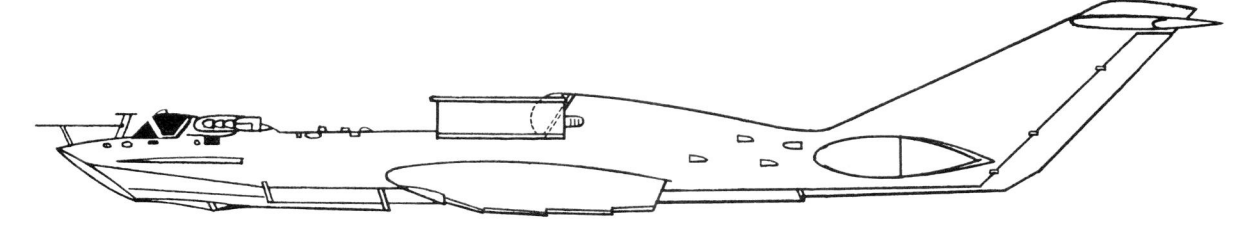

The SM-5 development vehicle.

A three-view of the SM-6 development vehicle, showing the hydroskis and beaching gear in deployed position.

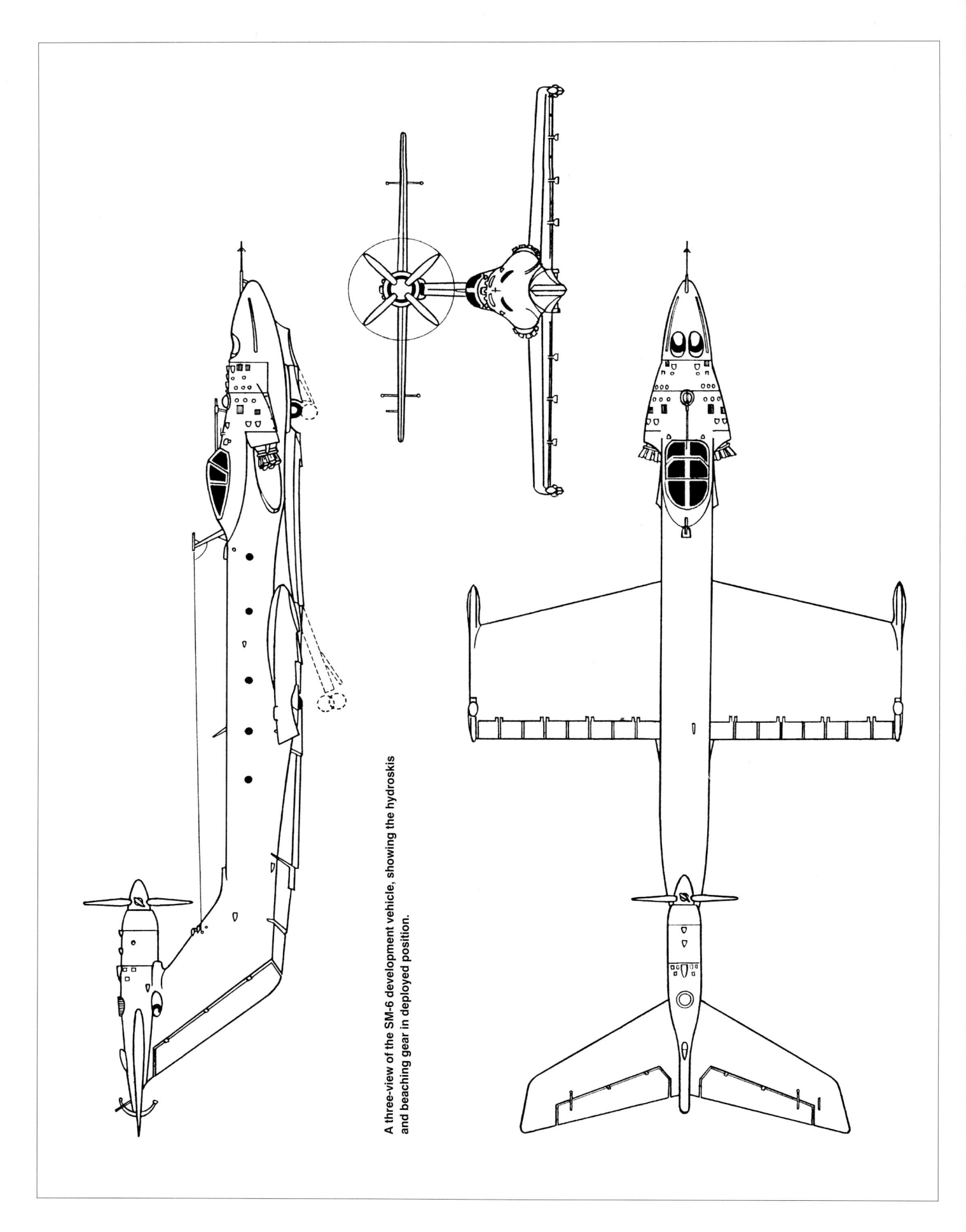

A three-view of the SM-8 development vehicle.

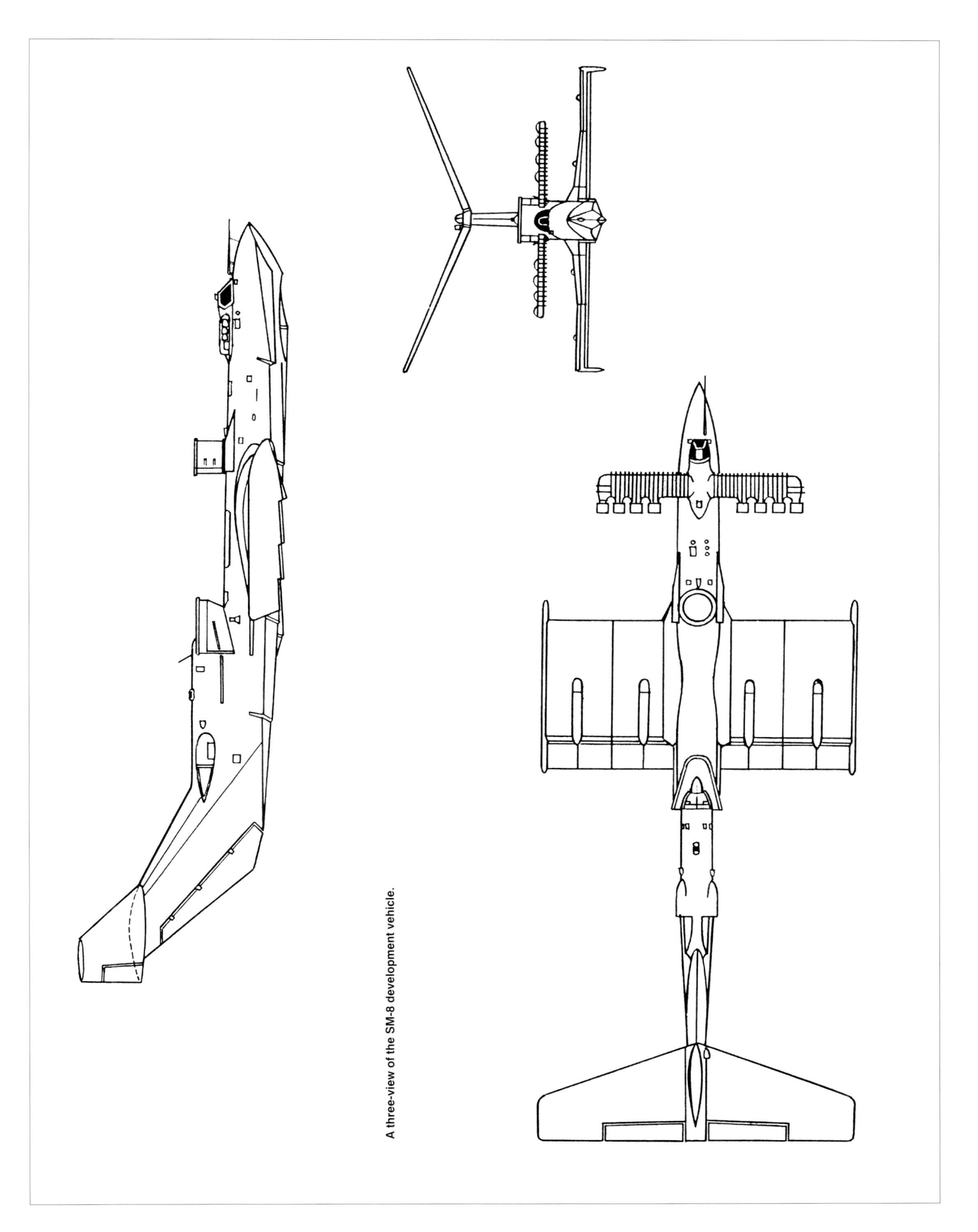

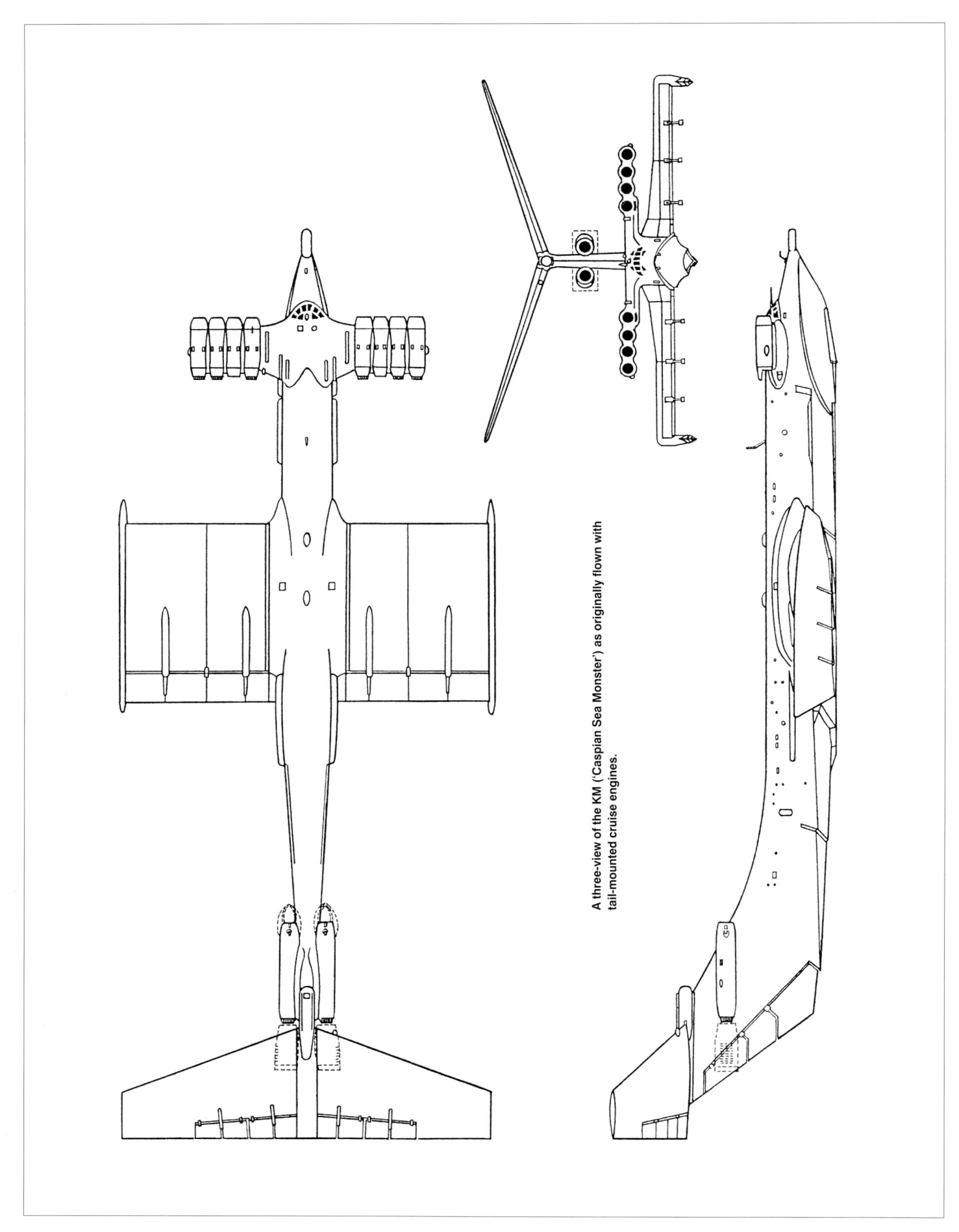

A three-view of the KM ('Caspian Sea Monster') as originally flown with tail-mounted cruise engines.

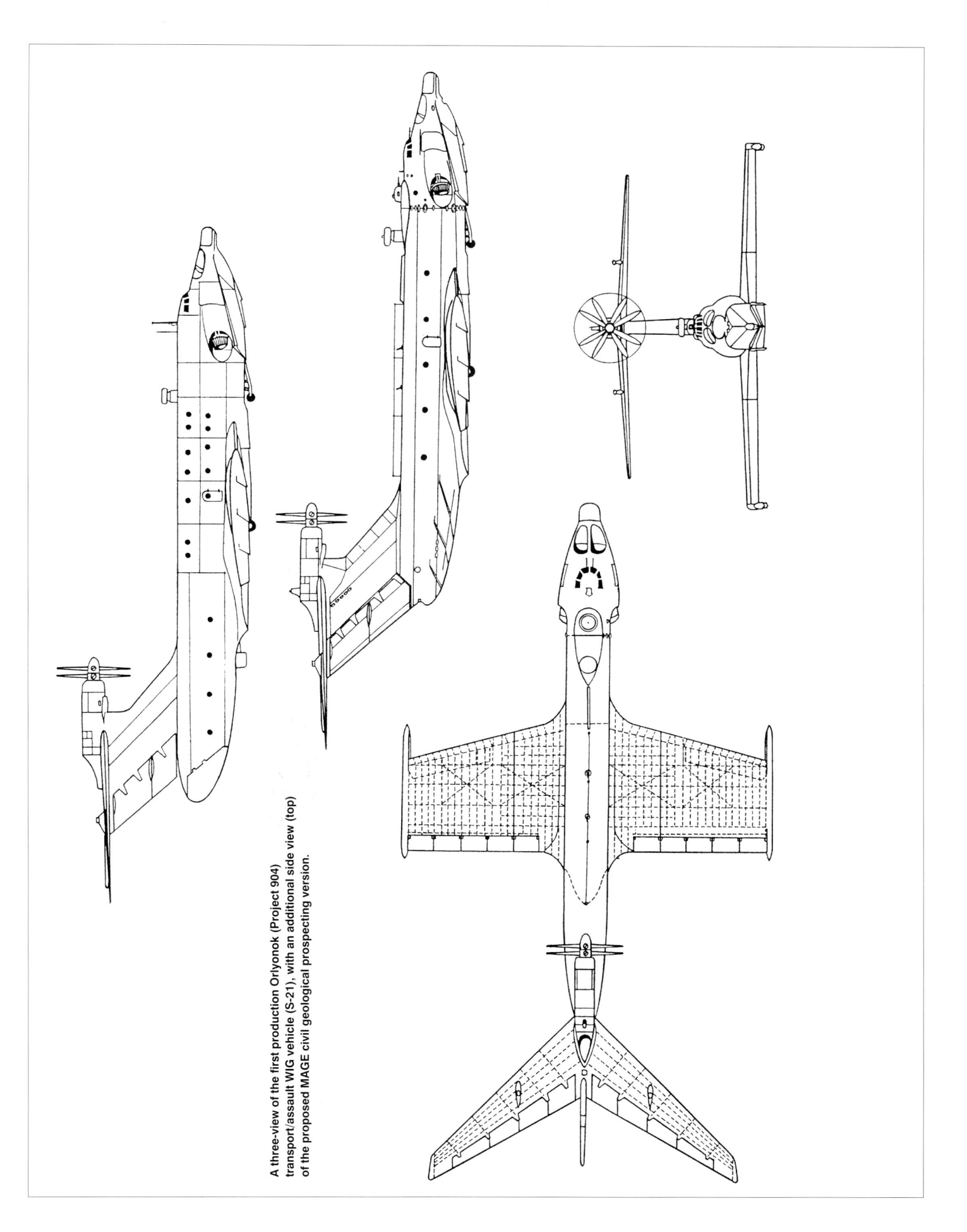

A three-view of the first production Orlyonok (Project 904) transport/assault WIG vehicle (S-21), with an additional side view (top) of the proposed MAGE civil geological prospecting version.

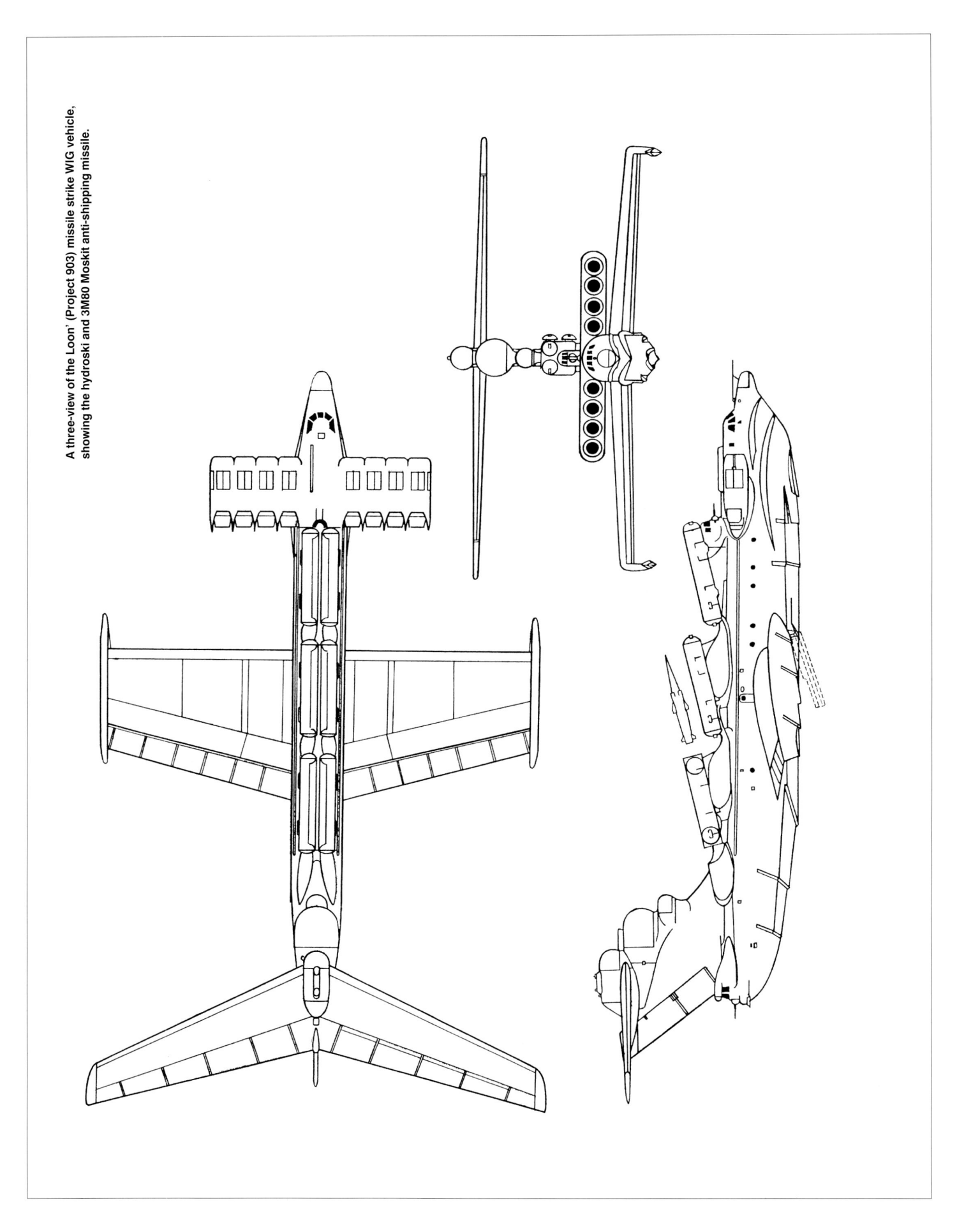

A three-view of the 'Loon' (Project 903) missile strike WIG vehicle, showing the hydroski and 3M80 Moskit anti-shipping missile.

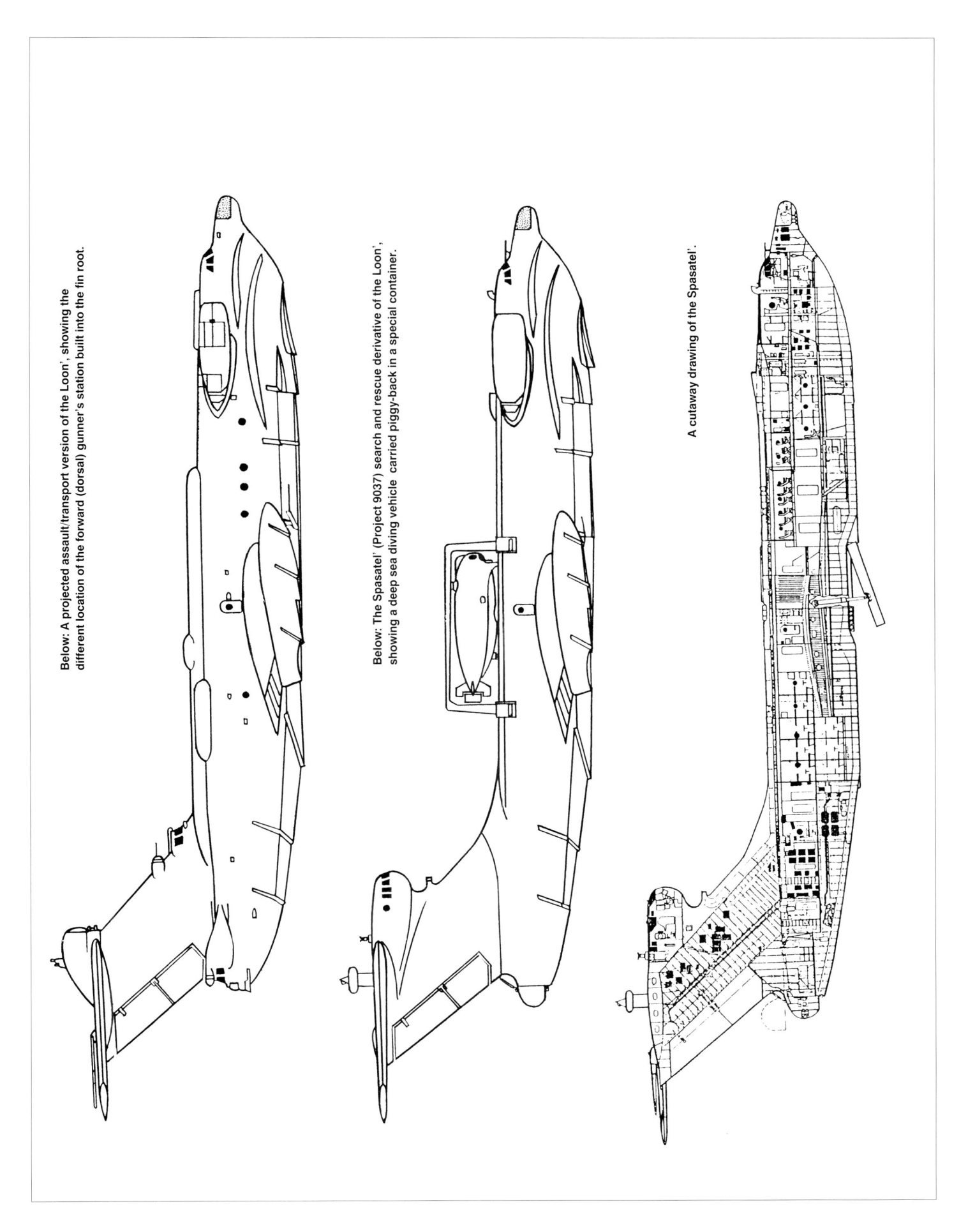

Below: A projected assault/transport version of the 'Loon', showing the different location of the forward (dorsal) gunner's station built into the fin root.

Below: The 'Spasatel' (Project 9037) search and rescue derivative of the 'Loon', showing a deep sea diving vehicle carried piggy-back in a special container.

A cutaway drawing of the 'Spasatel'.

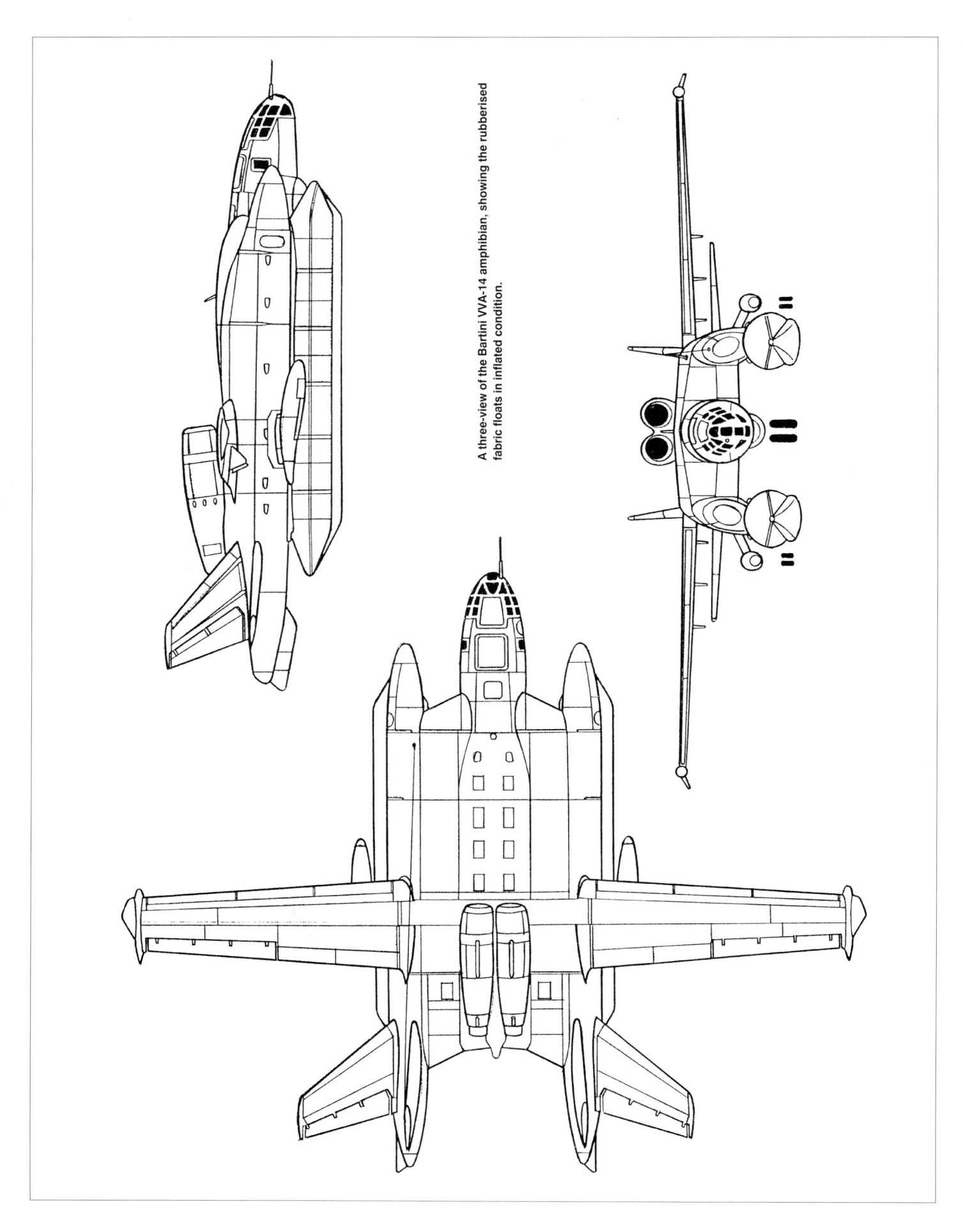

A three-view of the Bartini VVA-14 amphibian, showing the rubberised fabric floats in inflated condition.

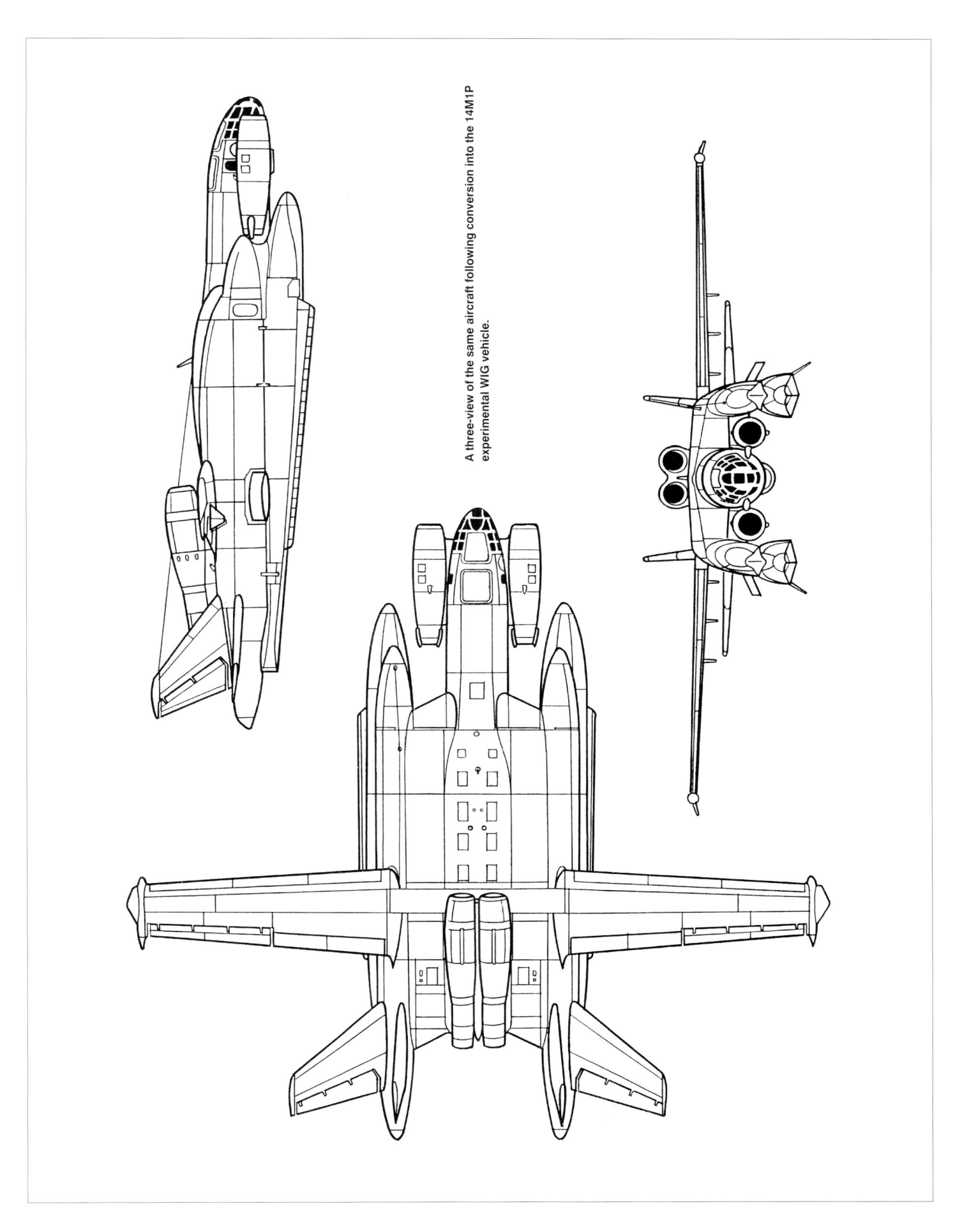

A three-view of the same aircraft following conversion into the 14M1P experimental WIG vehicle.

A three-view of the Beriyev Be-2500.

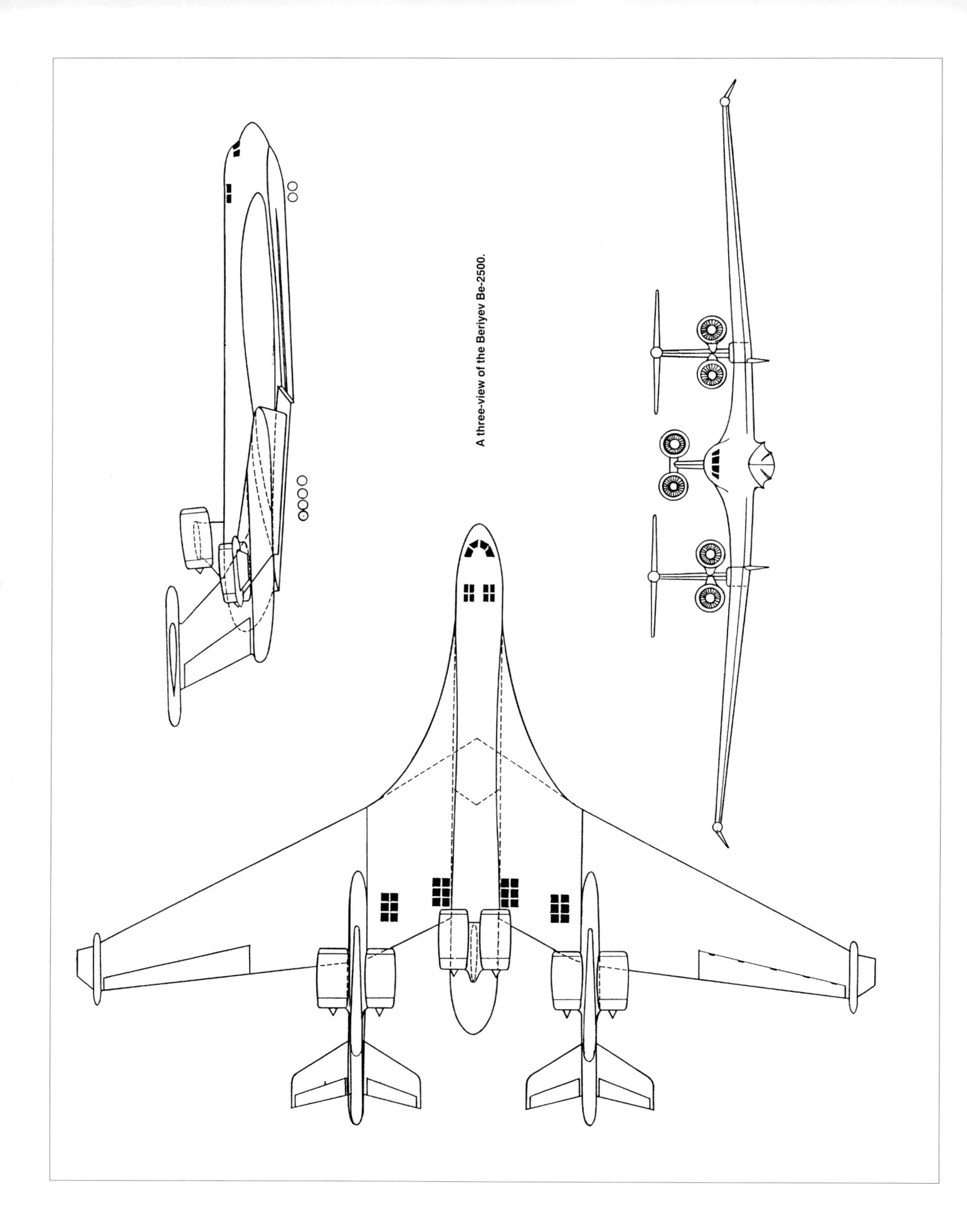

A three-view of the Be-2500P.

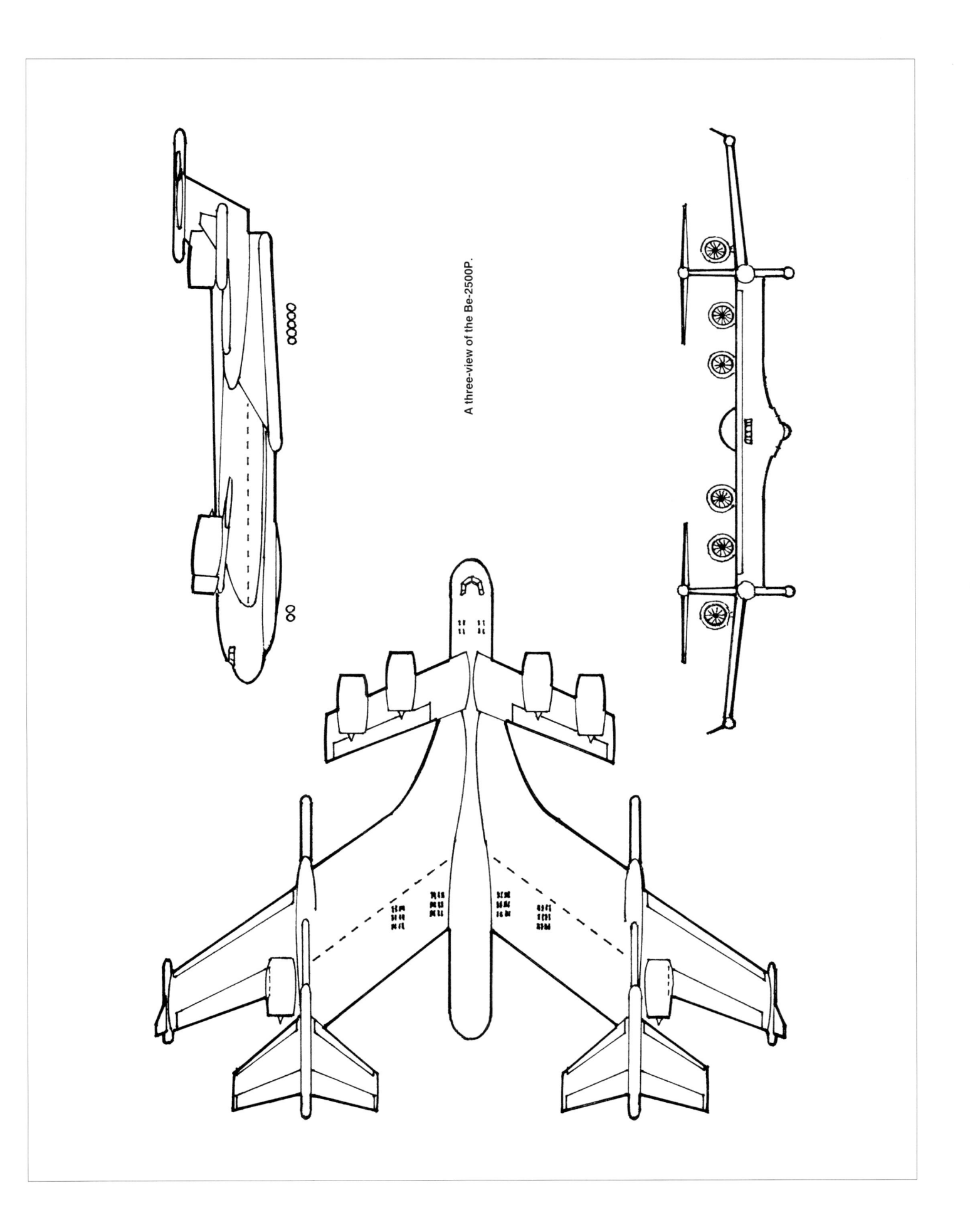

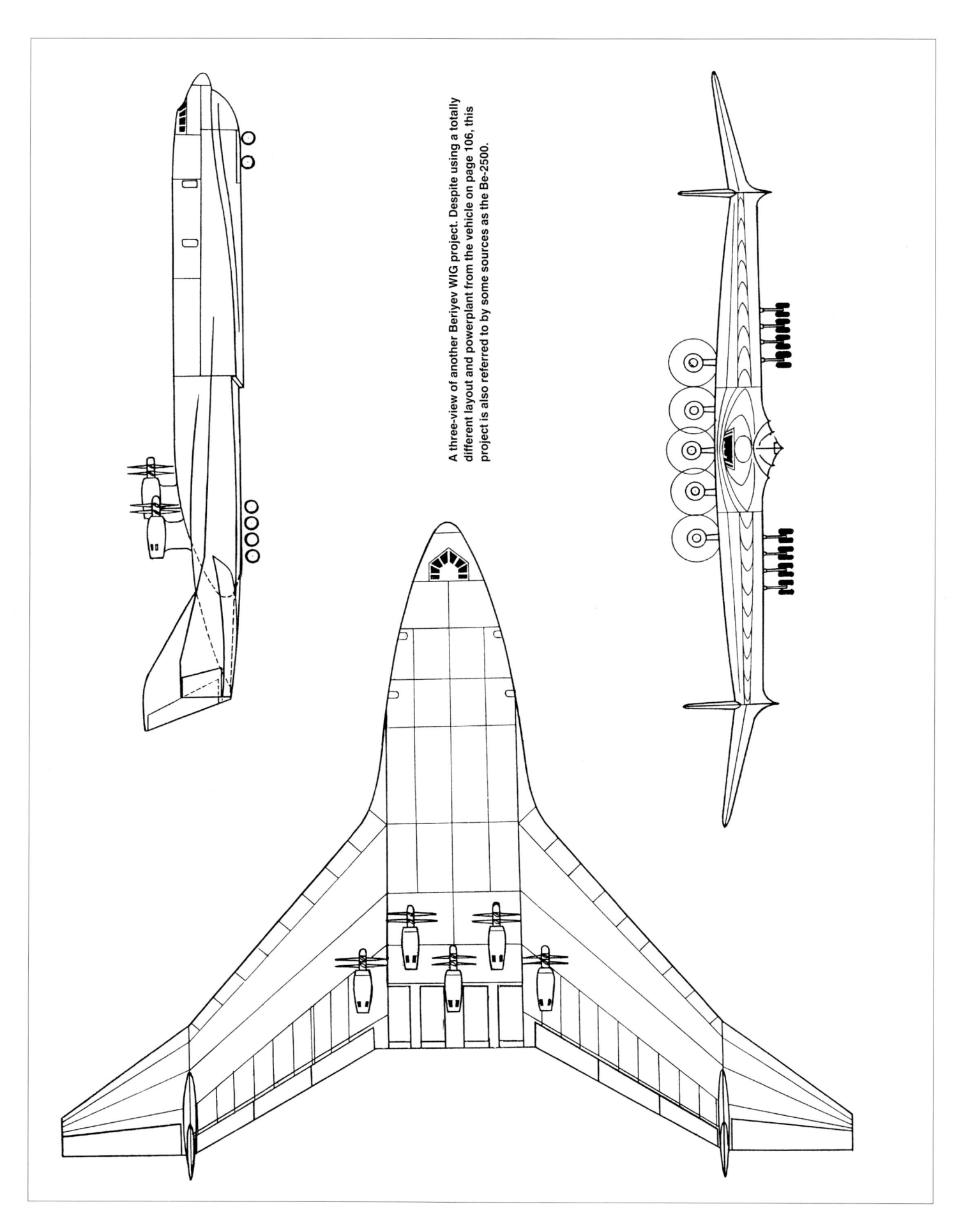

A three-view of another Beriyev WIG project. Despite using a totally different layout and powerplant from the vehicle on page 106, this project is also referred to by some sources as the Be-2500.

A three-view of the Alexeyev UT-1 training WIG vehicle. The upper side view shows the craft as first flown (before the retractable hydroski was fitted).

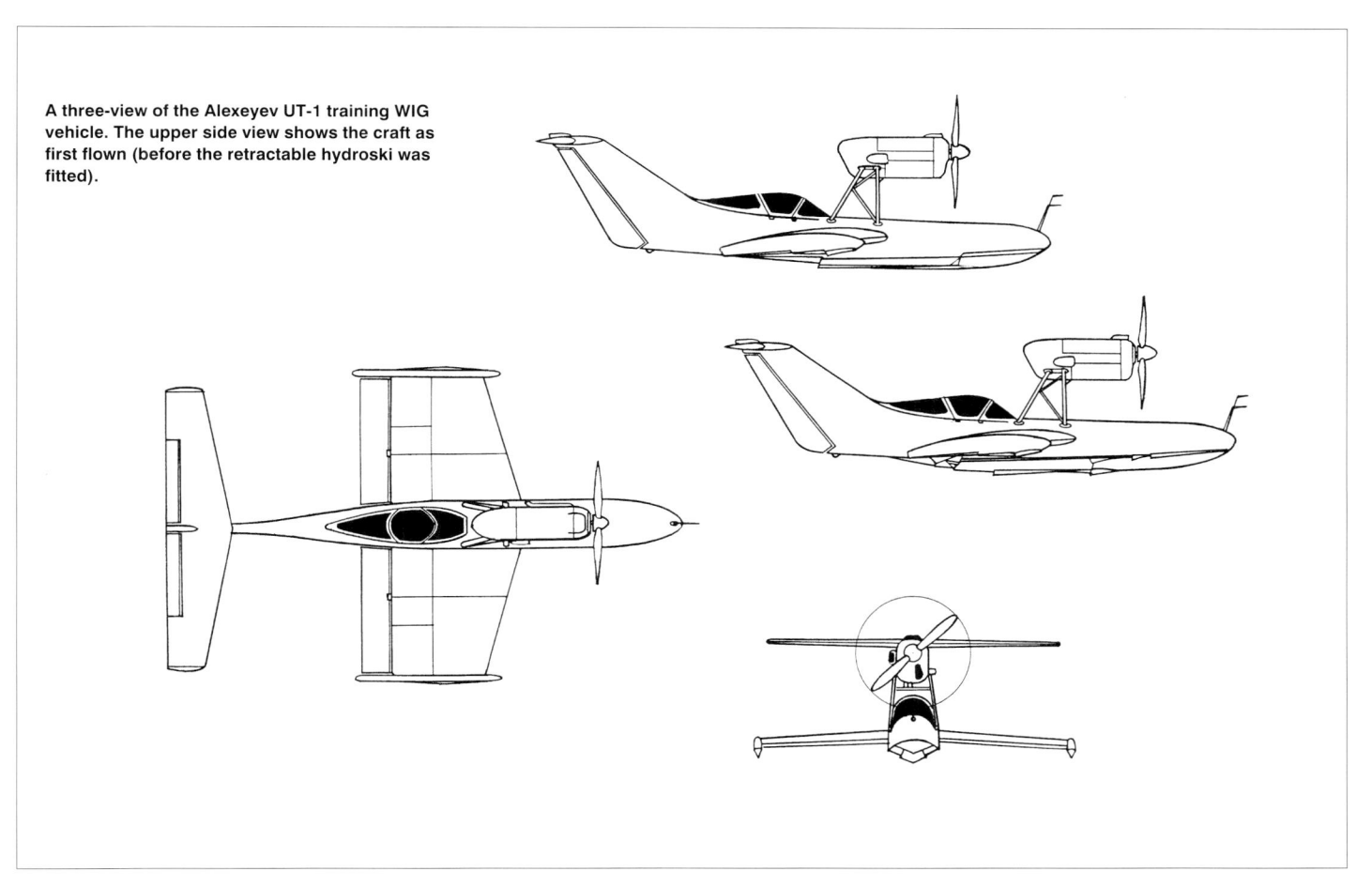

A three-view of the Alexeyev Strizh training WIG vehicle.

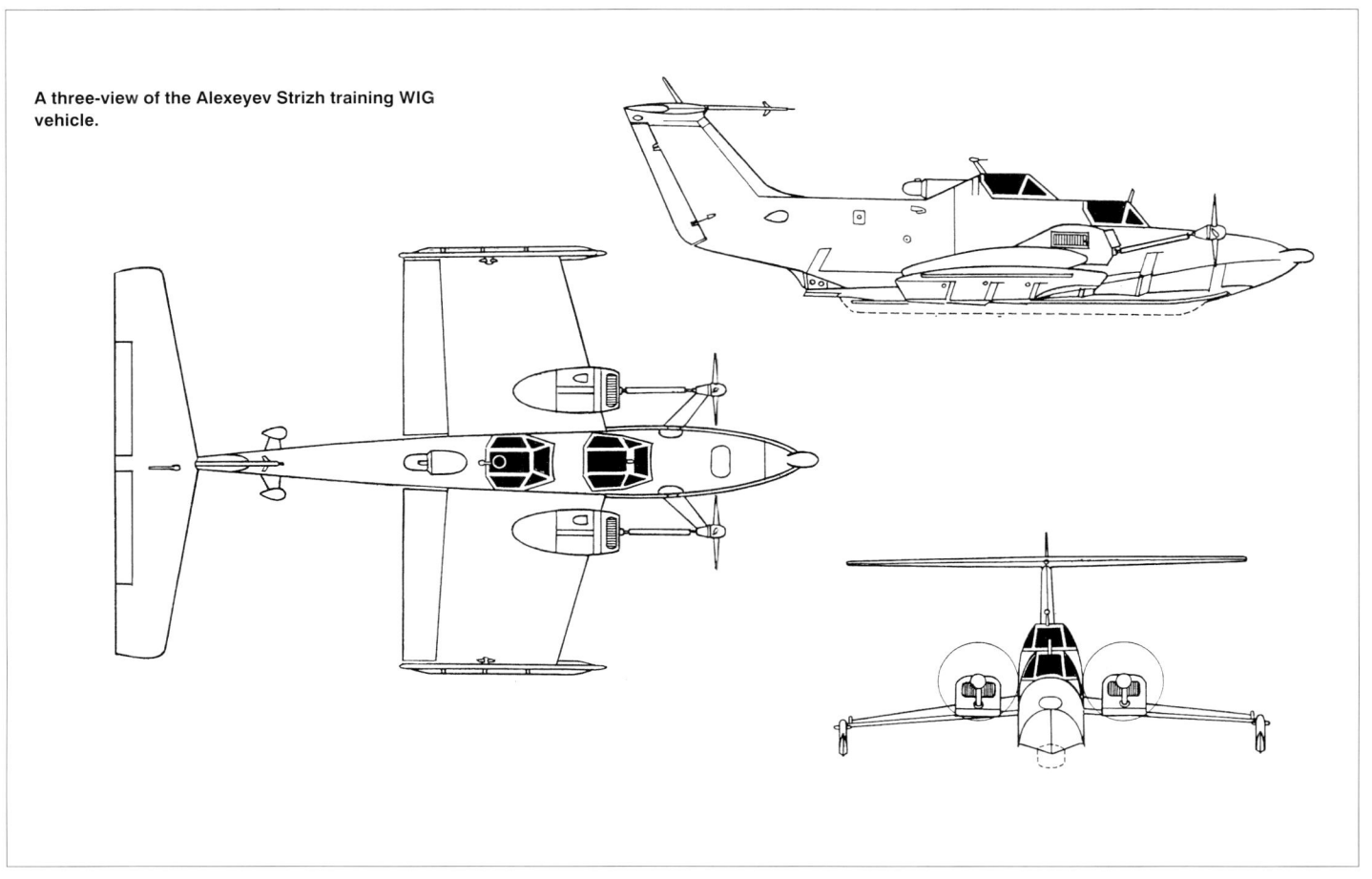

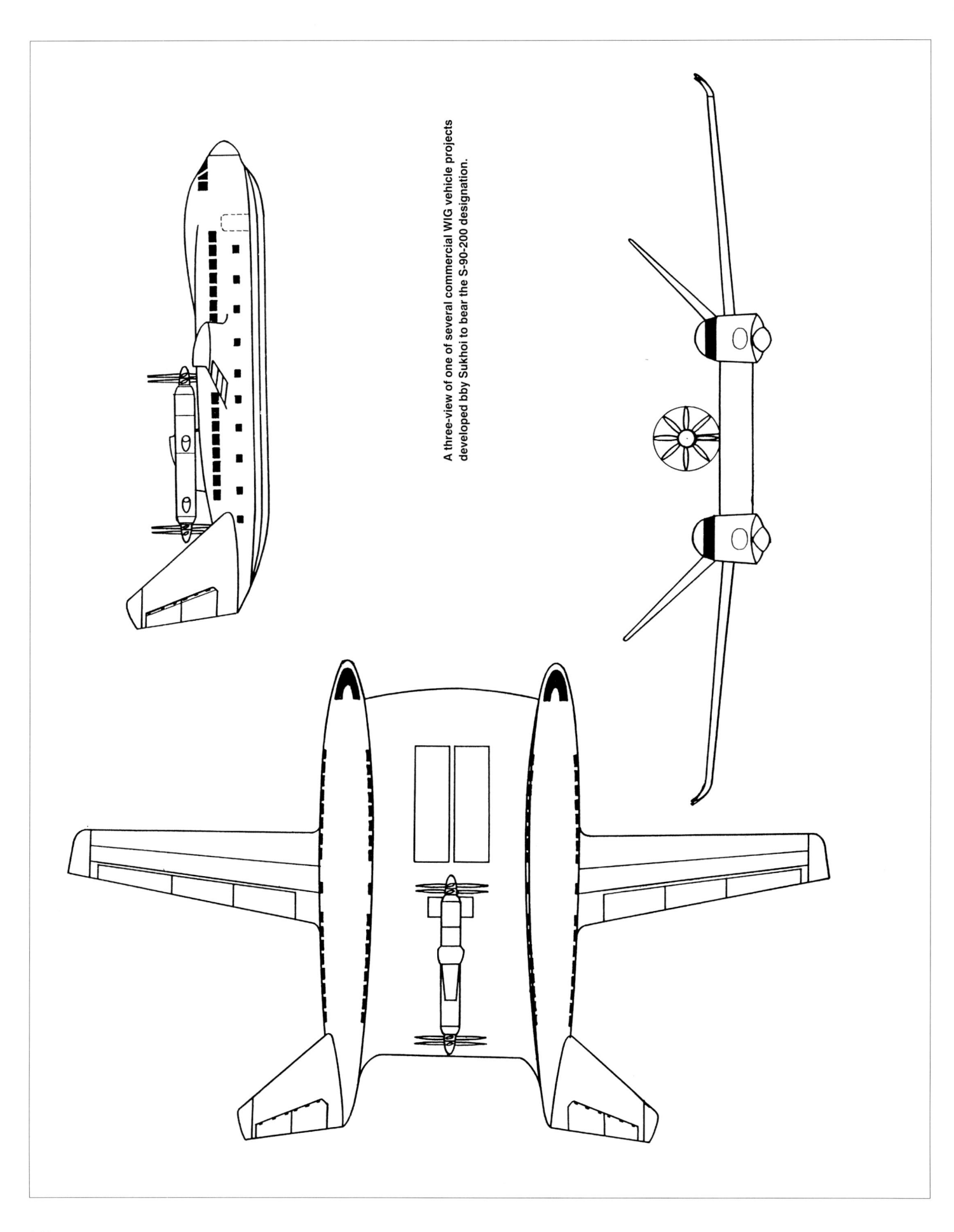

A three-view of one of several commercial WIG vehicle projects developed bby Sukhoi to bear the S-90-200 designation.

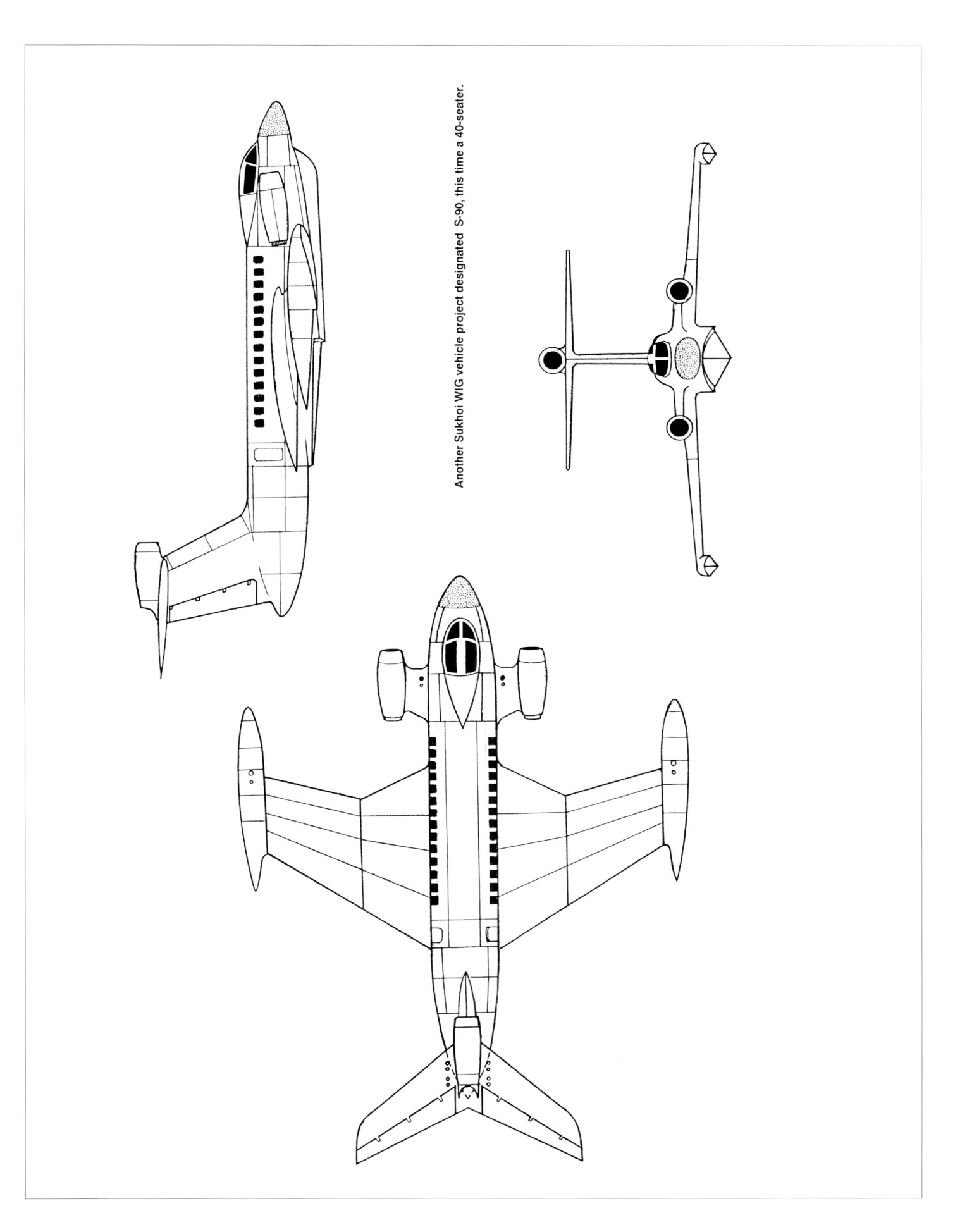

Another Sukhoi WIG vehicle project designated S-90, this time a 40-seater.

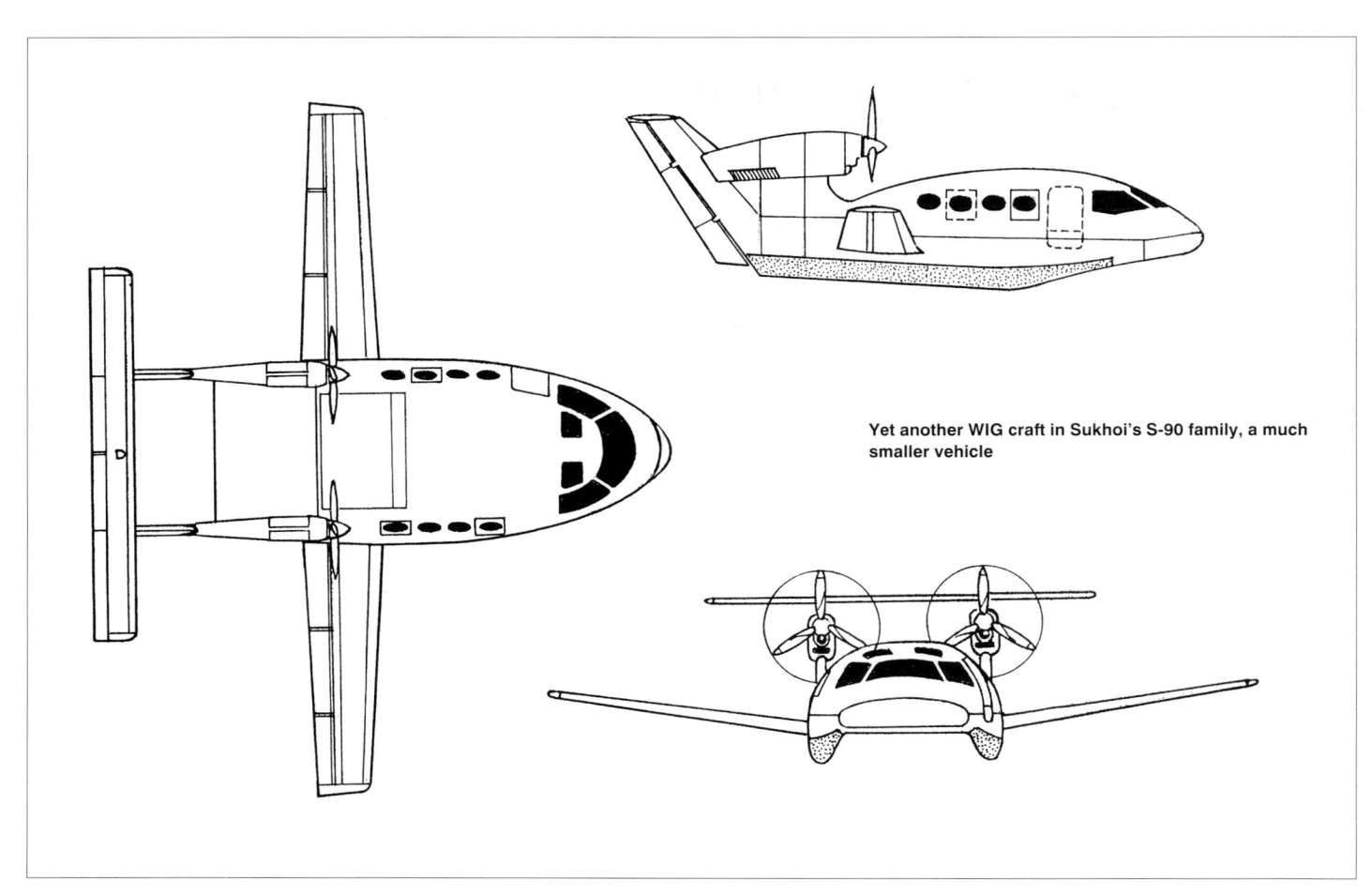

Yet another WIG craft in Sukhoi's S-90 family, a much smaller vehicle

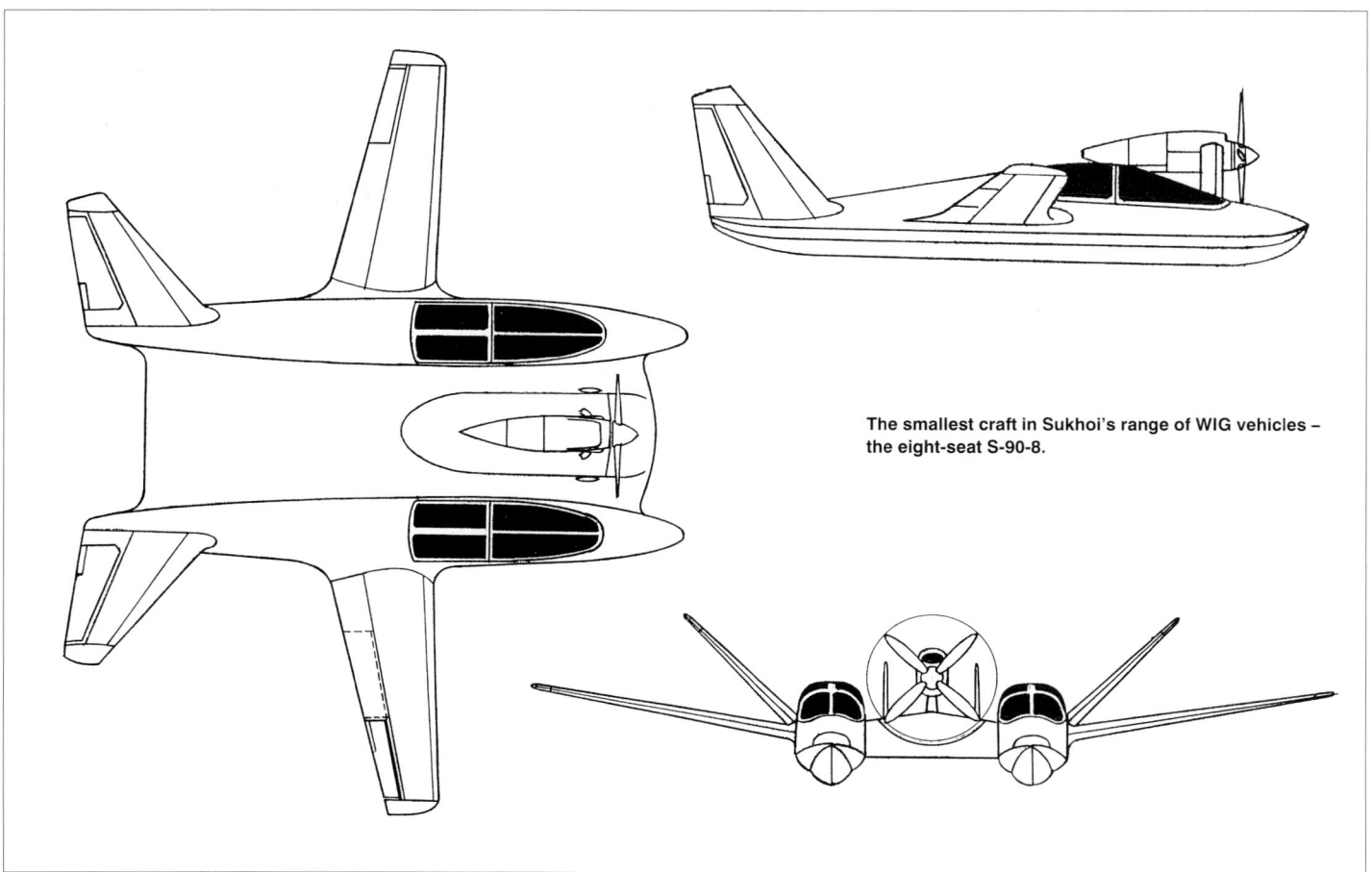

The smallest craft in Sukhoi's range of WIG vehicles – the eight-seat S-90-8.

Above: The Alexeyev KM in initial configuration with tail-mounted cruise engines and fin top radome. The craft was painted Navy grey, except for the red waterline and a thin blue cheatline.

Below: The third and final production Orlyonok (S-26) sitting on the hardstand in Kaspiysk in post-Soviet days (note the Russian Navy flag on the fin), with all the obvious signs of operational wear and tear. The cannons have been removed from the dorsal turret. The red-painted booster engine intakes are noteworthy.

Above: The S-26 starts up its cruise engine.
Below: Another view of the same craft at rest. The orange-painted MP-20 skylift based on a Skoda-706 lorry was used for inspecting the Orlyonok's tailplane.

Above: Close-up of the mighty Kuznetsov NK-12MK cruise engine with its AV-90 contraprops which make a very distinctive sound when running.
Below: The port wingtip, showing details of the flaps, ailerons and stabilising float-cum-endplate.

Above: The Orlyonok immediately after leaving the slipway at Kaspiysk. The wings are almost submerged at low speed, the upper surface only just visible. Below and opposite page, below: The S-26 makes a high-speed banking flypast for the benefit of the cameraman.

Above: The Orlyonok in a 'classic' posture, streaking not more than a dozen feet over the surface of the water. This photo illustrates the efficacy of the light grey camouflage worn by the type in Soviet/Russian Navy service.

Above and below: The Orlyonok at the moment of touchdown. The machine kicks up a tremendous cloud of spray which hides it almost completely for a couple of seconds as the Orlyonok decelerates.

Above: The S-26 demonstrates its ability to fly pretty high if necessary to clear an obstacle such as a ship.
Below: The inboard wingtip float almost touches the water during banked turns.

Above: Belching terrific flames and smoke, a 3M80 Moskit anti-shipping missile leaves the No. 2 (forward starboard) launch tube of the Loon' missile strike *ekranoplan*. The missile is obviously a training round, as indicated by the red and black paint job.

Below: The Loon' sits in storage at the Kaspiysk base, with maintenance platforms under the engine nacelles. Note the upper section of the rudder deflected differentially from the lower section.

Above: Konversiya at work. This model of the Spasatel' search and rescue WIG craft based on the Loon' was displayed at one of the Hydro Aviation Shows in Ghelendzhik. A striking high-visibility colour scheme like this one will in all probability be carried by the actual craft.

Below: Another view of the same model, the cutaway section revealing the on-board emergency hospital and rescue equipment storage hold, with an EMERCOM of Russia (Ministry for Emergency Control and Disaster Relief) display stand appropriately pictured in the background.

Above: Surrounded by scaffolding, the prototype of the Spasatel' awaits completion at the 'Volga' shipyard in Nizhniy Novgorod. The detachable outer wings have been temporarily placed on top of the fuselage, enabling the craft to be towed along rivers and canals to Lake Ladoga where testing will take place.

Wearing the false registration CCCP-10687, Bartini's ill-starred 14M1P WIG vehicle has been sitting for years at the Central Russian Air Force Museum in Monino near Moscow minus the outer wings and forward-mounted booster engines which are lying close at hand. There is hope that it may be restored yet.

Above: This model of a projected Beriyev ultra-heavy WIG flying boat was displayed twice at the Hydro Aviation Shows in Ghelendzhik as the Be-1200 (in 1996) and as the Be-2500 (in 1998).

The transparent sections afford a view of the Be-1200/Be-2500's freight holds. Interestingly, the vehicles stowed in the main freight hold include a Kamov Ka-50 Black Shark attack helicopter in a civil-style overall yellow colour scheme (!) and with folding rotors (?).

Above: The smartly painted Strizh training WIG vehicle in cruise flight. The legend on the fuselage reads AO TsKB SPK (Central Hydrofoil Design Bureau Joint-Stock Company).

Another view of the Strizh prototype. The orange-painted fairing aft of the elevated rear cockpit houses the 'black box'.

Above: The COMETEL EL-7S Ivolga prototype in the static park at the MAKS-2001 airshow in Zhukovskiy. This was the first time that a WIG vehicle intended for production and commercial operation was displayed publicly.

A view of the still unpainted EL-7 prototype flying at fairly high altitude for a WIG vehicle.

Above: A production Volga-2 dynamic air cushion vehicle 'parked' on the bank of the river after which it took its name. This example serialled 07 Red is probably a demonstrator owned by the 'Sokol' Nizhniy Novgorod Aircraft Factory whose logo is carried on the lower part of the fin.

A three-quarters rear view of Volga-2 '07 Red', showing the cooling louvres in the engine cowlings and the movable vanes directing the airflow.

126

Above: The driver's seat and instrument panel of the Volga-2. Note the side-stick, the rubber-bladed cooling fan, the overhead handle for training the roof-mounted searchlight and the triple windscreen wipers. The latter are a must because a lot of spray is flung up on the windscreen when the craft enters the water.

Close-up of the propeller/airflow control vane assemblies of the Volga-2.

We hope you enjoyed this book...

Midland Publishing titles are edited and designed by an experienced and enthusiastic team of specialists.

Further titles are in preparation but we always welcome ideas from authors or readers for books they would like to see published.

In addition, our associate, Midland Counties Publications, offers an exceptionally wide range of aviation, spaceflight, astronomy, military, naval and transport books and videos for sale by mail-order around the world.

For a copy of the appropriate catalogue, or to order further copies of this book, and any of many other Midland Publishing titles, please write, telephone, fax or e-mail to:

Midland Counties Publications
4 Watling Drive, Hinckley,
Leics, LE10 3EY, England

Tel: (+44) 01455 254 450
Fax: (+44) 01455 233 737
E-mail: midlandbooks@compuserve.com
www.midlandcountiessuperstore.com

US distribution by Specialty Press – see page 2.

Red Star Volume 1
SUKHOI S-37 & MIKOYAN MFI
Yefim Gordon

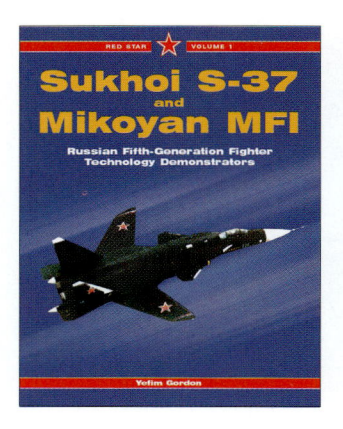

Conceived as an answer to the American ATF programme, the Mikoyan MFI (better known as the 1.42 or 1.44) and the Sukhoi S-37 Berkoot were developed as technology demonstrators. Both design bureaux used an approach that was quite different from Western fifth-generation fighter philosophy. This gives a detailed account of how these enigmatic aircraft were designed, built and flown. It includes structural descriptions of both types.

Sbk, 280 x 215 mm, 96pp, plus 8pp colour foldout, 12 b/w and 174 colour photos, drawings and colour artworks
1 85780 120 2   **£18.95/US $27.95**

Red Star Volume 2
FLANKERS: The New Generation
Yefim Gordon

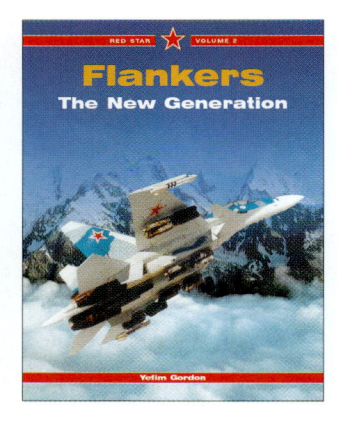

The multi-role Su-30 and Su-35 and thrust-vectoring Su-37 are described in detail, along with the 'big head' Su-23FN/Su-34 tactical bomber, the Su-27K (Su-33) shipborne fighter and its two-seat combat trainer derivative, the Su-27KUB. The book also describes the customised versions developed for foreign customers – the Su-30KI (Su-27KI), the Su-30MKI for India, the Su-30MKK for China and the latest Su-35UB.

Softback, 280 x 215 mm, 128 pages 252 colour photographs, plus 14 pages of colour artworks
1 85780 121 0   **£18.95/US $27.95**

Red Star Volume 3
POLIKARPOV'S I-16 FIGHTER
Yefim Gordon and Keith Dexter

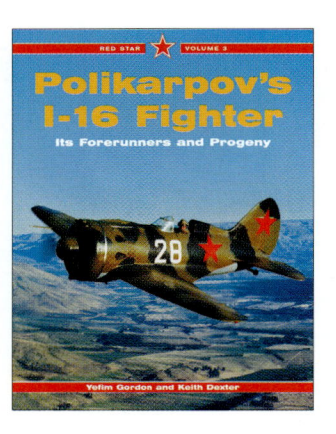

Often dismissed because it did not fare well against its more modern adversaries in the Second World War, Nikolay Polikarpov's I-16 was nevertheless an outstanding fighter – among other things, because it was the world's first monoplane fighter with a retractable undercarriage. Its capabilities were demonstrated effectively during the Spanish Civil War. Covers every variant, from development, unbuilt projects and the later designs that evolved from it.

Sbk, 280 x 215 mm, 128 pages, 185 b/w photographs, 17 pages of colour artworks, plus line drawings
1 85780 131 8   **£18.99/US $27.95**

Red Star Volume 4
EARLY SOVIET JET FIGHTERS
Yefim Gordon

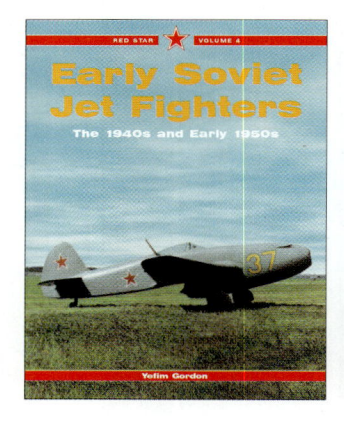

This charts the development and service history of the first-generation Soviet jet fighters designed by such renowned 'fighter makers' as Mikoyan, Yakovlev and Sukhoi, as well as design bureaux no longer in existence – the Lavochkin and Alekseyev OKBs, during the 1940s and early 1950s. Each type is detailed and compared to other contemporary jet fighters. As ever the extensive photo coverage includes much which is previously unseen.

Sbk, 280 x 215 mm, 144 pages 240 b/w and 9 colour photos, 8 pages of colour artworks
1 85780 139 3   **£19.99/US $29.95**

Red Star Volume 5
YAKOVLEV'S PISTON-ENGINED FIGHTERS
Yefim Gordon & Dmitriy Khazanov

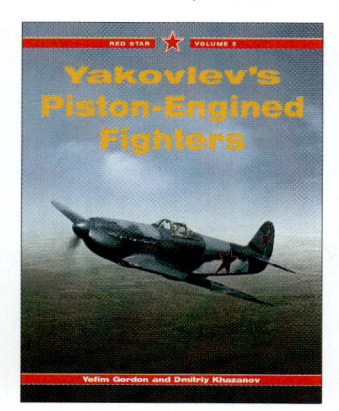

This authoritative monograph describes this entire family from the simple but rugged and agile Yak-1 through the Yak-7 (born as a trainer but eventually developed into a fighter) and the prolific and versatile Yak-9 to the most capable of the line, the Yak-3 with which even the aces of the Luftwaffe were reluctant to tangle. Yak piston fighters also served outside Russia and several examples can be seen in flying condition in the west.

Sbk, 280 x 215 mm, 144 pages, 313 b/w and 2 col photos, 7pp of colour artworks, 8pp of line drawings
1 85780 140 7   **£19.99/US $29.95**

Red Star Volume 6
POLIKARPOV'S BIPLANE FIGHTERS
Yefim Gordon and Keith Dexter

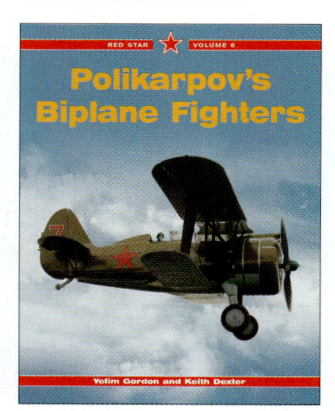

The development of Polikarpov's fighting biplanes including the 2I-N1, the I-3, and I-5, which paved the way for the I-15 which earned fame as the Chato during the Spanish Civil War and saw action against the Japanese; the I-15bis and the famous I-153 Chaika retractable gear gull-wing biplane. Details of combat use are given, plus structural descriptions, details of the ill-starred I-190, and of privately owned I-15bis and I-153s restored to fly.

Softback, 280 x 215 mm, 128 pages c250 b/w and colour photos; three-view drawings, 60+ colour side views
1 85780 141 5   **£18.99/US $27.95**

Red Star Volume 7
TUPOLEV Tu-4 SOVIET SUPERFORTRESS
Yefim Gordon and Vladimir Rigmant

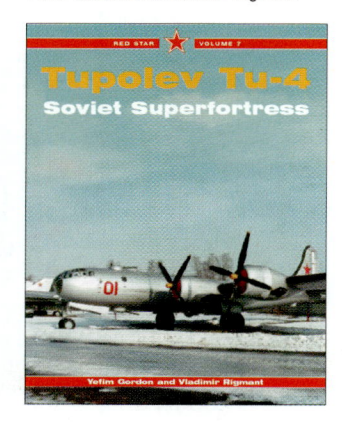

At the end of WW2, three Boeing B-29s fell into Soviet hands; from these came a Soviet copy of this famous bomber in the form of the Tu-4. This examines the evolution of the 'Superfortresski' and its further development into the Tu-70 transport. It also covers the civil airliner version, the Tu-75, and Tu-85, the last of Tupolev's piston-engined bombers. Also described are various experimental versions, including the Burlaki towed fighter programme.

Sbk, 280 x 215 mm, 128pp, 225 b/w and 9 colour photos, plus line drawings
1 85780 142 3   **£18.99/US $27.95**